African-American Experience

in World Mission: A Call Beyond Community

Editors

Vaughn J. Walston

Robert J. Stevens

William Carey Library
P.O. Box 40129
Pasadena, California 91114

Cooperative Mission Network of the African Dispersion (COMINAD)
P.O. Box 9756
Chesapeake, Virginia 23321

Published by
William Carey Library
P.O. Box 40129
Pasadena, California 91114
www.wclbooks.com

Published in conjunction with
Cooperative Mission Network of the African Dispersion (COMINAD)
P.O. Box 9756
Chesapeake, VA 23321
email: IAAMM@aol.com

Cover Design: Chad Upham
Cover photos courtesy of L. Foday Farrar and Brian Johnson

ISBN 0-87808-609-9

Printed in the United States of America

Foreword

The authors of this book took time to do research and interview African-Americans in relation to worldwide missions. It is not an exhaustive book, it is a presentation of the activity of past and the present world missions. Many denominations have a history of their own involvement in worldwide missions. But there are not many overall presentations of what all missions boards are doing.

This presentation helps to give us an overall picture of what is going on in the African-American worldwide involvement in missions. There are many people who are not aware of the great activity of our past in missions on the part of African-Americans. There were great outstanding men and women who are our role models in missions. There are some great outstanding men and women alive today, who are doing great exploits for our Lord and Savior Christ Jesus all over the world. If God's people read this book, they will realize that no one group has a monopoly on missions, and that God uses people of whose identity they may not be aware.

Most importantly, I believe that the readers of this book will realize what God has been doing, and that missions is not something new to the African-Americans. The reader gets a cross-section of life inside the context of African-Americans in missions. The reader will realize some of the difficulties, struggles, and hindrances of our past and present missionaries. This book reveals different attitudes and perceptions of missionaries in their various fields and personal actions. This book is not necessarily a textbook, but an exposure to the life of a great people in God's worldwide activity in reaching the lost with the Gospel of our Lord and Savior Jesus Christ.

Rev. Dr. Benjamin W. Johnson, Sr.
Nashville, Tennessee
June, 2002

Preface

This work is the product of an identified and confirmed need in the African-American community. As an African-American student of missions, a missions mobilizer, and short-term missionary, I desired to gain some understanding of the African-American heritage in missions. Equipped with only an awareness of a few resources which specifically addressed African-American missions involvement, I attended a conference on the subject. Finding the same need among the African-American missions community, I spoke about the issue with some faculty at Columbia Biblical Seminary (where I studied) and others with like mind. With good counsel, I embarked upon a faculty-directed study on the topic of mobilizing the African-American church for missions. Although my personal goal was to gain knowledge for my own enrichment, there was the excitement of developing a product that could serve as a resource to the African-American community and church/missions community at large. My research helped me produce a primary resource—the Bibliography of African-Americans in Missions (Appendix A)—a quick guide to literature on African-American mission involvement for an inquirer's own area of interest.

While networking with organizations through the Cooperative Missions Network of the African Dispersion (COMINAD), I met Robert Stevens with the U.S. Center for World Mission. Bob had an interest in introducing the course *Perspectives on the World Christian Movement* to the African-American church. I suggested that the course be contextualized by at least including articles representing the African-American heritage in missions. Excited about seeing the course represent the African-American church, we considered an anthology of readings to supplement the existing course material. That project evolved into the current work. My desire was additionally to create a resource that could serve the broader community beyond the *Perspectives* course. This book is a compilation of many of the articles collected during my research, with several newly written articles providing current or condensed information.

We hope that this work proves a useful guide to education and motivation toward greater missions involvement. Use this book as a missions anthology for academic use or dig into it as a curious searcher for good background into the rich heritage of African-Americans on task, on a mission, reaching beyond their own cultural constraints to take the Gospel to the ends of the earth.

Vaughn J. Walston

"Lord, why am I here." That was my prayer at the initial meeting of COMINAD (the Cooperative Mission Network of the African Dispersion) at Zoe Christian Fellowship in Whittier, CA, in March 1999. I met Vaughn Walston and Bobby Herron and both were eager to see African-American material put alongside the *Perspectives on the World Christian Movement* course that is offered in some 140 locations around the U.S. every year and sponsored by the U.S. Center for World Mission in Pasadena, CA. Within a week of the Whittier meeting, Vaughn drove to Raleigh, NC to say, "Its time to get working." He showed me all of the research he had done and our office said, "Yes, let's put this book together," offering our staff and equipment.

The first draft was shown to the next meeting of COMINAD in Atlanta in March 2000 and many valuable suggestions were made by a diverse representation of African-Americans involved in missions. These suggestions have been incorporated and the book has now become two volumes. The first volume covers briefly the biblical themes of missions, history of African-American involvement in missions, an understanding of the African-American harvest force, and a contemporary response by current missionaries to cross cultural issues.

Volume two will focus on biographical sketches of African-American pioneers in missions.

This book is intended not only for the African-American community to raise the level of mission awareness and involvement but also for the white community to understand the rich heritage of the African-American experience in world missions. So, with joy and anticipation COMINAD releases our first volume.

Robert J. Stevens

Acknowledgements

Special thanks to COMINAD (Cooperative Missions Network of the African Disperion) members for their contributions of articles, proofreading, consulting, editorial reviews and cover photos:

Elijah Adeoye, African Christian Fellowship, Norman, OK

Virgil Amos, Ambassadors Fellowship, Colorado Springs, CO

Clarice Banks, member, New Canaan Full Gospel Baptist Church, Garner, NC

Diane Becton, member, New Canaan Full Gospel Baptist Church, Garner, NC

Elder Don Canty, Director of Missions, New Birth Missionary Baptist Church, Atlanta, GA

L. Foday Farrar, Bishop overseer for missions for the Full Gospel Baptist Fellowship, cover photo credits, Garner, NC

Jennifer Furbert, COMINAD, Bermuda

Frank Gainer, African Christian Fellowship, COMINAD-Administrative Consultant, Indianapolis, IN

Bobby Herron, Impact Ministries, Campus Crusade for Christ, Santa Monica, CA

Ben Johnson, Christian Creative Ministries, Nashville, TN

Brian Johnson, National Coordinator of COMINAD, Virginia Beach, VA

Judy Laidley, Southeast Regional Office, U.S. Center for World Mission, Raleigh, NC

Glenn Mason, Director of Carver International Missions, Atlanta, GA

Courtney May, member New Canaan Full Gospel Baptist Church, Garner, NC

Amanda L. Meenke, YWAM, Elm Springs, AK

Christy Minger, Crusade Ministry, Chicago, IL

Shannon and Beth Newlin, Southeast Regional Office, U.S. Center for World Mission, Raleigh, NC

Joe and Peggy Raymond, Africa on Fire, Virginia Beach, VA

Jean Sorokin, Southeast Regional Office, U.S. Center for World Mission, Raleigh, NC

Bob and Ellen Stevens, Southeast Regional Office, U.S. Center for World Mission, Raleigh, NC

Jim Sutherland, Reconciliation Network, Chatanooga, TN

Jerry Thomas, God's Ambassadors, Eugene, OR

Ridley Usherwood, Professor Lee University, Cleveland, TN

Vaughn and Rebecca Walston, COMINAD, Orlando, FL

Jim Wilson, Wycliffe Bible Translators, Huntington Beach, CA

Daise Whaley, Retired Missionary with WEC to Ivory Coast, Africa, Philadelphia, PA

Cover design by Chad Upham, Pasadena, CA

Table of Contents

The Call Beyond Community

African-Americans' Historical Presence in Missions

African-Americans Crossing Cultures

Connecting to Africa and Other Nations

The African-American Church and African Mission in the 21st Century

The Call Beyond Community

Moving Beyond the Community

Rebecca Walston & RobertStevens

Rebecca A. Walston is currently working as an attorney while pursuing a Masters in Counseling. She has been involved in missions mobilizing since 1999, specializing in leadership development for short term teams.

Robert "Bob" J. Stevens has served as Southeast Regional Director of the U.S. Center for World Mission, since 1988 in Raleigh, NC. In the past 15 years he has helped coordinate and supervise 153 *Perspectives* classes in 11 states. Over 5100 people have taken the class in the Southeast with about 7 % of those working in long term mission among unreached people groups. Prior to that he served in campus ministry with Campus Crusade for Christ. Bob, his wife, Ellen, and their four children reside in Raleigh, NC. He is a graduate of NCSU with a B.S. in Chemical Engineering.

All first-person comments are by Rebecca Walston.

In 1992, when a jury acquitted the Los Angeles police officers who beat Rodney King, waves of shock and anger rang through much of the black community. That evening I sat at a community meeting at my church. The first half of the meeting, my pastor spoke of God's demonstrated commitment to correct injustice and protect His people despite racial prejudice from others. In the second hour, the floor was opened to those who wished to vent their responses to the decision in a civil, productive manner. As in the days of the civil rights movement, this moment sticks out in my mind as a symbol of the black church's continued commitment to find biblical solutions to our social and political condition as a people.

Acts 1:8 calls us to be His witnesses in Jerusalem, Judea, Samaria and even to the ends of the earth. In this verse, Christ calls the early Church to establish His Kingdom first in their own community of Jerusalem, and then to the surrounding community of Judea. But the Church is also called to move beyond geographical and cultural barriers and proclaim Christ in the neighboring culture of Samaria. And finally, the Church is commanded to go "even to the remotest part of the earth." The black church has a rich history and continued commitment to our community, our modern-day Jerusalem, but in Acts 1:8, we find an additional call beyond our own community. God calls us to declare the Gospel of a loving God far beyond our own community. God calls us to practice what some have termed "global evangelism" to be His witnesses even unto the ends of the earth.

A close look at Scripture reveals that moving beyond our communities and going to the ends of the earth has been God's plan from the beginning:

> Now the LORD said to Abram, "Go forth from your country, and from your relatives, and from your father's house, to the land which I will show you; And I will make you a great nation, and I will bless you, and make your name great; and so you shall be a blessing; And I will bless those who bless you, and the one who curses you I will curse; And in you all the families of the earth shall be blessed." (Gen. 12:1-3, NASB)

This promise to Abram, known as the Abrahamic Covenant, is repeated in Gen. 18:18 and 22:18 to Abraham, in

26:4 to Isaac, and in 28:14 to Jacob. At first glance, one might say that this charge applies only to Abraham and his lineage, and to the nation of Israel. However, the context in the introduction to the Bible is universal. The creation, fall, flood and Babel all point to universal conditions for man. Thus we can say that this plan applies to all nations, not simply the nation of Israel. God's plan is to bless all the nations of the world through those who have entered into a covenant relationship with him. God's specific ways of accomplishing this goal begins with Abraham and his seed. The seed immediately would be Isaac, then the Jewish nation, and finally Christ. "Now the promises were spoken to Abraham and to his seed. He does not say, "And to seeds," as referring to many, but rather to one, "And to your seed," that is Christ." (Gal. 3:16) Finally believers today are the seed of Abraham, as we see in Romans 4:13-16 (NAS),

> For the promise to Abraham or to his descendants that he would be heir of the world was not through the Law, but through the righteousness of faith. For if those who are of the Law are heirs, faith is made void and the promise is nullified; for the law brings about wrath, but where there is no law, neither is there violation. For this reason it is by faith, that it might be in accordance with grace, in order that the promise may be certain to all the descendants, not only to those who are of the Law, but also to those who are of the faith of Abraham, who is the father of us all.

So it is by faith that we are made heirs of the Abrahamic Covenant. "And if you belong to Christ, then you are Abraham's offspring, heirs according to the promise." (Gal. 3:29) What does this mean? Believers today are responsible to help fulfill the Abrahamic Covenant because we have become heirs of the promise by our faith. We are to be a blessing to all the nations, (Gen 12:3).

What is this blessing we have been commissioned to deliver? In Galatians 3:8, the concept of the Gospel is linked with that of blessing: "And the Scripture, foreseeing that God would justify the Gentiles through faith, preached before the Gospel to Abraham, saying, 'All the nations shall be blessed in you.'" The word blessing summarizes all of the Gospel. We are blessed with the Gospel to be a blessing (to bring the fullness of that Gospel) to all the families or nations on earth.

In Rev. 5:9 and 7:9 we find that this blessing of the Gospel will be extended to all nations and at the throne of God will be individuals from every nation, peoples, tribes and tongues declaring His glory.

> And they sang a new song, saying, 'Worthy art Thou to take the book, and to break its seals; for Thou wast slain, and didst purchase for God with Thy blood men from every tribe and tongue and people and nation.' (Rev. 5:9, NASB)

> After these things I looked, and behold, a great multitude, which no one could count, from every nation and all tribes and peoples and tongues, standing before the throne and before the Lamb, clothed in white robes...(Rev. 7:9, NASB)

God desires to share this love and joy with all the peoples on earth through all the peoples on earth. God has mandated through Abraham that His people are to be a blessing to every people. Instead of nation rising against nation in war, every nation should rise to give blessing to every nation by extending the Gospel of our incomparable Lord and Savior Jesus Christ that God may receive the worship proper for His glory.

Yet, even as we begin to understand God's call for us to demonstrate the Gospel to all peoples, both at home and abroad, there can arise a rather significant tension within. In light of the ever-present problems with race that still exist at home, how can I turn my energies to others? Am I not forsaking my brother whom I see daily? Though the tension is real, God's plan is not quite so simple. The call in Acts 1:8 is not an either/or proposition. We do not answer the call to the nations at the exclusion of home. God's plan for the Church, even the black church, is that we exalt His name in our community (our Jerusalem) and to the ends of the earth.

My brothers and sisters, could it be that precisely because of our struggles in America that God has called us to a unique place in His plan to reach every tribe and tongue? We as a people can relate to many of the oppressed peoples of the world as a result of our own struggle. I am not suggesting that

God orchestrated slavery and its horrors and repercussions. I am saying that what some meant for evil God can use for good, (Gen 50:20).

It is in the story of Joseph that I find this principle demonstrated. Like Joseph, who was sold into slavery, as a people, we too have been subjected to the effects of sin in such a way that our lives have been fundamentally altered. Like Joseph, we have been forced to live in the land of our affliction, never knowing the sanctity and safety of our native land. Yet, in the midst of all this Joseph realized that God had been with him. Scripture records that Joseph married and had two sons. The first he named Manasseh, meaning God has caused me to forget the toil of my Father's house. The second he named Ephraim, meaning God has caused me to prosper in the land of my affliction. As Joseph realizes God's provision and protection, God eventually uses him to bring deliverance from severe famine to both his family and the people of Egypt. Could it be, that despite the fact that we have suffered greatly at the hands of those who intended to do us harm, like Joseph, we have been given a special place in God's plan to redeem the nations unto Himself?

History is full of many African-Americans who answered this call and saw God use them and their cultural identity in unique ways. Their story needs to be told. This book will give you a glimpse of the black church's presence in missions abroad. We have overcome many obstacles to get to the nations. Yet we have had rich experiences and made significant contributions. As you read, you will enter the lives of some African-Americans who have served abroad. You will understand their call and realize cultural adjustments they faced as African-Americans. You will see where we are now and how we got to this point. You will also discover the battle we must fight in order to effectively mobilize the black church to make a global impact in this generation.

"One generation shall praise Thy works to another, and shall declare Thy mighty acts." (Ps. 145:4, NASB) Let us go forward and share this vision, share this story, share this joy that all peoples are invited to share in the blessing of Abraham by being a blessing to every kindred, and tongue, and people and nation to the glory of God! Our legacy is sure, our challenge is great, yet our God is greater.

Missions in the Local Church: Four Pastors' Perspectives

Edited by Rebecca Walston

For hundreds of years, the African-American Church has been the backbone of its community. The black church is our first and arguably only indigenous institution. The black church was a haven for the Underground Railroad and the foundation of the civil rights movement.

Against this backdrop of activism and support for the plight of African-Americans, how will the church balance its interests at home with its biblical mandate to take the Gospel to the world? Join us as we take a look at how the contemporary black church is responding to this mandate.

Pastor Gregory Alexander
  Rosedale Park Baptist Church, Detroit, MI
  US Chairman of the Board, Pan African Christian Exchange
Pastor Olah Moore
  Faith Community Church, Norfolk, VA
  former missionary to Nigeria, West Africa
Pastor Ron Horton
  Bethany Pembroke Chapel, Detroit, MI
  Dean, William Tyndale Bible Institute, Farmington Hills, MI
  (Representing three other pastors)
Missions Pastor Jack Gaines
  Calvary Evangelical Baptist Church, Portsmouth, VA

Please describe how you came to have a vision or a passion to serve God in missions and how you see yourself continuing this vision in the future.

Alexander: There are two experiences that stand out for me. First, at a very young age I can remember missionaries who came into our church and shared their stories about the mission field. Even as a youngster, their stories always fascinated me and began to spark an interest in me to be involved in missions. Second, when I was twelve, we had opportunity to go to a camp that specialized in training young people to survive on the missions field and at the end of that week I can remember coming back to our church and acknowledging that God had called me to ministry, particularly to have some involvement in missions on an on going basis.

Editor: Rebecca A. Walston is currently working as an attorney while pursuing a Masters in Counseling. She has been involved in missions mobilizing since 1999, specializing in leadership development for short term teams.

Transcribers: Amanda L. Meenk, YWAM, & Jean Sorokin, Southeast Regional Ofice, S Center for World Mission.

Moore: I knew a missionary, a young girl who grew up in our church, named Naomi Doles. She was a missionary in Liberia and God used her mightily. I was eight years old and I remember saying "I want to do that", and the Lord birthed that vision in me and I remember the next day going to school and our teacher asked each of us what we wanted to be and I said "a missionary". I didn't even know how to spell it. In fact, she thought I said "mercenary". But, ever since then there has been this passion in my heart to be a missionary and God continued to work that in me until I was in seminary. After seminary, I went to NIgeria for 11 years. Now being used of God to give vision to others on the mission field and having been on the mission field myself, I just believe that being a pastor now is just an interim step for me to be back in some mission.

Horton: I think my real vision of mission work really began to materialize when I first met Brian Johnson, director of COMINAD. We have been friends for about 28 years now. We both started out in the ministry together and he was a missionary. As time went on I began to see and to have a burden for those outside of my immediate community. The question had always been, especially in the black church, how do I go about trying to get others to see that missions outside of ourselves was something that God commissioned us to do? Matthew 28, talks about go[ing] and mak[ing] disciples in all the world. [The black church] has a community vision but not a world vision.

Gaines: I met Brian Johnson in 1992 and invited him to come and give a missions overview to our church. From that point on I have been heavily involved in what I call the biblical theology of missions—going both to Jerusalem, Judea and to the uttermost parts of the world at the same time. [Our church is] involved in prison ministry, college campuses, and outreach fellowships in the local church and the local community. Now we are [also] a part of "Adopt a Village" and we are supporting 23 other missionaries around the world.

As a pastor, what is your sense of your call to reach both your community and the world? Is it possible to do both?

Alexander: Certainly it is possible. Not only is it possible but it is what we have been called to do. Jesus' parting words in Acts 1:8 were that we were to be witnesses to Him in both Jerusalem, Judea, Samaria and the uttermost parts of the earth. I don't believe we should be doing one to the exclusion of the other. Because that is our call, our charge that we have been given, the church has to be involved in all of those areas of evangelism.

Moore: Our church had a unique tradition in that it came out of what was known then as the Colored Union Mission. It was natural for us to give immediate attention to the felt needs all around the church and yet what we always struggled with were our vows to reach out. We have had to be deliberate in structuring the ministry in the church to make sure that not only are the "Jerusalem" ministries taken care of, but especially those "to the uttermost parts of the earth". It is not only important that we understand that the Scriptures do not call us to do one, but that the Scriptures tell us to [reach] Jerusalem, Judea, Samaria and the uttermost parts of the world and to do all simultaneously.

Horton: My whole idea of missions is reaching all of these different components: the family, the community, the world. I honestly believe that God will bless the commission of reaching those who are lost if we have a focus that reaches all of these areas. It is a vision to be revealed. That's why as a church, in the black community, we have not reached across our own community lines to the world—because we are so contained by our own personal issues. Don't get me wrong, there are many issues, but I think that they have become so overwhelming and we have allowed ourselves to be so engrossed with those issues that we forget that two-thirds of the world has never heard the Gospel of Jesus Christ. So I think at this time God is beginning to raise up the awareness in these last days of the fact that there is a world without Christ. The Scripture says that until the Gospel is preached to all the world, Jesus will not return. So, this is what God is doing in the midst of us at just this point in time.

Gaines: Everyone seems to be hanging on Acts 1:8 and I know that's where our local assembly [our church] is. When you think about the relationship that the Jews had with Samaritans, they were undesirables. That's one facet that we are trying to implement in our local assembly. Our ministry is not only cross-cultural but also reaches out to those that society would call undesirables such as the inmates, those who are suffering from AIDS, or those in other similar situations. It is very important that we have that balance, I believe. Also, I believe that it is very important that we emphasize the fact, in our local assembly and especially in our black community, that overseas missions is not optional. A lot of times we think that because our situation is so rough right in our communities [we are] excused from foreign missions. But this is not an excuse. I think that it is our responsibility to go into our community and reeducate our people on the biblical theology of missions. I think that God right now has used that narrow definition of missions as applying only to our communities as an incubator to grow this powerful resource. I think that we are in the process of being used by the Lord to birth that resource into this biblical theology of missions in these times. And we thank God for the opportunity that He is giving us to be a part of this.

How important do you think it is to give financial support for those serving overseas? In what way can the African-American church develop this practice?

Alexander: One of the complaints that I hear on a regular basis whenever I am around African-American missionaries is how difficult it is for them to raise support while they are out on the mission field. I am certainly not one to be critical of the African-American church because I believe that it has done a tremendous job in terms of aiding the African-American community at home. But, we could do a better job of making our presence felt on the foreign mission field. So in addition to all the things that we have done, I believe that we can be of tremendous encour-

agement to those that are out on the foreign mission fields by realizing that we have a responsibility and an obligation to provide them financial support as well as prayer support and any other help that we can possibly give to encourage them.

Moore: After I graduated from seminary, I went on the mission field for 11 years. In those 11 years only one African-American church supported me and my family and that was the church that I grew up in, Faith Community Church. The only reason that they did it was because my father was a deacon and he said he was going to make sure that we didn't starve on the mission field. When I went to African-American churches, they were very supportive of my going to the mission field, but they did not have the internal financial discipline or infrastructure to support my family on a long-term basis. They took up tremendous one-time offerings that definitely met a need, but our month-to-month support on the mission field wasn't there. It wasn't that the African-American churches were not sympathetic as supporters, but this was something new to them. Things have changed and one of the reasons is, I believe, that a new type of teaching on stewardship and accountability by responsibility is presently taking place in African-American churches. Once we are taught to give differently and to give consistently for what God is doing not only locally, but around the world, I believe that the whole paradigm of giving from the African-American church would mirror some of the other communities in their giving.

Horton: In the church that I belong to, missionaries would go out with support given from individuals within the congregation. But it has always been an ongoing struggle in most black churches. I know that it has been a struggle in ours. Now that I am missions-minded I went to my own elders in church to find out what we have in place for missions. The interesting thing is that the [corporate giving] structure has always been whatever "the little old lady in the congregation would give to the brother" on the field. I was really amazed that there is nothing— nothing in place. So one of the reasons that I came to the COMINAD conference was to learn some things that I could do and try to put in place. Something that I am going to try to do when I get back is literally to put a mission fund in place and make it mandatory that 10 percent of everything that comes into the church's general fund goes into missions. I think the mindset in the African-American church has always been: "We kind of live day by day." I would come to the church and they would raise support and give me a beautiful offering, but later I was: 'Out of sight, out of mind.' We have always lived that way. I think we need to change the mindset [of the people]. I think that leadership has to initiate that change by putting things in place to help reeducate people on how they should be supporting those that are on the field. It's an ongoing task, I know, but it has to start somewhere.

Gaines: Again, I think it is very important to lend our financial support to those serving overseas. When I became a missions director, there were some things in place already. One of the structures that my pastor established when he came to our congregation of about 60 people, was that 10 percent of the morning offering would go towards missions. Also all of Wednesday-night Bible study offering and all of Sunday evening service offering would go towards missions. Now that we are running about 900 members, that is a significant amount of resources for missions. As a result we are sending support to approximately 23 missionaries around the world. We praise God for that and we would like to be a model. God says in the Word, "To whom much is given, much is required" (Luke 12:48). We are very sensitive to be obedient to what God has called us to do and to be very disciplined with the resources that He makes available to us.

Is there a specific passage of Scripture the Lord has used to sustain your vision to serve overseas?

Alexander: I stated earlier, when I was 12 years old I acknowledged God's call on my life to be involved in missions. But, I spent a number of years away from the Lord and it wasn't until I was about 30 that I actually I surrendered and rededicated my life to the Lord. I can remember the night when I told

the Lord that I would do with my life whatever He wanted me to do. Having said that prayer, I opened up my Bible to the book of Psalms and I began to read. And I told the Lord, "You're going to have to speak to me to let me know that You are confirming what I committed myself to doing." After what seemed like quite a long time—reading the scriptures and not hearing from God—I can remember saying, "Now how long is it going to take You to answer me?" He said to me, "I have already spoken to you." He directed me to go back to Psalm 2, verse 8, that says, "Ask of me and I will give you the heathens for your inheritance and the uttermost parts of the earth for your possession." I know that because He said it to me, somehow my life has been dedicated to make an impact on the world.

Moore: About eight years ago I preached through the book of Romans. At the end of Romans I ran across three verses that I had never seen before in my life. I have been on the mission field and knew it, but the Lord just opened up the understanding for me and ever since then I have been using this as my "ideal" of mission verses—Romans16: 25-27 says, "Now to Him Who is able to establish you by my Gospel and a proclamation of Jesus Christ according to the revelation of the mystery hidden from long ages past, but now revealed and made known through the prophetic writing by the command of the eternal God so that all nations might believe and obey Him. To the only wise God be glory, forever, through Jesus Christ. Amen." Just think, all of Scripture, everything that we teach has everything to do with the mandate, and that phrase grammatically is a result: "That all nations might believe and obey Him." All nations is ALL NATIONS. Obey means OBEY. It is not a suggestion. Yes, we hold on to Matthew 28, we hold on to Acts 1:8, but these last three verses in Romans really challenged my heart.

Horton: Olah 'knocked' my Acts 1:8. That's my verse, Acts 1:8—God has given me His Word on many occasions for my own personal call, but the call to this whole idea of missions really has taken place with me in the last, I guess, six or seven months. It has been a result of studying the book of Acts.

And that 1:8 is so essential in our growth. That's why I go back to that practical application for us, reaching the family, the community, and the world for Christ. I love Olah but that Acts 1:8, you see, is the whole essence. That's the vision that the Lord has given me as far as where we are as a local assembly, that we are to reach all aspects of the world, the community, and family.

Gaines: I heard a gentleman preach on Matthew 28 and he brought out something here that is very significant to me. It says in verse 16, "Then the disciples went to Galilee to the mountain where Jesus had told them to go. When they saw Him they worshipped Him, but some doubted." When those disciples doubted, Jesus responded with this. "Then Jesus came and to them and said, 'All authority is given to Me in heaven and in earth, now go.'" When I see what Jesus was trying to do to encourage and to motivate them to go, He revealed to them that all power and all authority has been given unto Him and we should be going with the utmost confidence with what we are doing. And, this scripture has motivated me.

Am I My Brother's Keeper?

The Search for African-American Presence in Missions

Michael Johnson

We've bought into the American dream of financial prosperity thinking that we deserve more, and we've missed God's desire to bless all peoples with the Gospel.

Michael Johnson and wife, Sandra, sold their home and cars, closed a busy and prosperous surgical practice, and moved to Kenya with their four children in 1990. The Johnsons since have been involved in a variety of ministries in Kenya. Most have revolved around hospital administration, surgical care for the extremely impoverished people of Kenya, work with street children providing health care to over 30,000 children in Nairobi, and the training of Kenyan physicians.

This article is the expanded text from a message given by Dr. Johnson at the COMINAD meeting at Zoe Christian Fellowship in Whittier, California in March 1999.

Genesis four gives an account of the first murder. We can see clearly Cain's motive in killing Abel. God had taken greater delight in the gift of Abel. Cain killed Abel because he was jealous of him. The biblical record says that God asked Cain of his brother's whereabouts. Cain replied, "I know not: Am I my brother's keeper?"

We address God with this same rhetorical question when we ask, "Is it our responsibility to do world missions?" Whose job is it to evangelize the world? Whose job is it to feed the hungry, clothe the naked, visit the sick and imprisoned? Whose job is it to encourage the downcast? Whose job is it to minister to the materially rich but spiritually impoverished?

This is the real question each of us is asking God when we consider whether we are called to missions. It is not the question of "Should I go to Africa, Asia, Europe or South America?" The question really is "Am I my brother's keeper?"

As mentioned above, this is not the first time God has heard this question. Abel was dead and hidden in the sand, having been killed by his brother, Cain. God was asking for some accountability and Cain tried to play a mind game on the Creator of the mind. "Who do You think you are...God or Somebody like that? Aren't You supposed to be in charge? If You know everything, why are You asking me where this guy Abel is? You find him! He is not in my charge...I am not his keeper!"

"Who do You think You are, God? I just got a new job and I finally got enough money to get cable television. I finally made it into a class of people that will allow me the prestige of owning a home. I just got a position that allows me to wear a tie and dress well. I just paid off my student loans. I finally got the kind of car I want and the kind of jewelry everyone else has. What has that trouble over there got to do with me over here? Don't I have enough trouble with my own people here? Let those folks take care of their own. I am not my brother's keeper."

"After all, those people don't even look like me. They believe different things. They have different traditions. What right do I have imposing my religion and my beliefs on them? I know this Jesus stuff is okay for me and my traditions, just let those folks be over there. I may call Him King of Kings and Lord of Lords, but I only meant that He is so around here. Those folks have their own beliefs. I am not really responsible for changing their worldview. I am not my brother's keeper. Or am I?"

The Lord Jehovah heard this argument from Cain. He left Cain with a mark on his head. This mark was a blessing and a curse. It assured Cain that no one would avenge Abel's blood, but it reminded them that Cain was a murderer.

We are our brother's keeper. When we ignore this calling, people look at us as members of the body of Christ and ask: "Aren't these the people who serve the God Who is supposed to help the helpless and feed the hungry and clothe the naked?" People watch us to see if we are wearing the mark of the cross of Christ or the mark of Cain. Am I my brother's keeper? God says you are. Who is your brother? "Anyone in need" is the answer Christ gives. As you meet the needs of people in Christ's name, you meet Christ Himself. For He Himself said, "When you do it to the least of these, you have done it unto me" (Matt 25:35-40).

I want to spell out for you the challenge I see for black Americans in missions. I will detail first of all a brief history of black Americans in missions and the challenges they faced. I will then give you a picture of what is happening in our community economically, academically, and professionally and identify our biggest challenge today. I will then give some details about the living conditions in Kenya and for those who are in need of the Savior. Finally, I will give you a detailed picture of how we can meet our commissioning as dictated by the Savior.

Where are the black Americans in missions? For too long this job of carrying Christ to the nations has been allocated almost exclusively to white missionaries. Current estimates are that there are more than 30,000 missionaries from the North America. Of them, about 200 are of African-American descent.

Why are we so few in numbers? Have we abandoned the call? Do we not read the same Gospel? Do we not share the same burden? Do we not identify with the downtrodden and outcast of the world? Are we not able to meet the call? Are we not prepared? Do we not have the resources? When we answer all of these questions we are still faced with the original query posed by Cain: "Am I my brother's keeper?"

Challenges in the Past

How do we find our place in this calling of missions? Do we have a history and a place of reference? Well, to be sure, the earliest American missionaries were of African descent. The first African-American missionary, George Liele, was a former slave who visited the West Indies to carry the Gospel of Christ. African-Americans have been at the forefront of missions even before the American Colonization Society to Liberia. This calling continued and was sustained in such agencies as the Union Missionary Society, formed in 1841 by the freed-man James Pennington, which sent African-American missionaries to Sierra Leone.

In the late 19th and early to mid 20th centuries, African-Americans were frequently hampered in their calling to missions because white agencies were fearful of them. Mary McLeod Bethune studied at the prodigious Moody Bible Institute of Chicago and applied to be a missionary in Africa. However, she was refused by white agencies that did not want African-Americans. Montrose Waite likewise was first accepted and worked with the Christian Missionary Alliance. He was later rejected as a missionary with this organization because of his color.

White mission boards were fearful that colonial governments during these early years might reject their agencies because free and outspoken people of color would undermine their economic interests. Furthermore, conservative boards were still uncomfortable allowing mixing of the races especially when this might result in people of color assuming administrative roles. To date, my family represents the only people of African origin in our agency's 80-plus-year history.

Missionary activity has always had a mixed agenda. Early missionaries from Europe to Africa and the Americas were frequently used by the colonial governments to soften up the natives in order to make them more accepting of economic conquest. European governments ravaged Africa in the name of Christ. Early American missionaries to the Native Americans, the so-called Indians, were used as an experiment by the U.S. government to make the Indians passive.

They even taught the Indians how to buy and use slaves for labor.

America itself had no colonies in Africa. However, it sought to establish such in the early 1800s. The American Colonization Society was founded in 1816 by the administration of President James Monroe wih the intent of establishing a colony in Liberia. The U.S. used former slaves as Christian missionaries to establish a presence in Africa. This was with dual intent. First, to rid the U.S. of freedmen or former slaves deemed a threat in the southern states to the institution of slavery. Second to establish a U.S. presence in Africa. Freed slaves were also seen as a menace in the northern states because they had the effrontery to expect to be treated as equals in society.

The propagation of the Gospel was frequently a side issue when we consider the history of mission activities of European and American churches in the 19th and 20th centuries. Economic, cultural, and military domination have been part and parcel of the package of benefits given to evangelized masses.

The fact that the Church is established in many parts of the world for profit is not a new phenomenon. Paul noted, "Some indeed preach Christ even of envy and strife and some also of good will...What then? Notwithstanding every way, whether it is pretense or in truth, Christ is preached" (Phil 1:15-18). The church is established in spite of missionary efforts in many instances.

Because of this very mixed history of good and bad in missions, many of us have avoided the call to serve God in this capacity. I myself recall the feelings of revulsion that swept over me when I considered going to work as an overseas missionary. I found myself recalling the horror stories I had heard. White men and women going to Africa and Asia and setting up for themselves little kingdoms in Jesus' name. I heard that these people even to this day continued to exploit people of color in order to live a good life in a kind of post-colonial era, having all of the good parts of the land.

I recalled pictures of Africans carrying heavy loads on their heads, sweating in the hot, humid malaria–infested jungles. They carried pianos in the hot, humid, snake infested jungles so the missionary could enjoy teaching them to sing "Jesus Loves Me" while the dumb African cooked in the hut outside their home. The missionary I saw in my mind was an older white man wearing a pith helmet, being carried on a cot or chair, lifted by four sweaty black men, all smiling despite the pain of carrying this black man's burden and singing "glory, glory, glory".

This picture was revolting to my every sensibility. How could I possibly associate myself with such a group of people? How could I stoop so low as to associate myself with a culture known for its exploitation of every culture it had encountered? How could I even identify myself with knowing the same God as they did? In fact, did we know the same God? How could I justify being a missionary? Is there any precedent for missions within my own people? Are there any people of color of whom it can be said they are missionaries?

These questions troubled me, as I am sure they trouble you. We need to consider this call of carrying the Gospel of Christ to all nations. Christ has indeed been preached by many people for many reasons. Nonetheless, Christ has been preached. I can say this much in defense of my white brothers and sisters; if they had never gone, many people of the world today would have no schools, no hospitals, and no development.

It is unfortunate that in carrying Christ, many of them carried their culture also. However, in the places where I have served in missions, white missionaries, despite their shortcomings, have done tremendous good. They are binding up wounds, providing for the present, and helping nations prepare for the future. Christ is, indeed, being preached. Many of our white brothers and sisters have sacrificed their health, careers, fortune, and their lives in bringing Jesus to the nations.

All of these facts notwithstanding, where do we fit in as a people? Is it our calling as African-Americans? Are we our brother's keeper? Do we have a role in missions, or is it the responsibility only of our white cohorts in Christ?

Today's Challenge

Are we able? Do we have the ability and resources? It is often argued that indeed we are our brother's keeper, but the problems are too big at home to even begin thinking about support overseas. A woman recently approached me and said, "Dr. Johnson, as soon as I hit the lottery, I am going to send you a big donation." Others have told me that I need to approach the millionaires in our society, the rich black people for support. I think by this that they mean the Michael Jordans and Oprah Winfreys of the world. It is amazing that some Christians think that people who have never professed Christ should support the work of evangelizing the world for Christ. Is it their job to do this work? Whose calling is this? Shouldn't the Christian to whom the Bible is written, be responsible for advancing the cause of Christ?

Whose job is it to support missionaries? We somehow have the mistaken notion that we must have a million dollars to perform the work. Quite frankly, of the $4,500 per month we raise for our support, the majority comes in $10 and $20 per month shares. The average black American church with 200 members or so could easily support our work if each member gave just $22 per month. That amounts to about seventy cents per day, or the amount we spend on cigarettes, sodas, cable television and other "essentials" of life.

Jesus was very clear on this subject of big gifts. He made it clear that the widow's mite was sufficient when given with a spirit of love (Mark 12:42). The God whom we serve was able to take the little boy's fish and bread and make a meal to feed thousands (John 6:9). Why are we hoarding the little bit we have? Why is it important for us to collect so many things of this world? Don't we recognize Paul's admonition that we are becoming dung collectors (Phil. 3:8)? We are storing up things in this life and not being rich towards God (Luke 12:21). What type of legacy are we building within our homes for our children to observe and to follow?

We show our children that we only give to God's work when it is convenient and not when it is inconvenient. We show God to be a God Who only requires us to give when we have everything in our home. We show our children and the world that unless our God has blessed us in the manner we feel is comfortable, we need not worry about giving to missions.

We now show God that we can't depend on Him to provide for us if we don't provide for ourselves. We tell the non–Christian world that providing for the poor around the world is only necessary when we have enough to buy all of our stuff at Christmas. We tell the non–Christian world that it is only necessary to give to the poor when we feel we are no longer poor. We are only our brother's keeper if God gives us enough. Otherwise it is the rich man's responsibility. It is the government's job. We can always just pray and let God do the work. Unless God gives me more, I am not my brother's keeper.

I wrestled with wanting more for myself. As a boy growing up in America, I wanted for so long to know if we were the poor people. I had heard that black people were poor. It was apparent to me that I was indeed black. I knew that having more was part of the American way of life. I learned this from the television, radio, and newspapers. Everyone wanted more. Everyone deserved more. Everyone could have more if they just worked long enough and hard enough.

I bought into this American dream of having more. I felt that if I studied hard and long in school I could achieve this American dream. Unfortunately or fortunately, I later learned that it takes more than just hard work; it takes a whole lot of grace when you are of a darker hue in this nation.

God provided for me sufficient grace in the form of a godly mother, grandmother and aunt. They taught me the importance of giving more versus getting more. They taught me how important it was to give and never stressed the getting part of this American dream. My mother showed me the importance of living a life that reflected God. That reflection of God she showed me was a God who gave His best to people, not because they deserved the best but because He was able to give the best. I learned very early on that getting and having is temporary and deadly, but giving and sharing is eternal and life giving.

We never get what we deserve. Cain did not get what he deserved when he killed his brother and arrogantly approached God with the question, "Am I my brother's keeper?" It was as though he was saying to God: "Why didn't you keep an eye on him, God. After all, if You had protected him, he would be all right!" My mother and my grandmother taught me that I needed to be responsible for the poor and helpless. We visited the poor in Chicago as I was growing up.

We took them food and money. We took in the homeless at times, black soldiers and sailors who were far away from home down south and had no family in the cold, cruel cities of the north. We learned very early on that we were indeed our brother's keeper.

My learning continued as I listened to Dr. Martin Luther King, Jr., expound upon the issues of not just black America, but a world that was caught up in corruption, war, hate, and civil unrest. Dr. King brought the Vietnam conflict to the forefront of black American thought when we were more settled in wrestling with the racism we faced in our own lives. He made us see that oppression anywhere in the world is just the same as oppression on our front door step.

I have often had to be reminded of my calling to my brother. Going through school in the '60s, '70s and '80s, was indeed a long time. While studying at Lawrence University in Wisconsin, the University of Michigan Medical School, and Graduate Hospital in Philadelphia for training in surgery, I often forgot about my brother.

It is easy to focus on your own comfort or discomfort when you are in the middle of things. I am reminded of the stories of soldiers in the World War II who would lay their bodies down on the barbed wires so that other comrades could climb over them to reach the enemy. Their bodies would be sliced through by razor-sharp pieces of metal and they would die in order that their brothers could defeat the enemy. They saw it was their duty to keep their brother. They laid aside their own discomfort, their very lives, to help accomplish the greater good of saving the nation of their brothers. It is easy to forget this in our times of discomfort.

As I finished training in surgery in Philadelphia, I shut out the horrors of the world around me and began to focus on me, myself and I. What did I want in life? What did I need in life? After all, don't I deserve more? I've been poor for so long!

That is our theme song as a people today. Don't we deserve more? Of course we do. Cain did not get all he deserved either, did he? What more did Cain deserve? Cain deserved hell. What more do we deserve? We deserve hell. But God who is rich in mercy for His great love for which He loved us, even when we were dead in our sins, hath quickened us together with Christ (Eph 2:4-5). God did not give us what we deserve; He gave us His only Son as the only way to eternal life.

But Lord, we have been poor for so long. We've been down for so long Lord. Don't you see our sad estate? Lord, give us more! We prayed for more. We prayed for freedom from slavery, the whip of the master, and the vicious reprisal of former slave owners after the Civil War. We prayed for relief from Jim Crow segregation, for jobs, and for voting rights. We prayed for fair employment, equal representation in government, fair courts, and good schools. These are important and necessary things. We need these things to survive.

As I came to the realization that I was given the privileges I had not for myself, but to give to others, my priorities started to change. Why had all of those people suffered for so long in order for me to get to where I am today? Right now, I admit people to hospitals and operate on those people in the very hospitals that 30 years ago I could not be treated in myself. Why has God given me such a legacy today? I believe He knew I would wake up one day and remember I am indeed my brother's keeper. God wants us to wake up today and remember that in the midst of all of our struggles, we are our brother's keeper.

Life in Other Places

You might ask, "Is the cost of living cheaper in Kenya?" I would answer, "Yes and no." What we consider to be essentials do not often figure into the Kenyan economy. There are many people in Kenya who have yet to board a motorized vehicle of any form. There are few homes in Kenya with electricity or indoor plumbing. There are few families having such luxuries as beds, blankets and pillows. The very idea of eating more than one meal per day is a luxury to many people in Kenya today, and very often that meal consists of nothing more than a handful of cornmeal. The newspapers of Kenya at the end of 1998 related stories of whole families and communities starving to death. Is the cost of living cheaper in Kenya? The life expectancy of Kenyans has dropped below 50 years of age. Living may be cheaper, but life is, too.

Life is cheaper in many parts of the world. so we turn off our cable television because we don't want to see just how cheap it is. As we in black America boast of the fact that African-American-owned companies that earned more than $32 billion in 1992, we continue to ignore the plight of a world that is facing economic meltdown. As we boast of spending close to $4 billion on foods and beverages from black-owned companies and continue to suffer from obesity, hypertension, diabetes, heart disease, and gallstones (all diseases from overeating) we resist the pictures of people huddled around a pot of boiled grass and tree leaves in Sudan, trying to feed their starving children.

We flush our toilets with cleaner water than most people of the world are drinking today. We buy $150 sneakers to wear to a $15 movie and eat $5 worth of popcorn and candy for a night on the town, while the average family in the world is trying to find a way to make a living for a day in the village. We take chances with our money, spending more on lotteries and casinos as a people, while most women in the world are taking a chance with their life even getting pregnant. They don't know if they will survive the pregnancy without a doctor in the village. In Nigeria, the oil-rich nation of West Africa, a woman who gets pregnant takes her life in her hands. If she becomes pregnant in January of this year with 100,000 other women, the likelihood is that 3,000 of them will die in pregnancy. Compare that to 9 out of 100,000 women who die during pregnancy in the U.S.

Parents in many parts of Kenya won't even take a chance at naming a child before two years of age because it might die of hunger or diarrhea. We scratch out the lucky Lotto number at the convenience store full of food, while they scratch the dust in the ground looking for food and water. Who has the better chance of winning? We lose at the lottery that day and go on to buy a Coke and a bag of chips. They lose at looking for food and water and go on to boil some grass and leaves or meat from a diseased cow that died in the field.

According to the 1996 U.S. census report, there are 34.2 million black people in America. The median income was $26,520 for that period. That means that the average black worker made in one year approximately what the average Kenyan would make in about 70 years, almost two lifetimes. Not two years, two lifetimes! The average Kenyan is paid a salary of $300 per year.

Consider also the persecution going on in Sudan. Farouk Aman, for instance, a 17-year-old boy living in southern Sudan, is a Christian. His chance of living to age 30 is very small since Christians in Southern Sudan are being chased on foot for hundreds of miles and executed by having their throats slit by their Muslim enemies. Their children are running into the hills to escape their Muslim captors and yet are being sold into slavery today, while we in black America boast that our black-owned car dealers sell over $6 billion per year of products we don't even produce. We would not walk the distance to work that these people are forced to run for their lives, yet we continue to try to buy the finest autos and ride in the latest style because we want to keep up with the Joneses.

Our brother is, of course, not just in Africa. God has never called us the brotherhood of Africans. We get sentimental and misty-eyed about helping out the poor African brother. We romanticize about the great kings and empires of Africa, forgetting that in order to have kings sitting on great thrones, there had to be some little people sitting in little outhouses. We have made Africa out to be a continent of nothing but great things when the Bible is quite clear that there is wickedness in every heart and every corner of the world.

Ps. 14:2-3 tells us that God looked down from heaven upon the children of men to see if there were any who did understand and seek God. They are all gone aside, they are all together become filthy; there is none that doeth good, no, not one. Even Africa at its glory was nothing but filthy rags, just as the rest of the world is without Jesus Christ as Savior and Lord.

We are not called just to Africa. We, as members of the body of Christ, are called to the world in need of the Savior. We are called not just to the materially impoverished of Africa, but the spiritually impoverished of Asia and Europe as well. Our brother is anyone who is in need of the Gospel of Christ. God would not give His only Son to accomplish such a limited activity as evangelizing Africa.

"For where your treasure is…"

God has given us all that we need to meet the needs of our brothers and sisters around the world. We have more than 9,000 physicians and tens of thousands of nurses who claim African descent. There are lawyers, architects, builders, teachers, preachers, artists, and entertainers by the tens of thousands, many of whom call Christ Lord and Savior and claim African descent.

A recent report in the *Philadelphia Inquirer* noted that more than 89,000 African-Americans graduate from college every year. When do we say we have enough education to help our brother? If we claim to know Him, He admonishes us in Luke 6:46 for calling Him "Lord" but not doing the things He says we should do. Jesus tells us that if we love Him, we will keep His commandments (John 14:15).

What is the black church doing in missions today? This is one of the most embarrassing points to be mentioned. One of the problems in the black church is our perspective on affirmative action. We don't mind affirmative action when it comes to our getting what we deserve from the government. However, when it comes to doing our fair share in missions, we feel the pie is too small to share. We don't want the "pie" of our income and members to be shared with some other ministries in some other place. Our pastors have the idea that if they support ministries other than those that are at the front door, they won't have enough money to place out a new welcome mat. We want to look good in the community. We want people to come to our church and note that the ministry is prospering and doing well. We feel we can't do that and support ministries overseas.

The typical African-American church budget might read something like this: "Church ministry to itself, 65%; building and maintenance, 26%; emergency fund, 4%; funds going outside of the church, 5%; of this, 4.2% for denominational expenses; United Negro College Fund, 0.4%; classic home missions, 0.4%; global Missions, 0%." This is an example drawn from a church in Tennessee. The total budget was $120,000 with a membership of 100-200 members.[1] More money is spent on the men's breakfasts and women's auxiliaries in the typical black church than is spent on the primary call of going into all of the world to win souls for the kingdom.

The African Methodist Episcopal, or AME Church, reported on its 8,000 congregations with 3.5 million members. As of 1993, the total overseas ministry income was $250,000. This represents seven cents per member per year or approximately $31 per church per year. The National Baptist Convention of the USA in 1992 was giving 40 cents per church member per year. When the cost of inflation is factored, this represents a 22 percent decline over 41 years since 1951.[2]

It is obvious that we as black people have put our money where our hearts are. The average amount spent on entertainment by black people in 1993 as recorded by the U.S. Department of Commerce is $772 yearly, per consumer. Compare this to a total of 22 cents we spend per year on missions as a people of Jesus Christ. Just where are our hearts and where are our treasures?

What are His commandments? Are we our brother's keeper? Who is my brother? "Who is my neighbor?," the rich young ruler asked Jesus in Luke 10:29. "Just who am I supposed to help, Lord?" Jesus responded to the man's question by reminding him that anyone in need was his neighbor. The man really didn't want to know the answer. Jesus told him to go and sell all he had and give to the poor and that he would find treasure in heaven.

The man went away crying because he had collected a lot of stuff and couldn't see selling it to meet the needs of the poor. Similarly, we really don't want to hear the answer to the question; "Am I my brother's keeper?" We are afraid we might leave the room in tears, too.

Conclusion

There is no getting around the fact that we are our brother's keeper. We have a call on our lives. If we claim Christ, we cannot avoid this call. Jesus was quite clear on this. He never said to wait until you have enough to satisfy your own desires and needs. Jesus never taught us to seek our own comfort first and then meet the needs of others less fortunate. Instead, He reminded us that our lives do not consist in the abundance of things we possess, but in being rich towards God (Luke 12:21).

Jesus tells us quite clearly that we are to be the "Word made flesh." We are the only Bible and the only Jesus some people of the world will ever see. Jesus made one visit here. When He comes back, it won't be to work miracles, forgive sins, or to call people to repentance. When Jesus comes back it will be to call the righteous home and judge the ungodly.

In the meantime, I am my brother's keeper and I need to be the word made flesh in my brother's presence. Jesus has sent us to work the miracles. He wants us to do just what He proclaimed as His own mission to preach the Gospel to the poor, to heal the broken-hearted, to preach deliverance to the captives and recovering of sight to the blind, to set at liberty them that are bruised (Luke 4:18). This is our calling! We are the Lord living among those who have yet to know Him as Lord. We are the Christ that the people of the world need to see.

I have given you a brief overview of missions. I have given you a few of the many details of the history of mission activities and mission life. We have reviewed what has happened in missionary activities overseas and here at home, both for those of us who claim African heritage and those who claim European lineage. We have seen that missionary activity has been a mixed blessing at times, even a mixed curse to many nations as the will of the strong has been imposed on the weak in the name of Christ.

We have learned that early white mission boards were a hindrance to our involvement because of their lack of understanding and fear of us. We are a people who understand what suffering is about, and our experience can minister to those who suffer around the world. But we've bought into the American dream of financial prosperity thinking that we deserve more, and we've missed God's desire to bless all peoples with the Gospel.

We have examined "Am I my brother's keeper?" and have no doubt about the answer. We have also learned that we have the resources to help our brother. Our brother is drowning in sin, and we dare not wait on the shore and yell for someone else to save him. We have it in our means to save our brother. We cannot stand on the shore and ask the World Bank, International Money Fund, United Nations, or U.S. military to save our brothers in Asia, Latin America, Europe and Africa. We are our brother's keeper.

We cannot say it is for one part of the body to do the saving. We, as the foot, cannot stand by and tell the liver to go save that drowning brother. We, as the hand, cannot stand by and tell the big toe to go pull that brother out of the water. We have to join in as the Body of Christ and save the brother from drowning. Our brother needs the whole Body to save him, not just the yellow part, nor just the red part, not just the white part or the black part.

We are our brother's keeper. Questioning our calling likens us to Cain who lived forever with a mark on his head as he neglected what God had given him to do. We don't want to bear the mark of a murderer. We want to bear the mark of God's salvation and His calling on our lives. That mark and that calling distinguish each of us as our brother's keeper.

Endnotes

1. James W. Sutherland, *African-American Underrepresentation in Intercultural Missions: Perceptions of Black Missionaries and the Theory of Survival/Security*, Ph.D. dissertation, Deerfield, IL: Trinity Evangelical Divinity School,1998, p.112.
2. www.rmni.org/africanamericanmissions.html

The Role of the African-American Church in Global Evangelization

Vaughn Walston

I t has been said that the African-American church is a sleeping giant. We have significant potential to do great things, but we are blinded by our drowsiness. We are involved in a great many things, but sometimes loose sight of the goal for which we exist. Many of our churches are on the forefront of preaching the Gospel and taking a stand for Christ. Others are heavily involved in community and economic development, building a foundation for our survival in our own neighborhoods. Yet we remain like a sleeping giant unawakened to our task of taking the Gospel in word and deed to the world.

The African-American church has both the resources and manpower to lend a strong voice in the missions world. Indeed, many say that African-Americans are in a position to become one of the most effective mission forces in the world today.

In this article, I will consider the role of the whole church in global evangelization.

Role of the Church

Before talking about mobilization, we must be clear on the task to which the church should be mobilized. Often we have great plans, but to reach inappropriate objectives. What is the purpose of the church? Why does this organic institution of God's people exist?

Part of the purpose of the church is to glorify God by *equipping* the saints for the work of the ministry. "And He gave some *as* apostles, and some *as* prophets, and some *as* evangelists, and some *as* pastors and teachers, for the equipping of the saints for the work of service, to the building up of the body of Christ;" Eph 4:11-12. Every member should be *growing* toward maturity in Christ and every member should be using their *giftedness* toward the completion of the *Great Commission* (Eph 4:13-16).[1] From these verses in Ephesians, we will look at four principles concerning the role of the church; equipping, growth toward maturity, giftedness, and the Great Commission. We will consider how these principles apply in the African-American church.

Equipping

Church leaders are not to function as dictators, but as equippers. Leaders do not do all the work, they equip the body to do the work (Eph 4:11,12). Since we are a body, we

Vaughn Walston is a missions mobilizer with The Impact Movement, a ministry of Campus Crusade for Christ. He earned his Master of Divinity in Missions at Columbia International Universtiy in 2000. He and his wife, Rebecca, reside in Orlando, FL.

all have functions. Rather than watching a few parts perform their function, we should all be set in motion to accomplish our unique tasks (1Cor 12:18).

Paul takes it a step further with Timothy. He admonishes Timothy to develop multiplying leaders. "And the things you have heard from me in the presence of many witnesses, these commit to faithful men, who will be able to teach others also," 2 Tim 2:2. Everyone will not be a leader, just as all are not to be teachers (James 3:1). But leaders and disciplers are to multiply themselves in order that the church may grow and mature. Everyone is to operate in his or her giftedness.

In the African-American church, equipping is usually accomplished through the preaching of the pastor and the Sunday school program. If we are going to see a fervor for missions in the African-American church, then it also must be integrated into those two primary components of the church. The education ministry of the church must include the basic equipping for ministry and such a ministry must include taking the gospel to the whole world, Matt 28:18-20.

Growth Toward Maturity

Ephesians 4:1 admonishes us to walk in a manner worthy of the calling with which we have been called. Ephesians 4:13 and 4:15 speak of us growing to maturity in Christ. Maturity does not come independently, but through the ministry of God's leaders and through unified use of our gifts to build one another (Eph 4:16).

Paul labored with and for the Colossians that they would mature. "And we proclaim Him, admonishing every man and teaching every man with all wisdom, that we may present every man complete in Christ. And for this purpose also I labor, striving according to His power, which mightily works within me," Col 1:28,29. In this capacity, he served to nurture the body. Nurture is a necessary part of bringing the church to maturity.

As we consider mobilizing the African-American church for global evangelization, we must consider how we are helping the body to mature in Christ so that we can be prepared to serve outside of the church in the community and world.

Giftedness

God has gifted each member of the body of Christ, the church, (1Cor 12:4-7). These gifts are often discovered in the context of the community of faith and discipleship. It is all our jobs to encourage others to operate within their giftedness. In discipleship, we should provoke others to find and operate within their giftedness.

The gifts given to all are for the edification of the church (1Cor 14:12). The parts of the body are to work together complementing one another to the completion of the task before us (1Cor 12:12-27). Too often, we use our giftedness in contrast rather than to complement. This causes the whole body to suffer (1Cor 12:26).

As the African-American church is involved in the community, we often deploy our gifts to aid our neighbors in community development. This same energy can be developed and channeled to the world. We have much to offer.

Great Commission

The Great Commission gives us the imperative to make disciples.

And Jesus came up and spoke to them, saying, "All authority has been given to Me in heaven and on earth. Go therefore and make disciples of all the nations, baptizing them in the name of the Father and the Son and the Holy Spirit, teaching them to observe all that I commanded you; and lo, I am with you always, even to the end of the age." Matt 28:18-20

The work of evangelism is central to this task, but it is not exclusive. After evangelism, a new convert must be incorporated into the body. They should be baptized into Christ and taught how to grow in Christ. This is the task of making disciples. It does not matter which terminology we use to define the process as long as we understand the whole process to be necessary in obeying the commission.

Before we can effectively make disciples of the nations, we must learn to be disciples and to make disciples of our neighbors. Many African-American churches have gotten away from this original charge and tend to focus more on social issues. As we focus on the "commission", the social issues will not be forgotten, but there will be a stronger foundation from which to address them. In order to fully engage the "commission", we must engage the world (all nations) with the message of the Gospel.

Conclusions

We have looked at the purpose of the church and the biblical mandate for reaching the world and making disciples of all nations. The whole church needs to be mobilized to accomplish the task.

Endnotes:

1 Adapted from Dwight Smith, *Mobilizing and Multiplying Local Churches*, (Saturation Church Planting International, 1998), 14.

African-Americans'
Historical Presence
in Missions

Black American Missionaries In Africa: 1821-1925

William Seraile

This paper will deal with the contribution of some black Americans as representatives of both white and black mission boards. It is impossible in the scope of this paper to cover completely the role of black missionaries in Africa. For a comprehensive coverage, readers are urged to consult the published Ph.D. dissertation of Wilbur Christian Harr: *The Negro as an American Protestant Missionary in Africa.*

The precise number of black missionaries working in Africa has never been documented. However, their overall influence was substantial as verified in contemporary missionary journals [for 1972].

Of the black missionaries, perhaps Lott Carey enjoys the most fame. Carey was a former slave who became interested in religious activities. His interest in the plight of Africa led to the formation of the African Missionary Society in Richmond, VA, in 1815.[1] When asked why he wanted to give up the comforts of America for Africa, Carey replied, "I am an African... I wish to go to a country where I shall be estimated by my merits--not by my complexion and I feel bound to labour for my suffering race."[2] Before his departure for Africa, Carey exclaimed, "I long to preach to the poor Africans the way of life and salvation."

In 1821, his expectations were achieved for he was sent to Africa by the American Baptist Missionary Union. Although this was a renowned white organization, a century later, Miles M. Fisher, adamantly contended that Carey was the first representative of a Negro missionary organization.[3] Fisher's viewpoint is a minority one, substantiated by shaky evidence.

Upon his arrival in West Africa, Carey established a mission among the Mandingoes in Sierra Leone. There he conducted religious services for those Africans liberated from slave ships. In the following year, Carey and a black reverend, Colin Teague, began a mission in Liberia under the auspices of the American Baptist Missionary Union.[4] Evidently Carey was an outstanding proselytizer, for according to a contemporary historian of the American Baptist Missions, Carey "commended the Gospel to their hearts [natives and emigrants] and consciences with unusual success." But although Carey was a great preacher he managed to have only six genuine converts by 1823.

William Seraile is a graduate of Teach College and Columbia University, and he was Lecturer at Herbert H. Lehman College in New York City. He formerly served for two years in the Peace Corps in Ethiopia.

From *The Social Studies*, Vol. LXIII, No. 5, Oct. 1972. Used by permission.

In 1828, Carey met an untimely death. By then, his Monrovia congregation had increased to 100 members. Undoubtedly the vast majority were emigrants who brought their religious faith from America, for Liberia was a hostile country. The explosion that killed Carey brought sorrow to his small congregation. The Richmond African Society saw fit to eulogize him: "through his instrumentality a considerable church has been collected together which seems to be in a prosperous and growing condition."[5] Evidently this was true, for the congregation at Monrovia grew to 200 under Teague's command.

Daniel Coker was another black American who departed for Africa in 1821. His arrival marked the beginning of mission work for the African Methodist Episcopalians.[6] Coker's tenure in West Africa ended with his death in 1846. His 25 years' service was unusual since many missionaries quickly succumbed in the malaria-infested colony of Sierra Leone.

Another hardy missionary was James M. Priest who journeyed to Liberia in 1843 under the auspices of the American Colonization Society. The Presbyterian Church acknowledged his services and upon his death in 1883 eulogized his "forty years of exemplary Christian life."[7]

Carey's missionary endeavors made him the most famous of the early 19th century missionaries, but the latter half of the century, honors would go to William Sheppard. Beginning in 1887, Sheppard "consistently urged the Presbyterian Executive Committee of Foreign [sic] Missions to send him to Africa."[8] His persistence paid off, for in April, 1891, Sheppard and Samuel Lapsley, a white missionary, started a mission at Luebo, Congo.

The Presbyterians were pleased with their integrated team. In 1903, Dr. Williams of the Upper Kongo [Congo] Mission wrote to the *Missionary Review of the World*, "in connection with our Luebo Presbyterian Mission we have eight Negro Missionaries.... We have never had a word of complaint from our white Missionaries nor from the natives concerning the acceptability of the Negro Missionaries. Mr. Sheppard is a fellow of the Royal Geographic Society, and the other Negro Missionaries all have fairly good education, one of them being a physician."[9]

The tragic death of Mr. Lapsley left the guidance of the Luebo Mission primarily under Sheppard's control. As Sheppard discovered, it was no easy task to convert people to Christianity. In fact, it was four years before a single convert was made. Miraculously, five men were converted and trained to be native missionaries.[10] Although the figures were not documented, Sheppard stated in 1917 that there were 15,000 church members in the Upper Congo, as well as 160 native ministers in training.[11] These figures do seem remarkable and probably account for Brussels and London considering Mr. Sheppard to be one of the greatest of African missionaries.

Another missionary of note was Samuel Crowther. Although not an American, he is worth a brief description. Born into the Yoruba tribe of Nigeria, Crowther was captured in an 1821 slave raid. He was liberated on the high seas by a British slave runner and taken to Sierra Leone. After adopting the "white man's religion," Crowther began to perform mission work along the Niger River in Nigeria. His work was so exemplary that in 1864 the United Church of England and Ireland made him a bishop.[12] This is, indeed, a major feat for an African who conceivably could have lived and died as a plantation slave.

Although brutally treated as slaves and denied equality as freemen [in U.S.], blacks were given much responsibility in mission work. Even though their missionary work was exemplary, it must be noted that the majority of black missionaries were sent to Africa by white missionary boards. And not all black missionaries were men. In 1835, the Protestant Episcopal Church appointed Mr. and Mrs. James M. Thompson to African mission work.[13] Mrs. Thompson proved to be hardy in her own right: she survived her husband and served faithfully until her death in 1865.

The dominance of black missionaries began to show prominently in the Protestant missions' overseas staffs. In 1935, Methodists sent blacks to work along side the new black colonists. In less than 20 years, the entire

Methodist mission staff in Africa was black. Evidently this monopoly was based on the Foreign Mission Board's decision in 1838 that "if properly educated...there must be many [blacks who] would make efficient missionaries to the lands of their forefathers."[14]

This belief was held also by the Presbyterians, for in 1868 they reported a mission staff of 13 in Liberia, 12 of whom were Black.

Even Southern Baptists subscribed to this theory. They believed that whites should remain in Africa only long enough to train blacks to accept responsibilities. This became a reality in the late 1850s when the Foreign Mission Board reported 19 missionaries in Liberia and all were black.[15]

In 1853, the bandwagon grew heavier when Bishop Payne of the American Protestant Episcopal Church admitted that "Africa must be evangelized chiefly by her own children."[16] In that year, nearly all the missionaries and teachers in Liberia were blacks who had control of the schools and churches and who determined the "direction of the intellectual, moral, and religious training of the youth."[17]

Less one be misled, blacks were not granted the privilege of doing mission work because they possessed superior intellect, but because whites thought they possessed greater resistance to the malaria infested climate of West Africa. A typical comment of the times was the one offered by Mr. Sherman, a white missionary, who was obliged to leave Liberia because of poor health. In his words, there "is a fearful mortality among African missionaries. If the white man cannot live [there] to evangelize [Africans]... educated colored men... must... be the only instrumentality employed in the conversion of [Africans]."[18]

In 1868, Sen. Frelinghuysen of NJ said that whites could not survive in Liberia, therefore, "it is left to the [black man] to enjoy the honor" of civilizing and Christianizing Africans.[19] On the eve of Appomattox, Rev. P. D. Gurley wrote "the [African] climate is fatal to the white man." Gurley suggested that "if Africa is... to be redeemed, it must be through... colored men [for] past experience proves colonies of colored people are the only means

whereby the blessings of the Christian people can be carried to... Africa."[20]

Obviously, many blacks, too, succumbed to malaria, but evidently enough survived to perpetuate a belief that blacks were better suited to the adverse climate. This is indicated by the Massachusetts Colonization Society reporting in 1893 that the vast majority of missionaries in Liberia "are not men... sent out as missionaries, but men or children of men, whom we have sent out as emigrants".[21] In that same year, the American Colonization Society reported that of the 52 ordained ministers in Liberia, only two were sent from the United States as missionaries; the rest were furnished by Liberia.

Liberia proved to be a fertile ground for proselytizing blacks. Mr. Duryee, a white man, addressed the American Colonization Society in 1882 with these words: "the banner of the cross is there upheld... by Negroes themselves."[22] The key words of his address were "[a] church with pastor and people of the same race is worth a hundred holding on to some foreign missionary as its only source of life, and ready to sink into... heathenism if disease strikes the exile down."[23]

Although words of praise came from many diverse religious bodies, Africa was not being entirely evangelized by black men. We must remember that the majority of blacks were sent by white mission boards, thus they controlled the number sent and determined the sites for mission work. In this context, Liberia played a large role in Black missionary work. But this was expected since Liberia was a black republic. The source of this praise must be examined also. Much of it came from the national or from state colonization societies. These organizations had a vital interest in the achievement of black emigrants. Consequently, the role of the black missionary was highly publicized.

After 1900 Jim Crowism, lynchings, and disfranchisement became a way of life for black Americans. Not surprisingly, mistrust and hostility were directed towards black missionaries. No longer were white mission boards full of praise for blacks. Opposition to black missionaries became so widespread that the Negro Mission Boards lamented "it has not been a matter of placing [a Negro] with a preponderance of personnel of another race. Rather, it has been the problem of securing opportunity and representation adequate for a constructive contribution to the Christianization of Africa."[24] Blacks were acceptable to Methodists, Presbyterians, and Southern Baptists during the 19th century, but by 1910, the Sudan United Mission's hostility towards the thought of using blacks as African missionaries was typical of the white missionary boards. By 1920 the honeymoon had ended and the marriage was dead. In that year, the president of the Lott Carey Mission Board lamented that "we are shut out from large areas by the strong arm of human laws." He emphasized, "We find little welcome in our fatherland save in the Republic of Liberia."

Why the turnabout? One answer was politics. Belgium, that admirer of William Sheppard, admitted its reluctance to admit black missionaries into the Congo—"We must keep Garveyism out of Africa." [Marcus] Garvey, who said "Africa for Africans," created a fear in the minds of whites. What if black missionaries slipped in their political philosophy between morning prayers and afternoon catechism?

Garvey wanted the British to give up their West African territories. Of course, they would not, but they wanted to keep all potential troublemakers out. In 1925, Dr. J. F. East, Corresponding Secretary of the National Baptist Convention (Black), stated that the British feared American blacks educating and Christianizing Africans because the African would advance as quickly as had the black American since the Civil War. Naturally this would jeopardize the colonial system.

The fear of black Americans stirring up latent political desires was indicated when the Union of South Africa refused entry permits to black missionaries unless a white man controlled the mission, thus curtailing any political activity on the part of black missionaries. Although Garvey was considered a buffoon by many Americans, black and white, his philosophy was frightening to African colonial governments. They feared that black missionaries would preach the gospel of Marcus Garvey instead of St. Matthew to Africans and cause agitation among the oppressed blacks in Africa.

Although politics was the primary reason for excluding black missionaries, some white mission boards raised the question of "whether American Protestant Missionary Societies can send Negroes to Africa and accomplish missionary service." In light of the black missionary's past contribution to African missionary work, the fear behind the question was unfounded. As long as qualified blacks were sent to Africa, the fear was an imaginary, instead of a real one.

The issue of continual widespread use of black American missionaries, in light of Garveyism and Pan-Africanism, was placed on the agenda of the 1926 International Missionary Conference. Dr. Hope, black President of Morehouse College and a delegate of the American Baptist Foreign Mission Society, stated "those who have a desire to give service to Africa ought to be given a chance."[25] The plea was a simple one, yet most of the white missionaries present felt that it was not the right time to press African colonial governments to admit more Black missionaries. However, a small minority insisted that Africa had hard-working Blacks whose actions might pave the way for others.

Prior to adjournment, the Conference drew up six recommendations, two of which were pertinent. First, blacks should be "encouraged by missionary societies to play an important part in the evangelization, medical service, and education of Africa, and that the number of their missionaries should be increased as qualified candidates are available." Second, "assistance should be given by white missionaries to qualified American Negroes working in Africa... of the same missionary status [society]."

Unfortunately, colonial governments were not about to alter their viewpoint. Save for Liberia, black missionaries, like black jockeys, were to pass into history.

In conclusion, black missionaries made a contribution to African mission work as individuals instead of in a collective sense. It appears that blacks met resistance when they began to arrive in Africa as members of black mission boards. The black mission boards became active during the rise of Garveyism and the culminating fear over his philosophy provided colonial governments with an excuse to exclude black missionaries from Africa.

Evidence indicates that the black missionary was extremely active in Liberia and Sierra Leone. His mission work in Angola, South Africa, and the Congo was sporadic. A useful guide is that where the climate was suitable for the European or white American, the black missionary was mainly excluded. This accounts for the virtual non-placement of black missionaries in the highlands of East Africa. During certain periods of time, the black missionary was in dominance, but at no time was this dominance any more than a regional one.

Endnotes

1 Archibald Alexander, *A History of Colonization of the Western Coast of Africa*, Ayer Company Publishers, Inc., p. 243.

2 Ibid., p. 244.

3 Miles Mark Fisher. "Lott Carey, The Colonizing Missionary," The Journal of Negro History. 7:381, (October, 1922).

4 David Christy. *Ethiopia: Her Gloom and Glory*, self published pamphlet, 1857, p. 200.

5 Alexander, op. cit., p. 254.

6 L. L. Berry, *A Century of Missions of the African Methodist Episcopal Church: 1840-1940*, p. 7.

7 Wilbur Christian Harr, *The Negro as an American Protestant Missionary in Africa*, Chicago, IL: Univerty of Chicago, 1945, Ph.D. dissertation, microfilm, p. 30.

8 Ruth M. Slade, *English-Speaking Missions in the Congo Independent State: 1878-1908*, p. 104.

9 "The Negro as a Missionary," *The Missionary Review of the World*, 26:946, (December, 1903).

10 William H. Sheppard, "An African's Work for Africa," *The Missionary Review of the World*, 29, (October, 1906).

11 William H. Sheppard, *Presbyterian Pioneers in The Congo*, p. 151.

12 Jesse Page, *Samuel Crowther: The Slave Boy Who Became Bishop of the Niger*, p. 30.

13 Harr, op. cit., p. 22.

14 Ibid., p. 29.

15 Christy, op. cit., p. 203.

16 Ibid., p. 206.

17 Ibid., p. 208.

18 Ibid., p. 203.

19 *Fifty-First Annual Report of the American Colonization Society*, (January 20-21, 1873), p. 22.

20 John H. B. Latrobe, and Phinehas D. Gurley, *American Colonization Society Addresses,1864*, p. 15.

African Missions and
The African-American Christian Churches

Sylvia M. Jacobs

Sylvia Marie Jacobs was born in 1946 in OH. She received her BS and MBA from Wayne State University, MI, and her Ph.D. from Howard University, DC. Her memberships include: Delta Sigma Theta, Association for the Study of African American Life and ASALH History, Southeastern Regional Seminar in African Studies Association of Black Women Historians, National Council of Negro Women, Inc., Southern Poverty Law Center, Committee of the Status of Minority Historians and Minority History, Organization of American Historians, and Organization of African Studies Association.

She has received numerous achievements and awards for her works.

Sylvia Jacobs resides with her family in Durham, NC and is Professor, Department of History, North Carolina Central University, NC.

From Encyclopedia of African-American Religions. *New York: Garland Publishing, 1993. Eds. Murphy, Meton, and Ward, pp. 10-23. Used by permission*

At the beginning of the 19th century, American Protestant missionary societies began to focus on foreign mission work. White Congregationalists, Baptists, Methodists, Episcopalians, and Presbyterians all had organized foreign mission societies by 1840. The first foreign mission society in the U.S. was the interdenominational American Board of Commissioners for Foreign Missions, formed in 1810. However, with the rise of denominationalism, all the non-Congregationalists withdrew from the ABCFM and founded their own separate mission societies.

A number of American mission societies began to support mission work in Africa in the early 19th century. By that date, Africa was seen as a legitimate area for proselytizing and American-based churches established mission stations there. American boards regarded Africans as "uncivilized and un-Christian" and they sought financial support from congregations at home by evoking a picture of the ignorant, unclothed, diseased, and generally benighted African.

The idea that "civilization" meant Westernization enjoyed a special vogue in mid-19th century missiology. Christianity and "civilization" were inseparable. Racially inferior Africans could never attain the heights of Western "civilization"; they might receive all the spiritual blessings of Christianity but still remain within their own inferior culture. Therefore, any study of Christianity in Africa since 1800 must involve an analysis of these perceptions.

During the American Protestant missionary movement in Africa, black Americans assumed a role in the evangelization of Africa. Many African Americans accepted the contemporary theory of "providential design," the idea that blacks had been brought to America for slavery so that they might be Christianized and "civilized" to return to Africa with the light of "civilization." Basically, African Americans endorsed the Western image of Africa as a "Dark Continent."

In the latter half of the 19th century European governments shifted their interest in Africa from the slave trade to colonization. Hence, the late 19th and early 20th centuries witnessed the partitioning of Africa with the subsequent establishment of European colonial rule. During this period, a small segment of the African American community addressed themselves to the issue of the impact of European colonialism in Africa. Generally, they concluded that as long as the interests and welfare of Africans were being considered, European activities on the continent could be beneficial to Africa and Africans.

Black Americans also supported mission work in Africa, believing that this religious and cultural exposure would help make the continent more acceptable to the world. Neither the black masses nor their leaders have ever forgotten their ancestral homeland and during the height of the missionary movement, black churches expressed their interest in the continent by sending missionaries there, just as white churches were doing. After 1870 African-Americans could not resist the call to serve, and black churches became involved in African mission work. Although African-Americans were assigned to fields other than Africa by both white and black church boards, the majority saw their destiny in Africa and volunteered to work there.

The earliest plan contemplated for the use of black American missionaries in Africa was the one proposed by Samuel Hopkins of Newport, RI. Soon after his installation in 1770, Hopkins, a prominent clergy of the First Congregational Church of Newport, formulated a plan that contained both missionary and emigration features. Actually, the missionary tradition had its roots in the emigration movement. Hopkins' plan called for the selection and education of American free blacks as Christian ministers who would then emigrate to Africa and teach Africans the doctrines and duties of Christianity.

Two candidates, both members of the First Congregational Church, were selected to be trained for this purpose and went to Princeton University (Princeton, NJ) to study theology in order to prepare themselves as missionaries. With the British occupation of Newport during the American Revolutionary War, Hopkins' pastoral work was interrupted. He was unable to put his plan into effect. After 1791 Hopkins sought to renew his plan, but his death in 1803 ended his emigration missionary dreams. At that time none of his emigrant-missionaries had completed their education. However, it is believed that at least two of his candidates later went to Liberia under a similar plan of the American Colonization Society (ACS).

On December 28, 1816, the constitution of the ACS was adopted. The ACS was dedicated to repatriating blacks to Africa but it also was committed to African mission work. The philosophy of the ACS carried a strong missionizing theme. As such, a free black minister of the African Methodist Episcopal Church (AME) emigrating to Liberia became the first African American missionary in Africa.

On February 6, 1820, Daniel Coker, from Baltimore, MD, along with 90 others, left New York, NY, harbor, on the ship the *Elizabeth*, as the first party of emigrants sent by the ACS to what would become Liberia. Coker was sent to Africa, a year before Lott Carey, as a missionary with a subsidy from the Maryland Colonization Society. Daniel Coker was the first African American to leave for Africa with a clear missionary purpose, although he had not been appointed by any particular missionary board. Ten days after the ship left New York, Coker organized the first foreign branch of the AME Church on board the ship. Coker first settled in Liberia but later transferred to Sierra Leone.

In 1815 Lott Carey helped to establish the Richmond African Baptist Missionary Society and was elected as its recording secretary. Carey, born a slave, purchased his freedom and eventually became a leader in the First Baptist Church of Richmond. On May 1, 1819, Carey was appointed as a missionary by the General Missionary Convention of the Baptist Denomination in the United States of America for Foreign Missions. It had been formed in 1814, but soon was known as the Triennial Convention because it met every three years. The Triennial Convention was later renamed the American Baptist Foreign Mission Society and is today the American Baptist Churches in the U.S.A. This appointment set the stage for the beginning of Baptist mission work in Africa. Carey, then, was also both an emigrant and a missionary.

The First Baptist Church of Monrovia [Liberia] was organized in Richmond, VA, on January 11, 1821 by ACS emigrants who 12 days later sailed to Africa on the *Nautilus*. The group first settled in Sierra Leone because ACS agents had not yet purchased land in Liberia. However, in 1822 they moved to

Cape Mesurado, the first settlement in Liberia and the present-day site of Monrovia. Carey established the first Baptist church in Monrovia, Providence Baptist Church.

The Methodists: Independent black-led churches began mission activity in Africa in the nineteenth century and began to appoint blacks as missionaries in their ancestral homeland. The largest number of African American missionaries sent to Africa by black boards went during the late 19th and early 20th centuries.

The AME Church was organized as a separate branch of Methodism in 1816. Its foreign mission outreach began in 1820 when Daniel Coker organized the first AME Church in Sierra Leone. That church, however, was abandoned after Coker's death. In 1822 Charles Butler was appointed the first official AME missionary but he never left the United States for his assignment. John Boggs became the earliest commissioned AME missionary to reach Africa in 1824, serving in Liberia. However, there is no available information on the extent of the work that he established.

In 1844 the General Conference of the AME Church authorized the organization of the Parent Home and Foreign Missionary Society as the central agency for the operation of missions, but the society did not begin to function actively until 1864, when a Board of Missions was established and a Secretary of Missions was elected. Ultimately, two women's auxiliaries were formed. In 1874 the Woman's Parent Mite Missionary Society was organized in Philadelphia. The Woman's Home and Foreign Missionary Society was established in South Bend, IN, in 1898 as a result of Bishop Henry McNeal Turner's visit to South Africa where he saw the need for black missionaries, and because of southern AME women's dissatisfaction with northern leadership in the Mite Missionary Society. The Woman's Parent Mite Missionary Society supported the work of the church in Haiti, Santo Domingo, Liberia, Sierra Leone, Barbados, Demarara, the Bahamas, the Virgin Islands, Trinidad, and Jamaica. The Woman's Home and Foreign Missionary Society supervised AME missions in southern Africa.

Africa was set apart as a foreign mission field by the General Conference of the AME Church in 1856 and John R. V. Morgan was appointed missionary pastor to Liberia. Little is known of his activities except that he returned to the U.S. because his work was not supported by the church.

The first permanent AME mission in Africa was established in 1878. On April 21 of that year Samuel E. Flegler sailed from Charleston to Liberia on the *Azor* with over 206 other SC emigrants. Flegler led this AME congregation to Liberia where they settled at Brewerville, sixty miles in the interior of Liberia. Their settlement marked the formal beginning of AME churches in Africa. Initially sponsored by the Morris Brown AME Church in Charleston, the Liberian AME Church eventually was recognized by the national church conference. Flegler returned to SC in 1881.

The permanent work of the AME Church in Sierra Leone began in 1886 when John Richard Frederick was appointed as the first officially sponsored AME missionary to that country. Frederick was sent to Africa by the New England Conference of the AME Church but most of his financial support was contributed by the Ohio Conference. He sailed on November 20, 1886.

Frederick was quite successful during his first few years in Sierra Leone and he soon spread his work into the interior. He was the first AME missionary to work extensively with indigenous Africans rather than with emigrants. After his arrival in Sierra Leone in 1887 he worked with educational and social welfare projects.

Frederick became friends with the West Indian emigrant Edward Blyden, who was living in Sierra Leone at the time. With Blyden and James "Holy" Johnson, Frederick helped found the Dress Reform Society, which had the goal of encouraging westernized Africans to reject European dress in favor of traditional African attire. Frederick remained one of Blyden's closest friends and was chosen to preach the sermon at Blyden's funeral in 1912.

Frederick got along well with Africans, so much so that some interior ethnic groups pleaded for him to open a mission station in their towns. He began training Africans as missionaries and also as ministers. He founded Bethel AME Church and Allen AME Church in Sierra Leone. In 1890 Frederick started AME missions at Mange and Magbele. He adjusted well to Sierra Leone and remained there for the rest of his life.

By 1897 Frederick had become disillusioned over AME commitment to support the mission in Sierra Leone. He felt that he was faced with a lack of moral and financial support from the AME Church and withdrew from the church. He joined the British Wesleyan Methodist Church.

The year after Frederick's arrival in Sierra Leone in 1887, Sarah Gorham, 56 years of age, became the first woman missionary of the AME Church appointed to a foreign field. In 1880 Gorham visited relatives who had emigrated to Liberia and she spent a year traveling throughout the country preaching and comforting the needy. It was on this trip that she became interested in African mission work. She returned to the U.S. in 1881 and settled in Boston, MA, where she joined Charles Street AME Church. In 1888 Gorham offered her services to the AME Church as a missionary. Although sponsored by the AME Woman's Parent Mite Missionary Society, most of Gorham's financial support, like John Frederick's, came from the Ohio Conference.

Soon after her arrival in Freetown, Sierra Leone, in September of 1888 Gorham traveled to Magbele, where she was active in the Allen AME Church. She worked at Magbele, 100 miles from Freetown, among Temne women and girls. It was at Magbele that she established the Sarah Gorham Mission School, which gave both religious and industrial training. In 1891 she traveled back to the U.S. to recuperate and regain her health. She later returned to Sierra Leone.

In July of 1894 Gorham was bedridden with malaria. She died on August 10 in Freetown. On her tombstone was inscribed: "She was early impressed that she should go to Africa as a missionary and that her life['s] work should be there. She crossed the ocean five times, and ended her mission on the soil and among the people she so desired to benefit."

In November of 1891 Bishop Turner reached Freetown and organized the Sierra Leone Annual Conference in the Zion AME Church. This was the first annual conference of the church established in Africa. Two weeks later he initiated the Liberia Annual Conference in Muhlenberg.

The years between 1892 and 1900 also witnessed the rise and growth of the AME Church in South Africa. The late 19th and early 20th centuries saw the emergence of the independent church movement, or Ethiopianism, in South Africa. European missionaries in South Africa unwittingly sowed the seeds of discontent among African religious leaders by refusing to promote indigenous clergy to positions of responsibility and by not heeding the African cries for self-determination in church government. During the early 1880s African evangelists began to secede from established churches in South Africa. The seeds of Ethiopianism had been sown. On November 5, 1893, Mangena Maake Mokone formed his own church, the Ethiopian Church.

In 1895 the Ethiopian Church of South Africa began negotiations for affiliation with the American-based AME Church. The Ethiopian Church believed that union with the AME Church would help them evangelize the continent of Africa. On June 19, 1896, the Ethiopian Church of South Africa became the 14th Episcopal District of the AME Church, with James Mata Dwane as its general superintendent. Bishop Turner visited the recently constituted 14th District in 1898 and ordained more than 50 AME ministers.

However, the failure of the AME Church to fund a proposed training school in the Cape Colony for educating South African AME church members, and the belief that the Ethiopian Church's absorption into the AME Church undercut the Ethiopian spirit of self-reliance led Dwane to secede from the AME Church on October 6, 1899. In 1900, Dwane's group, the Order of Ethiopia, was accepted into the Anglican Church.

In 1900 Levi Jenkins Coppin was elected the first bishop of South Africa and was assigned to the 14th Episcopal District (Cape Colony and the Transvaal). Coppin was born free in Frederick, MD, on December 24, 1848.

His mother was a very religious woman who gave him religious training and taught him to read and write. He was graduated from Protestant Episcopal Divinity School (Philadelphia, PA) in 1887. The son of AME parents, Coppin joined the church in 1865, was licensed to preach in 1876, ordained a deacon in 1879 and an elder in 1880, and elected the 13th bishop in 1900. In 1881 he married his second wife, Fanny Jackson.

Fanny M. Jackson Coppin, one of America's first black women to be graduated from college, was born a slave in Washington, DC, in 1837. After her aunt, Sarah Clark, bought her freedom, she was educated in MA and RI, then earned an A.B. degree in 1865 and an A.M. degree in 1890 from Oberlin College (Oberlin, OH). Between 1865 and 1902 she taught at and eventually became principal of the Institute for Colored Youth in Philadelphia. From 1883 to 1892 she served as president of the AME's Woman's Home and Foreign Missionary Society.

Levi Coppin first arrived in Cape Town alone on February 19, 1901, and departed for the United States on December 26. In November 1902 he returned with his wife, Fanny. Missionary headquarters were located in Cape Town, although the Coppins frequently traveled into the interior.

Levi Coppin was prohibited by the South African government from visiting the Orange Free State and Transvaal Republics, but he traveled throughout Cape Colony and into Basutoland (today Botswana) and Southern Rhodesia (today Zimbabwe) to establish missions and spread the Gospel. He married almost 100 couples and baptized over 100 adults and children. During their stay in South Africa, Fanny Coppin directed most of her attention in Cape Town and the rural areas to organizing black South African women into Women's Christian Temperance Union societies and into women's Mite Missionary Societies.

One of the permanent results of the Coppins' missionary stay in South Africa was the establishment of Bethel Institute at Cape Town. An old building was converted into a school and mission house. They left South Africa in the spring of 1904. A Fanny Jackson Coppin Girls' Hall was named in her honor at Wilberforce Institute in Evaton, South Africa.

By the beginning of the 20th century the AME Church was definitely mission-minded. The church was united in an effort to support the cause of missions in Africa and elsewhere.

The second-largest independent black Methodist denomination in the U.S. in the 19th century was the African Methodist Episcopal Zion Church (AMEZ). A conference in October 1820 officially organized the AMEZ denomination. In 1876 the AMEZ Church began its foreign missionary activities in Liberia. In that year Andrew Cartwright of NC arrived at Brewerville. On January 7, 1876, Cartwright, his mother, Mary Cartwright, his first wife, Rosanna Cartwright (full name unknown) of Elizabeth City, NC, and their two daughters, Anne Marie and Lucy Cartwright, emigrated to Liberia.

Andrew Cartwright combined the positions of emigrant and missionary even though the AMEZ Church did not officially sponsor his mission. He organized the first AMEZ churches on the African continent in Brewerville on February 7, 1878, and in Clay Ashland in November 1878. He also established a mission at Cape Palmas in 1879. By 1880 he reported another church at Antherton.

Andrew Cartwright sent a formal report to the AMEZ General Conference assembled in Montgomery, AL, in 1880. It was at this meeting that concrete plans for AMEZ work in Africa were made with the formation of the General Home and Foreign Mission Board and the Ladies' Mission Society. The church sponsored Livingstone College in Salisbury, NC, and was encouraged to train missionaries for Africa.

Andrew Cartwright returned to America in order to arouse the mission interest of the members of his denomination. At the AMEZ General Conference of 1884 he officially was confirmed as the church's first missionary to Liberia. Cartwright's first wife had died in Liberia in 1880, and before he left the U.S. he married Carrie Annie S. (full name unknown) of Plymouth, NC in 1885. The two returned to Liberia.

In 1886, Andrew Cartwright organized a church at Cape Palmas, but a shortage of funds caused it to close. Two years later he started the first foreign mission school of the AMEZ Church, with both male and female students. Carrie Cartwright worked as a missionary teacher in the school.

Andrew Cartwright felt that he should have been acknowledged by the AMEZ Church as superintendent of African missions, but the church's response was that there was no need for the election of a missionary bishop at that time. The church viewed him as a poor administrator who had not expanded the mission. Andrew Cartwright served in Liberia until his death in Liberia on January 14, 1903, but his mission never grew much beyond an individual effort.

However, in 1896 John Bryan Small was elected AMEZ Bishop to Africa, the West Indies, and three home conferences. Small was born and educated in Barbados. He joined the British army as a clerk and was stationed in the West African country of the Gold Coast (today Ghana) for three years, but he also traveled along the western coast from Sierra Leone to Nigeria. He resigned from the army because of British policies toward the Asante kingdom. On a number of occasions in the 19th century the British had battled with the Asante, who wanted to prevent foreign domination of the coastal trade.

In 1871 Small came to the U.S., joined the AMEZ Church, and pursued his original career as a preacher. In 1896 the church decided to appoint a bishop to Africa, the West Indies, and three home conferences, and because of Small's experience in Africa, he was elected. He chose as his ecclesiastical motto, "For bleeding Africa."

On June 22, 1896, Bishop Small and his wife, Mary Julia Blair Small, left the U.S.. As bishop, John Small visited Sierra Leone, Liberia, and the Gold Coast but he centered his work in the Gold Coast. His most outstanding contribution to AMEZ mission work in Africa was his efforts to train indigenous African church leadership. He discouraged the church from sending more black American missionaries to Africa and concentrated on sending young Africans to be trained as missionaries at the AMEZ Church's Livingstone College. Between 1897 and 1900 Small had enrolled at least four students from the Gold Coast at Livingstone College. The most notable was James E. K. Aggrey who was destined to become famous in the 20th century as an educator and African nationalist.

Under Bishop Small's administration, AMEZ work in Africa took on new life. Steady and substantial progress was made in the formation of new organizations and the establishment of schools. By 1900 the mission could claim one school with 45 students, and two churches with 71 full members. In 1901 Small founded the Zion Missionary Seer in the Gold Coast to stimulate work in foreign fields. Bishop Small returned to the U.S. in 1904. He died on January 15, 1915, with these words from his deathbed: "Don't let my African work fail."

By the beginning of the 20th century the AMEZ Church had established itself in the Gold Coast. There had developed in the church a widespread interest in missionary expansion in Africa. Like the AME Church, the AMEZ Church concentrated on adding African members from already converted English-speaking areas such as Liberia, Sierra Leone, the Gold Coast, or South Africa.

This was not the case with the smaller black Methodist church. In the early 20th century the Colored Methodist Episcopal (CME) Church would join with the Methodist Episcopal Church, South (MECS) to open a mission station in French-speaking Belgian Congo (today Democratic Republic of Congo).

The Methodist Episcopal Church (today a constituent part of the United Methodist Church) was one of the earliest missionary societies in Africa. The church sent its first missionary, Melville Beveridge Cox, to Liberia in 1833. But Cox died four months after his arrival, with his dying words forming the backbone of future American Methodist missionary work in Africa: "Though a thousand fall, let not Africa be given up." With the division of the Methodist Episcopal Church in 1844, the Liberian field fell to the Methodist Episcopal Church, North. Thereafter, the Methodist Episcopal Church, South

(MECS) did not initiate African mission work until 1910.

The CME Church (today the Christian Methodist Episcopal Church) was organized in Jackson, TN, on December 15, 1870. At its inception the church was made up of ex-slaves who had been members of the MECS. The CME Church sought cooperation and assistance from southern whites and continued close association with the MECS. The CME Women's Missionary Society was founded in May 1894 at Fort Valley, GA, by Lucius Holsey and it became an organized missionary department in July of 1898.

For two decades before 1910, leaders of the Southern Presbyterian Church repeatedly had asked the MECS to enter the Congo and cooperate with them in the evangelization of Central Africa. The Southern Presbyterian Church's African adventure had begun in 1890 when two pioneer missionaries—a white, Samuel N. Lapsley, and a black, William Henry Sheppard—established the American Presbyterian Congo Mission at Luebo. Four years before the beginning of World War I, the MECS decided to investigate the possibility of sending missionaries to Africa and asked the CME Church to join in the effort. Neither the MECS nor the CME Church had missions in Africa at that time.

Certainly, one of the considerations of the MECS was the desirability of securing the co-operation of the CME Church prior to entering African mission work. The MECS would furnish a large share of the financial support and a portion of the leadership while the CME Church would furnish the principal number of workers. As one CME minister explained, "The purpose of the great Methodist Episcopal Church, South, is to do its bit for African missions through the Colored Methodist Episcopal Church! If we furnish the men and women, the parent Church will furnish the means." Basically, this statement summarized the proposed relationship that the MECS and the CME Church were to have in Africa, and the nature of the union.

At the 16th meeting of the Board of Missions of the MECS, held in Nashville, TN, in May 1906, a resolution was adopted affirming that the members of the board supported the opening of a mission in Africa, and the

matter was referred to committee. From 1906 to 1910, the church discussed and studied the issue, resulting in a number of young men and women of the MECS volunteering for missionary service. At the same time, interest was stimulated among the students and faculty of the CME's Paine College in Augusta, GA, which led to a discussion of the role of the CME Church in the evangelization of Africa, and the possibility of cooperation between the MECS and the CME Church in the opening of a mission in Africa. These events were followed by an offer for service by Rev. John W. Gilbert, professor of Greek at Paine College and assistant secretary of the Board of Education for work among blacks of the MECS.

During the 1910 General Conference of the CME Church, which convened at Augusta, GA, Dr. W. R. Lambuth, Fraternal Messenger to the CME Church from the MECS, delivered an address which suggested that the CME Church should cooperate with the MECS in establishing a mission in Africa. At the end of Lambuth's speech, resolutions were adopted requesting the College of Bishops of the CME Church to appoint a committee to investigate the plan. Lambuth felt that Prof. Gilbert's offer to serve in Africa, along with two other Paine College graduates, immensely strengthened the appeal to both churches.

When the Board of Missions of the MECS met in 1910, the secretary presented the report of the committee to which had been referred the question of opening a mission in Africa. The committee resolved that the Board of Missions should take immediate and definite steps toward the establishment of a mission in Africa and confer with the CME Church concerning an alliance in this missionary effort. Gilbert, Fraternal Delegate to this conference from the CME Church, was invited to address the board on this subject. The committee's report was adopted unanimously.

The resolution of the committee was endorsed by the 1910 General Conference of the MECS. Still, by the 1911 annual meeting, no further action had been taken to inaugurate these recommendations. The College of Bishops, however, appointed Lambuth to lead an expedition to Africa. A Board of African Missions was set up to raise funds and secure qualified candidates for the proposed mission. Lambuth arranged to visit Central Africa in 1911.

For the two Methodist churches, Lambuth of the MECS and Gilbert of the CME Church were the logical persons to make the trip to Africa. Accordingly, the MECS in 1911 commissioned the pair to proceed to the Congo to investigate the possibility of establishing a mission in the country. This action represented the first biracial attempt to cooperate in the formation of an American mission in Africa, although there were many examples of interracial collaboration through the use of black and white missionaries, such as the Southern Presbyterian Church in the Congo or the American Board of Commissioners for Foreign Missions (Congregationalist) in Angola and Southern Rhodesia.

Walter Russell Lambuth had been born on November 10, 1854, in Shanghai, China, the son of missionary parents, James William and Mary Isabella McClellan Lambuth. He earned a B.D. degree and an M.D. degree in the U.S., and served intermittently from 1877 to 1891 as a medical missionary of the MECS in China and Japan. On May 16, 1910, at the 16th General Conference of the church, Lambuth was elected bishop. Three days later he was ordained. Bishop Lambuth died at Yokohama, Japan, on September 26, 1921.

John Wesley Gilbert was born on January 9, 1865, in Hephzibah, GA, to Gabriel and Sarah (full name unknown) Gilbert, farm hands. Early in his teens Gilbert went to Augusta, GA, where he entered the public schools and later was the first student at and a graduate of Paine Institute. He also studied at the Atlanta Baptist Seminary (now Morehouse College, Atlanta, GA) and Brown University (Providence, RI), and at the American School of Classics in Athens, Greece. Gilbert, in 1888, became the first Black teacher at Paine Institute and College, where he taught Greek. In 1895 he entered the ministry of the CME Church. From 1913 to 1914, he served as the third president of Miles College (Birmingham, Alabama). Reverend Gilbert died in Augusta, Georgia on November 18, 1923.

The relationship between the MECS, the CME Church, and Paine College was noteworthy. Paine Institute was established in 1882 at Augusta, GA, and chartered in 1883, adopting its present name in 1903. Its original mission was to train African American ministers and teachers. It represented a unique experiment in southern interracial cooperation. It was assisted financially and was operated by both the CME and the MECS. Almost from its beginning, Paine's faculty was interracial and international. The trustees were chosen equally from both churches. It was understandable, then, that out of this environment would come an attempt at Methodist missionary union in Africa.

For Lambuth and Gilbert, the years 1911-1912 were spent in travel and study. Gilbert, the CME Church's first commissioned missionary to Africa, met Lambuth in London and they sailed for the Congo from Antwerp, Belgium, on October 14, 1911. They arrived at Matadi, on the Lower Congo River, 21 days later, on November 5. The following morning they began a two-day railroad journey to Stanley Pool where they remained for 10 days. From this point they traveled nearly 900 miles by boat on the Upper Congo, Kasai, and Lulua Rivers, reaching the American Presbyterian Congo Mission at Luebo on December 7. They were welcomed at Luebo and observed the results of 21 years of missionary work.

After spending two weeks at Luebo, and with the advice of the Presbyterian missionaries, Lambuth and Gilbert, with 60 carriers, started inland to find a location for their new mission. On February 1, 1912, after a 41 day march by foot, they reached the village of Wembo Niama (or Wembo Nyama) in the Atetela region. The village of Chief Wembo Niama was located about four degrees south of the equator between the 24 and 25 degrees longitude and bounded by the Lubefu, Lomami, and Lukanye Rivers. Lambuth and Gilbert were invited to the house of the chief where they remained for four days. Because of the urgings of the chief, and the belief that the hand of God had shaped their course, the two church leaders determined to plant the mission station at this place. Lambuth and

Gilbert, after seven months in the Congo, returned to the U.S. in the spring of 1912.

Upon their return, Bishop Lambuth reported at the 67th meeting of the Board of Missions of the MECS that there was a great opportunity in the Congo for evangelization. He revealed that Belgian authorities were friendly and seemed willing to grant Americans the privileges of missionary work among Africans. A land concession had been ceded to the church in the Atetela region.

Gilbert, after his arrival in the U.S., offered himself to the Board of Missions of the MECS as a candidate for African mission work and was accepted. Both Lambuth and Gilbert assumed that Gilbert would go back to the Congo to help establish the mission. For a while after 1912, the CME Church continued to be eager about cooperating with the MECS in this venture.

The MECS's Congo Mission was launched officially at the meeting of the Board of Missions in May 1913. The work was to begin in the village of Wembo Niama. Three white missionaries and their wives were accepted by the Committee on Candidates and scheduled to sail for Europe in late 1913 in order to hear lectures on tropical life, the care of health, and missionary methods and policies. Bishop Lambuth was to join the group in Antwerp, Belgium, and then they would all proceed to the Congo. With these missionaries, and "with the entrance into that field at a later date of Prof. and Mrs. J. W. Gilbert, representatives of the Colored Methodist Episcopal Church," Lambuth believed that the MECS would be able to establish a strong and viable mission.

On November 8, 1913, Bishop Lambuth and the party of six missionaries set sail from Antwerp without Prof. Gilbert, to open the MECS's Congo Mission. They arrived at Matadi on November 28 and reached Luebo on Christmas Eve day. With the full cooperation of the nearby American Presbyterian Congo Mission, the Methodist Episcopal Congo Mission was organized on February 12, 1914, at Wembo Niama, and the missionary dream of the MECS in Africa became a reality.

At the 1914 General Conference of the CME Church in St. Louis, Rev. Gilbert made an appeal for CME cooperation with the MECS. But despite Gilbert's plea, and a prior interest in placing Africa under special Episcopal superintendency, by the time the CME Church met in 1914, it was indifferent to the idea. This spirit of detachment made it impossible for the conference to recommend a bishop for Africa, despite assurances from the MECS that it would assist the CME Church in supervision of the African work.

At the 1918 meeting of the General Conference of the CME Church, the body turned its attention to the development of educational programs, an area that the church always had given first priority. In 1918 Rev. Gilbert was elected the first editor of Sunday School materials of the CME Church. In the 1922 Episcopal address CME bishops spoke of African missions, affirming, "we wish to say, with all emphasis, that we are in thorough sympathy with [the idea of missions], but we do not see where we can get men and money for such an enterprise at this time, when other older and better equipped churches find it a trying task to foster the missions which they have projected in that land [Africa]." Obviously, the idea of a union between the CME Church and the MECS was dead by this date.

As it was conceived, the unification scheme of an African mission of the MECS and the CME Church never had a chance of getting beyond the planning stages. Although Bishop Lambuth and Professor Gilbert made a propitious trip to the Congo, nothing ever could have come of the idea of combining MECS finances with CME Church labor.

In spite of the initial support of both churches, probably the greatest obstacle was the Belgian government, which refused to issue permits to African Americans seeking to reside in the Belgian Congo.

As early as 1878 King Leopold of Belgium and his concessionary companies had shown an interest in using African Americans as workers in the Congo. However, during the 1890s two African-American—the historian, George Washington Williams, and the missionary, William Henry Sheppard—led a campaign, which depicted Leopoldian rule in the Congo as exploitative. This did not ensure an attitude of trust of black Americans by Congo authorities. The reluctant Belgian government had been forced to assume control of the Congo in 1908, after years of worldwide condemnation of the atrocities of the Leopoldian regime. In addition, in 1909 Sheppard, of the American Presbyterian Congo Mission, was tried in Leopoldville for libel against a Belgian concessionary company operating in the Congo. Although Sheppard was found innocent, soon after the trial he returned to the U.S. permanently. From this date onward, Belgian officials discouraged and limited black American missionaries from work in the Congo. Bolstering their exclusionary policy were recent uprisings in Kenya, Nyasaland (today Malawi), South Africa, Southwest Africa (today Namibia), and Tanganyika (today Tanzania), some of which the European colonialists erroneously tied to African-American missionary activity. This atmosphere helps to explain why the Belgians dissuaded American churches from using African-Americans in their African missions, particularly well educated blacks such as Gilbert.

There is also evidence that such an interracial enterprise was opposed by some leaders in the MECS and the CME Church. One CME member explained why: "Perhaps the colored church was not quite ready for such responsibility. Perhaps the white church was not quite Christian enough to treat Negroes as brothers as Bishop Lambuth had done." In the end, it was not feasible to carry out the plan of cooperation between the MECS and the CME Church. The suspicions of the Belgian government and the attitude of some MECS and CME Church administrators help to explain why the scheme of the two churches in 1911-1912 to open a Congo mission never materialized.

The Baptists: Black American Baptists also became involved in African mission work in the 19th century. The result of this missionary consciousness among black Baptists was the organization and spread of many independent regional organizations throughout the U.S., including the Providence Baptist Association formed in 1835 and based in OH; the Wood River Baptist Association created in 1838 in IL; the General Association of West-

ern States and Territories organized in 1873; and the New England Baptist Missionary Convention established in 1874.

In 1840 black Baptists from the New England and middle Atlantic states met to organize the first national black Baptist missionary group, the American Baptist Missionary Convention. The second national black Baptist missionary organization, the Northwestern and Southern Baptist Convention, was formed in 1864 to serve those areas not reached by the American Baptist Missionary Convention. In 1866 the American Baptist Missionary Convention and the Northwestern and Southern Baptist Convention joined to form the Consolidated American Baptist Missionary Convention. Although the Consolidated Baptists had home missions they made no efforts in foreign missions. In 1878 the work of the Consolidated American Baptist Missionary Convention terminated and in 1880 the Baptist Foreign Mission Convention of the U.S. (BFMC) was organized.

Interest among black Baptists in African missions came from the efforts at organization from southern black Baptists, particularly in the southeastern states of SC, NC, and VA. In 1878, the Baptist Educational, Missionary, and Sunday-School Convention of SC, founded in 1866, resolved unanimously to send a missionary to Africa. The group selected Harrison N. Bouey as its missionary appointee. Bouey was born on August 4, 1849, in Columbia County, GA, but he grew up in Augusta. He was converted in 1870, ordained in 1876, and completed the theology course at Augusta Institute (moved to Atlanta in 1879 to become Atlanta Baptist Seminary, today Morehouse College). He worked as a public school teacher in Augusta.

On April 21, 1878, Bouey, a bachelor, sailed to Liberia on the *Azor* with the group of 206 SC emigrants including the AME missionary Samuel E. Flegler. Bouey retorted: "Go to Africa? Yes, my Lord commands, and I am afraid not to go." During his two-year stay in Monrovia, Bouey worked among the Gola people. While there he helped construct a road outside Royesville, 18 miles northwest of Monrovia, which came to be called the "Bouey Road." Bouey also helped organize the Liberia Baptist Missionary Convention. The two Baptist churches established by the SC emigrants were accepted into the Liberia Baptist Missionary Convention in December 1879. Bouey returned to the U.S. in 1880. He settled in Selma, AL, and served as the first vice president of the BFMC.

In April 1882 Bouey married Laura P. Logan of Charleston, SC. He served as pastor and superintendent of missions for Missouri Baptists. After the death of his wife in 1897 Bouey again sailed to Africa in January 1902 but returned to America in 1905. On December 11, 1906, Bouey and three of his four sons returned to Africa. His elder son later joined them. Bouey continued to work in Liberia as a National Baptist Convention missionary until his death on December 15, 1909, at Cape Mount. He was buried on the banks of Lake Peause alongside Hattie J. Pressley and, allegedly, Henderson McKinney, although McKinney's grave has not been found there.

In 1879 the Black Baptist State Convention of NC followed the lead of SC and appointed James O. Hayes as a missionary to Liberia. Hayes went to Africa as a missionary emigrant, as had Lott Carey and Harrison Bouey.

Hayes had been born in eastern NC. He was one of the first students to enter Shaw University (Raleigh, NC), graduating from the scientific department in May 1879. Hayes did not sail to Liberia until June 1881. He was one of the founders and the first teacher of Ricks Institute in Montserrado County. In 1883 he married Ada Ellen Merritt.

When the Lott Carey Foreign Mission Convention (LCC) opened its first mission in Brewerville, Liberia, in 1897, Hayes became its first missionary. He had affiliated with the convention immediately after its founding that year. Hayes pastored a church in Brewerville to which an industrial school was added to train Liberian youth. He served as a member of the Liberia Baptist Missionary Convention.

During the years 1880 to 1883 the Baptist Foreign Mission Convention laid the foundations for future missionary endeavors and the movement for African missions gained momentum. From 1883 to 1886 the African mission movement of the BFMC experienced success. In 1883 the BFMC commissioned six

missionaries to Liberia: William W. Colley and his wife (name unknown), James H. and Hattie J. Harris Pressley, John J. Coles, and Henderson McKinney.

William W. Colley headed this mission party, which sailed in December 1883. Colley was born a slave on February 12, 1847, probably in Winchester, VA. He attended Richmond Institute and was graduated in 1887 (chartered in 1876, name changed to Richmond Theological Seminary in 1886, united with Wayland Seminary in 1897 under the name Virginia Union University). Colley was accepted for African mission work in 1875 by the Southern Baptist Convention and worked at Lagos and Abeokuta in southern Nigeria. In Lagos he helped erect a chapel and residence. When he was recalled in 1879 the Lagos mission had 24 members.

Back in the U.S. Colley helped organize the BFMC and served as its first corresponding secretary from November 1880 to December 1883, when he sailed to Liberia. In Liberia the six pioneer missionaries established the Bendoo Baptist Mission at Grand Cape Mount among the Vai people of western Liberia. Colley began publication, at his own expense, of the periodical *African Missions*. He returned to America in 1886 because of poor health.

James Pressley, also a graduate of Richmond Institute, and Hattie Pressley of VA arrived in Liberia in December 1883 with the BFMC pioneer party. Hattie Pressley helped with the establishment of the Bendoo Baptist Mission. Reverend Pressley organized a Baptist church among the Vai people and baptized more than 100 persons.

But the mission had problems from the beginning; the foremost one was health. Hattie Pressley was pregnant when she arrived in Liberia but she lost the baby. And less than a year after their arrival Hattie Pressley died of fever on August 15, 1884. She was the first BFMC missionary to die in Africa and was buried in Liberia.

Rev. Pressley was sick most of his two years in Liberia. Weakened by periodic bouts with fever and disheartened by his child's and wife's deaths, he returned to the U.S. in 1885 as an invalid. In a poem entitled "The Cry of the Heathen," published in 1896, Rev.

Pressley emphasized a continuing need for missions by erroneously portraying Africa as devoid of any religious development:

Hear the voice of Ethiopia
 Coming from that distant land;
Would you answer to that crying?
 Give to them a helping hand.
Don't you hear that heathen mother,
 Praying to the gods of stone?
Trying to heal a heart of trouble,
 A heart by sin and sorrow torn.

In this land we have our Jesus,
 Who will save us when we die;
When we leave this world of trouble
 We shall live with Him on high.
But they know no God of mercy,
 Who will hear them when they pray;
There they have no loving Jesus,
 Who will take their sins away.
Thus they die in awful darkness,
 Die without the Gospel light;
Die without the love of Jesus,
 Die and sink to endless night.
If you cannot go and teach them,
 You can help those who are there,
You can with a cry of pity.
 Carry them to God in prayer.

John J. Coles was born on April 26, 1856, in Shattersburg, VA. Coles entered Richmond Institute in 1878 and was graduated five years later, in 1883. He was licensed to preach by the Baptist Church on July 14, 1878, and ordained on November 4, 1883. On December 1, 1883, he sailed to Liberia with the BFMC pioneer party. Coles was assisted financially by the New York Colonization Society.

Coles and McKinney entered Liberia College to study Arabic under Edward Blyden. Coles was first stationed at the Bendoo Baptist Mission and was elected president of the mission on January 20, 1885. Having learned the Vai language, he preached to the people without an interpreter. A book that Coles wrote during his mission work in Liberia, *Africa in Brief*, was published in 1886. The same year he returned to America, traveling throughout the South lecturing on the need for financial support of the BFMC Liberian mission.

While on furlough in the U.S. he met and on December 21, 1886, married Lucy A. Henry of Memphis, TN. The pair traveled to Liberia in early 1887 accompanied by four other missionaries, Edgar (or Egbert) B. and Mattie E. (full name unknown) Topp, and James J. Diggs and his wife (name unknown). Upon his return to Liberia John Coles was assigned to the Bendoo and Jundoo stations where he organized and maintained a school for African boys. Lucy Coles aided her husband in the work at the Bendoo and Jundoo stations where she taught at the mission school.

The ill health of Rev. Coles forced the couple to leave Africa in 1893. Financial problems forced the Bendoo Baptist Mission to be closed after their departure. The old mission houses were sold for lumber. Upon their return to the U.S., John Coles was elected the third corresponding secretary of the BFMC but he died a few months after his election. Lucy Coles was elected to finish his unexpired term, which she did until 1895 when the National Baptist Convention, U.S.A., Inc., was organized.

The sixth and final missionary who was commissioned by the BFMC in 1883 was Henderson (nickname Hence) McKinney. McKinney was born in Edwards, MS, in 1860. In May 1883 the first graduation was held at Natchez Seminary and McKinney was one of the first seven students to receive a high school diploma. The coeducational school was founded at Natchez, MS, in 1877 and was operated as a private church school by the American Baptist Home Mission Society until 1938. In the fall of 1883 Natchez Seminary was moved to Jackson, MS, and by common consent, the institution's name was changed to Jackson College, in honor of Andrew Jackson, for whom Jackson, MS, was named (today, Jackson State University; Jackson, MS).

On December 1, 1883, McKinney traveled to Africa in the party with William Colley. McKinney also was supported by the New York Colonization Society. Before his departure, McKinney cautioned: "Fear not the African climate, for God in the form of man visited Africa long ago."

McKinney received additional seminary training, and learned Arabic at Liberia College under the West Indian emigrant Edward Blyden. In 1884 McKinney was appointed as an active missionary. He opened the Marfa station near Grand Cape Mount. On April 15, 1887, McKinney died at his post. He had set out on a mission tour in the interior of Liberia and apparently died in a ferry accident. A Liberian chief had entrusted to McKinney a young Liberian man to be sent to the U.S. to be educated. But before final arrangements could be completed, McKinney died. Edgar (or Egbert) Topp later brought the young man to Jackson College as the school's first foreign student. From 1887 to 1894, a time of nationwide economic difficulty, the African mission movement of the BFMC declined because of the limitation of financial resources.

In 1895 the Baptist Foreign Mission Convention of the U.S. joined with the American National Baptist Convention (organized in 1886) and the Baptist National Educational Convention (established in 1893) to form the National Baptist Convention of America (NBC). The National Baptist Convention split into two conventions in 1915, the National Baptist Convention and the National Baptist Convention of the U.S.A., Incorporated.

R. A. Jackson, an independent Baptist missionary in South Africa, affiliated with the National Baptist Convention in 1896. Jackson, a Baptist preacher from Arkansas, financed his own way to South Africa in 1894 and established a mission at Cape Town. He later was joined by Joseph I. Buchanan, a Black sailor from Baltimore, MD.

As an independent missionary, Jackson traveled 25,000 miles into the interior, and within four years he had founded five mission stations. In 1896 the NBC agreed to sponsor Rev. Jackson as their superintendent of South African work. His brightest convert, John Tule, was elected an official missionary by the NBC and later was educated in the U.S.. Tule and his American-born wife, Mamie Branton Tule of NC, returned to South Africa in 1897 as missionaries of the NBC and the Lott Carey Convention.

In July 1897 Jackson and his wife (name unknown) took a six-month furlough in the U.S.. For a short time in 1898 Jackson defected to the Lott Carey Convention because of inadequate financial support from the NBC. But by 1900 Jackson had withdrawn from the LCC. The Jacksons remained at their post until October 1906 when they permanently returned to the U.S..

In 1897, a majority of the VA and NC delegates of the newly formed National Baptist Convention met in Washington, D.C., where they set up the Lott Carey Foreign Mission Convention (later the Lott Carey Baptist Home and Foreign Mission Convention). Separation centered on the issues of the declining importance of foreign missions in the National Baptist Convention, and a desire by these delegates for black control of mission work without any cooperation with white Baptists.

In the early years the LCC cooperated with other Baptist boards engaged in mission work in foreign fields. In 1900 the LCC agreed to join with the American Baptist Missionary Union (ABMU) to mutually support Rev. Clinton Boone and Eva Boone in the Congo.

Clinton Caldwell Boone was born on May 9, 1873, in Winton, NC. At the age of 19 he entered Waters Normal Institute in Winton. Scholarships helped him to complete Waters Institute and Richmond Theological Seminary. He was graduated from the seminary on May 21, 1900, with a B.D. degree. It was probably in Richmond that he met Eva Roberta Coles, his first wife, and Rachel A. Tharps, his second wife, both of whom were graduates of Hartshorn Memorial College (Richmond), which was opened in 1883. On January 16, 1901, Boone married his first wife.

Eva Roberta Coles was born on January 8, 1880, in Charlottesville, VA. Although it has been claimed in some publications that she was the daughter of the missionary couple John J. and Lucy A. Henry Coles, this was not likely since the Coleses did not marry until December 21, 1886. Coles taught in Charlottesville before marrying Clinton Boone.

The Boones left New York on April 13, 1901, reaching the Palabala station in the Katanga province of the Congo on May 24.

They went out under the auspices of the ABMU (today the American Baptist Churches in the U.S.A.) in cooperation with the LCC.

Clinton Boone preached and taught the Congolese in their own language. Eva Boone took charge of the infant class and conducted the kindergarten. She was one of the first ABMU missionaries to advance the idea of a sewing school. Despite the difficulty of enlisting African women, who saw sewing as men's work, Eva Boone enrolled more than 40 women in her sewing group before her death. After several weeks of illness, brought on by a poisonous bite, Eva Boone died on December 8, 1902, barely 22 years old, and was buried at Palabala.

In 1905 Clinton Boone was transferred to Lukunga, where he assisted in building a new station. He spent five years in the Congo and in 1906 he returned to America. He took the medical course at Leonard Medical School, Shaw University (Raleigh, NC), which he completed in 1910.

The same year Boone traveled to Liberia as a LCC medical missionary. He first was stationed at Brewerville but later was transferred to Monrovia where he opened a day school. In 1918 he became minister of Providence Baptist Church, which had been organized in 1822 by Lott Carey.

After nine years in Liberia, he returned to the U.S. and allegedly took a course in mechanical dentistry at Bodee Dental School (New York City). Boone received training both as a physician and a dentist at the expense of the LCC. His education equipped him as one of the best-prepared missionaries ever sent out by any convention.

In 1919 Boone married Rachel Tharps. Rachel A. Tharps was born in Richmond, VA. After graduation from Hartshorn Memorial College, she became a schoolteacher in Richmond. The Boones traveled to Monrovia, Liberia in 1920 as LCC missionaries. Clinton Boone worked as a medical and dental missionary, and as pastor of Providence Baptist Church. Rachel Boone opened a school in the city.

The Boones and their two children (both born in Liberia) left the country in 1926 and returned to America permanently. Reflecting on his mission work in Africa. Rev. Boone reminisced: "I do not regret a single sacrifice that I have made for the redemption of Africa and if I had 10,000 other lives I would be delighted to spend them all to lift up the fallen and care for the dying in Africa."

In 1908 the LCC agreed to co-sponsor, with the NBC, D. E. Murff in South Africa. D. E. Murff was born on May 17, 1857, in Laurensville, MS. He attended Wayland Seminary (opened in Washington, D.C., in 1865, moved to Richmond, VA, in 1899 after merging, into Virginia Union University). On December 11, 1906, Rev. Murff sailed to South Africa with his wife Mattie E. Wilson Murff, who had been born in Natchez, MS, on May 15, 1867. The Murffs took up NBC work in Cape Town.

During his superintendency, Rev. Murff assisted in laying the foundation for the Shiloh Baptist Church and finished building a school house. Mattie Murff was a faithful and efficient assistant to her husband. The couple returned to America in July 1910 because of impaired health.

Also in 1908 the LCC appointed three new missionaries to Liberia. Cora and William Thomas sailed to Liberia as LCC missionaries in December 1908, arriving in January 1909. G. D. Gayles arrived in mid-1909.

Cora Ann Pair was born in Knightdale, Wake County, NC, on September 8, 1875. She was graduated from Shaw University (Raleigh, NC) in 1895 with a higher English diploma. Between 1904 and 1906, she took post-graduate courses in missionary training at the theological school of Fisk University (Nashville, TN). Before going to Africa Pair acted as principal of an orphanage for black children in Oxford, NC. In November 1908 Cora Pair married William Thomas.

William Henry Thomas was born on March 31, 1881, in Duncans Parish of Trelawny, Jamaica. He completed his elementary and secondary education in Jamaica but came to the United States as a young man to continue his higher education. He was graduated from Shaw University in 1908 with an A.B. degree and B.Th. degree. Pair and Thomas had met at Shaw University. Cora Thomas was sponsored by the Woman's Baptist Missionary Convention of North Carolina.

The couple was stationed at Brewerville, Liberia. Shortly after their arrival, William Thomas became a naturalized Liberian citizen. At Brewerville, Rev. Thomas served as LCC superintendent of the mission as well as a preacher and teacher. For 33 years he served as principal of the Baptist boarding high school in Brewerville. He extended the work of the convention into journalism and for a while operated the only printing press among black Baptists in Liberia. In 1909 he began publication of the *Watchman,* a monthly paper of the Brewerville station.

Cora Thomas encouraged the LCC mission board to establish an industrial school, which was later named the Lott Carey Mission School. She taught hundreds of boys and girls and young women and men at the school. After Rev. Thomas' death on September 4, 1942, Cora Thomas was appointed superintendent of the mission, succeeding her husband. She served in that capacity for four years. In 1946 she left Liberia because of failing health. Cora Thomas returned to Liberia in 1951 with the Lott Carey Pilgrimage Group. After a severe attack of malaria, she died at Brewerville on May 10, 1952. She was buried on the Lott Carey Mission School campus next to her husband.

The third missionary that the LCC appointed to Liberia in 1908 was G. D. Gayles of Baltimore, MD. Gayles' travel expenses were paid by Baptists in his home city. He arrived in Liberia in mid-1909 and was also stationed at Brewerville.

The paucity of financial resources of the LCC and NBC tended to limit their missionary activities in Africa. By 1915 the LCC had placed most of its American-born missionaries in West Africa, primarily in Liberia. In that country the LCC could build upon the foundation laid by James Hayes. NBC missionaries, by that date, had served in South Africa, Liberia, and Nyasaland.

The African mission work of African-American churches changed after 1920. By the end of World War I, European imperialists had occupied the entire continent of Africa except for Liberia and Ethiopia. These colonialists believed that the African American presence in Africa caused unrest among Africans. European officials felt that black missionaries were dangerous to the maintenance of law and order in Africa because Africans might identify with their better educated and more politically conscious brothers and sisters. The European powers feared that these black American missionaries might unwittingly, or wittingly, encourage political revolts among Africans. By that date, the general consensus of European governments in Africa was that African American missionaries upset the status quo and caused too many disruptions to warrant their effectiveness in the "civilizing mission" in Africa.

During the 40 year period between 1920 and 1960 very few black American missionaries not already stationed in Africa were assigned there by white boards. Black boards continued to send African American missionaries to Africa, but their efforts basically were confined to several countries. After 1960 black Americans were again appointed as missionaries to Africa, but by that date African indigenous missionaries made up the majority of missionaries on the continent and these Africans replaced foreign missionaries.

Between 1820 and 1980, from 250,000 to 350,000 Americans served as missionaries in Africa. Black Americans represented an infinitesimal percentage of that figure. During this period probably no more than 600 African-Americans, sent out by over two dozen missionary societies served in sub-Saharan countries. About half of these were sent out by black church boards. Of the total 600, at least half were women, with about two-thirds of these unmarried commissioned missionaries and one-third "missionary wives." Over 50 percent of all the black American missionaries who were stationed in Africa before 1980 served in Liberia and another 25 percent served in three other West African countries, Ghana, Nigeria, and Sierra Leone.

African-Americans served as missionaries in a total of 20 sub-Saharan countries. Because language was a crucial determinant to placement, 13 of these colonies or countries were English-speaking. There were five French-speaking colonies and two Portuguese-speaking colonies with black American missionaries. None were assigned to German; Italian; or Spanish-speaking colonies.

The significance of the mission work of African-American churches in Africa was that it helped to bridge the chasm between Africans on the continent and African-Americans that had been created by the slave trade. Black boards had fewer missionaries stationed in Africa than white boards because less financial resources were available for mission support. Therefore, since a smaller number of missionaries were sent to Africa by black boards during the 19th and 20th centuries, in comparison to the numbers sent by white boards, any contribution that these missionaries of black boards made to African mission work was as individuals more so than in a collective or denominational sense.

Regardless of how historians assess the impact of the mission movement on Africa, African-American churches felt that they had a "special" relationship and "special" obligation to Africa and Africans. This belief was a significant if not the determinative factor in their motivations for African mission work, and in their continued interest and multiple activities on the continent.

Bibliography

Adams, C. C., and Talley, Marshall A. *Negro Baptists and Foreign Missions*. Philadelphia, PA: Foreign Mission Board of the National Baptist Convention, U.S.A., Inc., 1944. 94 pp.

Berry, Lewellyn L. *A Century of Missions of the African Methodist Episcopal Church, 1840-1940*. New York: Gutenberg Printing Co., 1942. 333 pp.

Boone, Clinton C. *Congo As I Saw It*. New York: J. J. Little and Ives Co., 1927. 96 pp.

Liberia As I Know It. Richmond, VA: 1929. 152 pp. Rept.: Westport, CT: Negro Universities Press, 1970. 151 pp.

Bradley, David Henry. *A History of the AME Zion Church*. 2 vols. Nashville, TN: Parthenon Press, 1956. 1970.

Cade, John, *Holsey: The Incomparable*. New York: Pageant Press, 1964. 221 pp.

Calhoun, E. Clayton. *Of Men Who Ventured Much and Far: The Congo Quest of Dr. Gilbert and Bishop Lambuth*. Atlanta, GA: Institute Press, 1961. 153 pp.

Cannon, James. *History of Southern Methodist Missions*. Nashville, TN: Cokesbury Press, 1926. 356 pp.

Cauthen, Baker J., ed. *Advance: A History of Southern Baptist Foreign Missions*. Nashville, TN: Broadman Press, 1970. 329 pp.

Chirenje, J. Mutero. *Ethiopianism and Afro-Americans in Southern Africa, 1883-1916*. Baton Rouge, LA: Louisiana State University Press, 1997. 231 pp.

Colclough, Joseph C. *The Spirit of John Wesley Gilbert*. Nashville, TN: Cokesbury Press, 1925.

Coles, John J., *Africa in Brief*. New York: New York Freeman Steam Printing Establishment, 1886.

Coppin, Fanny Jackson. *Reminiscences of School Life and Hints on Teaching*. Philadelphia, PA: AME Book Concern, 1913. 191 pp.. Rept.: New York: Garland Publishing, 1987. 191 pp.

Coppin, Levi J. *Observations of Persons and Things in South Africa, 1900-1904*. Philadelphia, PA: AME Book Concern, 1904. 205 pp.

Fitts, Leroy. *Lott Carey: First Black Missionary to Africa*. Valley Forge, PA: Judson Press, 1978. 159 pp.

Freeman, Edward A. *The Epoch of Negro Baptists and the Foreign Mission Board*. Kansas City, MO: Central Seminary Press, 1953. 301 pp.

Gregg, Howard D. *History of the African Methodist Episcopal Church: The Black Church in Action.* Nashville, TN: AMEC Sunday School Union, 1980. 523 pp.

Harvey, William J. ,III. *Bridges of Faith Across the Seas: The Story of the Foreign Mission Board, National Baptist Convention, USA, Inc.* Philadelphia, PA: Foreign Mission Board, National Baptist Convention, U.S.A., Inc., 1989. 523 pp.

Hervey, G. Winfred. *The Story of Baptist Missions in Foreign Lands.* St. Louis, MO: Chancy R. Barns, 1884.

Hood, J. W. *One Hundred Years of the African Methodist Episcopal Church.* New York: A.M.E. Book Concern, 1895.

Jacobs, Sylvia M., ed. *Black Americans and the Missionary Movement in Africa.* Contributions in Afro-American and African Studies, #66. Westport, CT: Greenwood Press, 1982. 255 pp.

Jenifer, John T. *Centennial Retrospect History of the African Methodist Episcopal Church.* Nashville, TN: AME Sunday School Union, 1916. 454 pp.

Jordan, Artishia Wilkerson. *The African Methodist Episcopal Church in Africa.* N.p., n.d.

Jordan, Lewis Garnett. *In Our Stead: Facts About Foreign Missions.* Philadelphia, PA: 1913.

Negro Baptist History, U.S.A. Nashville, TN: Sunday School Publishing Board, 1930. 394 pp.

On Two Hemispheres. Nashville, TN: 1935.

Pebbles From An African Beach. Philadelphia, PA: Lisle-Carey Press, 1918.

Up the Ladder in Foreign Missions. Nashville, TN: National Baptist Publishing Board, 1901. 269 pp.

Lakey, Othal Hawthorne. *The Rise of "Colored Methodism." A Study of the Background and the Beginnings of the Christian Methodist Episcopal Church.* Dallas, TX: Crescendo Book Publications, 1972. 128 pp.

Lambuth, Walter Russell. *Winning the World for Christ: A Study in Dynamics.* New York: Fleming H. Revell Company, 1915. 245 pp.

Martin, Sandy D. *Black Baptists and African Missions.* Macon, GA: Mercer University Press, 1989. 242 pp.

McAfee, Sara Jane. *History of the Woman's Missionary Society in the Colored Methodist Episcopal Church.* Jackson, TN: Publishing House C.M.E. Church, 1934.

Merriam, Edmund F. *A History of American Baptist Missions.* Philadelphia, PA: American Baptist Publication Society, 1900.

Payne, Daniel A. *History of the AME Church.* Nashville, TN: Publishing House of the AME Sunday School Union, 1891. 218 pp.

Pelt, Owen D., and Smith, Ralph Lee. *The Story of the National Baptists.* New York: Vantage Press, 1960. 272 pp.

Pinson, William W. *Walter Russell Lambuth, Prophet and Pioneer.* Nashville, TN: Vantage Press, 1925. 261 pp.

Reeve, Thomas E. *In Wembo Nyama's Land, A Story of the Thrilling Experiences in Establishing the Methodist Mission Among the Atetela.* Nashville, TN: Publishing House of the M.E. Church, South, 1923.

Rux, Mattie, and Ransome, Mary M. *History of the Woman's Auxiliary to the Lott Carey Baptist Foreign Mission Convention, 1900-1956.* N.p., n.d.

Smith, Charles Spencer. *A History of the African Methodist Episcopal Church.* Philadelphia, PA: Book Concern of the AME Church, 1922. 570 pp.

Tupper, Henry Allen. *Foreign Missions of the Southern Baptist Convention.* Philadelphia, PA: American Baptist Publication Society, 1880.

Walls, William Jacob. *The African Methodist Episcopal Zion Church: Reality of the Black Church.* Charlotte, NC: AME Zion Publishing House, 1974. 669 pp.

Williams, Walter L. *Black Americans and the Evangelization of Africa, 1877-1900.* Madison, WI: University of Wisconsin Press, 1982. 259 pp.

A Brief Historical Survey of African–American Involvement in International Missions[1]

David Cornelius

> Somewhere in the struggle, the vision for world evangelization that many of the early black Christian leaders had exhibited became blurred.

For much of the 20th century, American Christians as a whole have felt that African-Americans are not interested in international missions. This opinion is based, in part, on the observation that very few African-Americans serve as long-term (two years or more) international missionaries. Only a handful of the more than 40,000 American Christian missionaries serving long-term are African Americans. Most churches with predominately African-American membership have given little emphasis to international missions. Instead, they have preferred to carry out the mandates of The Great Commission at local, regional and national levels. International missions has been left, for the most part, in the hands of white Christians.

While the observations which led to this opinion are accurate, the conclusion is not necessarily true. The fact is that African-American Christians are interested in international missions and the overarching mandate of our Lord's command to make disciples of all nations. Many African-American Christians do feel the responsibility to make Christ known to the world. In fact, African-Americans have been (historically) and continue to be (at an accelerating rate) involved in international missions.

African-Americans in International Missions

The historic involvement of African-Americans in international missions may be seen as far back as the 18th century. "The foreign mission motif predates home missions in general among black Baptists."[2] From the time slaves began accepting Christianity, it was in their hearts to carry the Gospel of Christ not only back to their fatherlands, but also to other parts of the world. According to historical records, African-American missionaries went not only to Africa in the 18th and 19th centuries, but to Canada and the Caribbean islands as well. Though the ability to carry out their convictions has varied over the years, this missionary theme has endured throughout the history of the African-American church.

African-American Pentecostals in International Missions

Though it is the largest African-American Pentecostal denomination, the missionary endeavors of the Church of God in Christ (or COGIC, founded in 1907) were largely domestic

David Cornelius is the Director of African American Church Relations and Co-Director of the International Volunteer Fellowship of the International Mission Board, Southern Baptist Convention in Richmond, VA. For nine years he served as a missionary in Nigeria.

before the end of World War II. In fact, it was only after the civil rights period that the COGIC began to emphasize international missions in Africa and the Caribbean. The fastest growing segment of Christianity in African countries has consisted of African independent church movements. These are usually Pentecostal in form. At present, the membership of COGIC International is estimated to be about a half million. COGIC missionaries are also active in esatblishing churches in the Caribbean region.[3]

African-American Methodists in International Missions

Both the African Methodist Episcopal (AME) and African Methodist Episcopal Zion (AMEZ) denominations started missionary work in Africa during the 19th century. The denominations established work in West Africa in the early years, and in South Africa toward the end of the 19th century.

Rev. Daniel Coker, who had been pastor of the Bethel AME Church, Baltimore, MD, has the distinction of being the first African-American Methodist missionary to serve in Africa. He sailed to Sierra Leone in 1820, only a few months before Baptist missionary, Rev. Lott Carey (sometimes spelled Cary) left VA for Liberia.[4] Coker, under the auspices of the American Colonization Society (ACS), formed the first AME church aboard ship and was ready to operate in Sierra Leone.[5]

It was through Rev. Andrew Cartwright that the AMEZ Church started missionary work in Africa, Liberia, in 1878. Today, the denomination has missionary work going on in at least four countries, Ghana, Guyana, Liberia, and Nigeria. In addition, there are a number of AME Zion churches in Canada.

The third major African-American Methodist denomination, the Christian Methodist Episcopal Church (CME), began its formal missionary work in Africa in 1911 as a joint venture with the Methodist Episcopal Church, South. The CME denomination (formerly known as the Colored Methodist Episcopal Church) initially focused on educating Africans in church colleges in the U.S. They chose Zaire, what is now the Republic of Congo, as their first international mission field and have since sponsored missionary efforts in South Africa, West Africa and (as have the other two black Methodist denominations) the Caribbean.

African-American Baptists in International Missions

Although Methodists are older as a denomination among African-Americans, Baptists have a more extensive record in the area of international missions. George Liele and Prince Williams were pioneer African-Americans in the area of international missions.

Rev. George Liele (sometimes spelled, Lisle), a freed slave and preacher from SC, left the U.S. for Jamaica in 1783. By 1784, he had founded the First Baptist Church of Kingston, Jamaica. It is interesting to note that just as the spread of the Gospel in New Testament times was due, in part, to persecution (Acts 8:1), so Liele left the country of his birth for fear of being persecuted through re-enslavedment.

Another freed slave from SC, Rev. Prince Williams, was the first African-American Baptist missionary to the Bahama Islands. He left Saint Augustine, FL some time following the Revolutionary War. Around 1790, he organized a Baptist church in Nassau. In 1801 he secured land and built a small house of worship. He called the new organization the Bethel Baptist Mission.[6]

By 1790, David George, Hector Peters, and Sampson Calvert, all had gone to Africa and begun preaching on its West Coast. However, it was not until Lott Carey came on the scene that a more structured approach to international missions began to emerge.

Lott Carey was born in Charles City County, VA (about 30 miles southeast of Richmond) in 1780. Around 1800 he moved to Richmond where he worked in the tobacco warehouse district. Over the next few years, through his own saving and with help from some sympathetic white people, he raised enough money to purchase both his freedom and that of his family. He learned to read and write by attending a night school conducted by William Crane, a deacon of the First Baptist Church of Richmond.

Through William Crane, Carey became aware of the ministry of Luther Rice. This, along with several other influences in his life, had a profound impact upon his ministry.[7] Carey became a powerful and well known preacher. In 1815, he led in organizing the African Baptist Foreign Missionary Society, the first organization for international missions founded by African-Americans in the U.S.[8]

Through the intervention of William Crane and the Richmond Baptist Missionary Society, the General Missionary Convention of the Baptist Denomination in the U.S. of America for Foreign Missions,[9] which had been organized in 1814, agreed to support Carey and Colin Teague (a free African-American preacher who shared Carey's desire to preach the gospel to the Africans). On January 16, 1821, after several years of working toward fulfilling his dream of preaching the Gospel to the Africans, Carey, along with Teague and their families, sailed for Liberia.

The funds for their journey came from several sources, including contributions from their own pockets (some $1,500 from the sale of Carey's farm), the African Baptist Foreign Missionary Society, some white people who were sympathetic to his cause, and the American Colonization Society. Shortly after their arrival in Liberia they established the Providence Baptist Church.[10]

Carey labored and established a colony in which he served as chief political, religious and military leader, and a medical officer. In spite of the difficulties faced, he felt that Africa was the best place for him and his family (and any black persons who did not want the hue of their skin to hinder their advancement in the society in which they lived). Because of his stands on various issues, he incurred the disfavor of some of the colonial rulers. Carey died in an explosion in 1828.[11]

In the years before the Emancipation Proclamation, African-American Christians continuously exhibited an interest in participating in international missions. During the 19th century prior to 1863, African-Americans (primarily those who were free) made numerous attempts to establish a national entity that would enable them to carry out missionary work, both domestically and internationally, more effectively. A major hindrance to success was lack of finances. On occasions, they requested assistance from white Christians and their organizations. In some cases,

assistance was given; in others, it was refused. Occasionally there was disagreement as to whether or not to join with white-controlled missionary societies in order to carry out the work. In some cases, the two races did work together; in others, blacks chose to work independently, expressing concern that whites would dominate the relationship and decide what would be done with little or no consideration of what their black partners wanted.

During the years 1843-1845, the long-standing tension between northern and southern Christians over the issue of slavery came to a head. It resulted in separation of both the Methodist and Baptist denominations into basically two groups: pro-slavery and antislavery. For the Baptists, it meant the rupture of the fragile alliance between Northerners (who were mostly anti-slavery), and Southerners (who were mostly proslavery) in the Triennial Convention. On May 8, 1845, a new convention, the Southern Baptist Convention (SBC), was born from this rupture.

Early on, the young SBC sought to show that, in spite of the stand of both individuals and member congregations on the slavery issue, they possessed great interest in the spiritual welfare of blacks and slaves. Before the inaugural meeting was over, two boards had been established. One, the Board for Domestic Missions, was to focus on evangelizing inhabitants of the U.S., including blacks and Indians. The other, the Foreign Mission Board, was to focus on helping Southern Baptists to evangelize overseas.

By 1846, a year after the founding of its Foreign Mission Board, the new convention had appointed two African-Americans as missionaries, John Day and A.L. Jones. Over the next 40 years, the board either appointed or gave support to at least 62 black missionaries.[12] The vast majority of these served in Africa.

African-American Baptists in International Missions: Post Emancipation Proclamation

Soon after the effective date of the Emancipation Proclamation, Jan. 1, 1863, African-Americans who had been freed from slavery by the Proclamation began leaving white

Baptist churches and organizing their own churches and associations. Driven in part by a desire to become more efficient and effective in evangelizing Africa, black Baptists continued to try to organize a national convention, a movement which had pre-Emancipation roots. Attempts at forming a national convention were hindered, at least in part, by regionalism. Efforts to organize at the state and regional level were more successful. However, even these successes were relatively short-lived. It would not be until 1895 that black Baptists would succeed in organizing an enduring national convention.

During the period between 1863 and 1895, African-Americans continued seeking to 'flesh out' what they believed to be their God-given mandate of sending missionaries to evangelize Africa. A number of outstanding African-American missionaries, serving in the tradition of Lott Carey, Colin Teague and Harrison N. Bouey,[13] moved these efforts forward. Among them were men such as Solomon Cosby, and a Virginia-born preacher named William W. Colley.

Colley is recognized as the only African-American Baptist to have served as an appointed missionary of both a white administered missionary-sending agency and a black administered missionary-sending agency. W. W. Colley was appointed by the Foreign Mission Board, SBC, in 1875 to serve in West Africa as the assistant to W. J. David, a white missionary from Mississippi. In November 1879, he returned to the U.S. with the conviction that more blacks should be involved in international missions, especially in Africa.

As he traveled back and forth across the country, mostly in southern states, he urged black Baptists to take an independent course in mission work and form their own sending agency.[14] Colley's effort is considered the primary force in the founding of the Baptist Foreign Mission Convention (BFMC) on November 24, 1880. The BFMC became one of three conventions that merged in 1895 to form the National Baptist Convention of the USA, Inc., the first truly national convention of black Baptists in the U.S.[15]

Colley was among the first six missionaries appointed by the BFMC in 1883. He, along with his wife, Joseph, and Hattie Presley,

John J. Cole, and Henderson McKinney, was sent to West Africa. It has been said, speaking of missionaries in those days, that Africa was the white man's graveyard, referring to the many white missionaries who died as a result of disease contracted while serving in Africa. It may also be said that Africa was the black man's graveyard. Of the first dozen missionaries sent to Africa by the BFMC, 11 either died on the field or became so ill that they had to return to the U.S. The popular notion held by both whites and blacks that African-Americans could tolerate the conditions in Africa better than whites was proven to be in error.

The years during which the BFMC operated (1880-1895) were characterized by waxing and waning of both interest and support. During the early years, there was great excitement over the work being done in Africa. As the years passed and hardship and tragedy struck, causing one missionary after another to leave the field, interest seemed to decline. During the entire existence of the BFMC, those states which had missionaries on the field whom they could claim as their own seemed to give stronger support to the convention. There were other factors in the decreasing support.

As early as 1886, a decline in support for the BFMC could be seen. By 1888, the convention's work was severly impaired. By the early 1890s, the convention's work, for all practical purposes, did not exist. Several factors may have contributed to this declining support:

I. Prior to the founding of the BFMC, a number of states appointed and sent their own missionaries. Even after the founding of the convention, this practice continued.

II. There were those who chose to work with white missionary societies and organizations, believing these groups to be the more "legitimate" channels for Baptists to do missionary work since they had been established for some time.

III. During the late 1880s, the economy was especially bad for African-Americans. In addition to the country's economic slump, segregation and discrimination were having a devastating impact on African-Americans.

IV. Complaints from missionaries on the field that they were not being paid in a timely manner, or that they were not receiving support at all, may have contributed to a decline in black Baptists' confidence in the convention's governing board.

V. During those periods of time when there were no BFMC missionaries on the field, the support was noticeably less. By 1894, the Convention had no missionaries on the field. No doubt, this had a devastating impact on the support given to the Convention.

In the end, it was the founding of such agencies as the Foreign Mission Board of the National Baptist Convention of the U.S.A., Inc. and the Lott Carey Baptist Foreign (and Home) Mission Convention that has continued to foster the international missions efforts of black Baptists in the U.S.

Where Do We Go From Here?

It has been shown, though in summary fashion, that African-Americans are not newcomers in the area of international missions. Nor is it true that African-Americans are not interested in international missions.

Historically, there have been factors that have worked against their full participation in the international missions arena. As a result, throughout much of their history, African-Americans have achieved neither their full desire nor their full potential in the international missions arena. Many of those hindering factors have been eliminated, but others remain.

During the years of slavery, many who had the desire to serve as international missionaries could not for obvious reasons. As African-Americans began to shed the chains of slavery, they also began to go to foreign lands with the Gospel. Over the past two centuries, African-Americans have been involved in international missions both by working in partnership with white Christians and by forming their own conventions and agencies. There have been periods when white Christians did not want increasing numbers of African-Americans serving on international mission fields alongside them. There have been times when African-Ameri-

can participation was discouraged by governmental actions: refusal of visas, unreasonably high fees for visas, some colonial governments even refused to honor lawfully obtained visas for certain African countries when they were in power.

In the midst of post-Emancipation activity of African-American Christians to evangelize Africa, there was also the struggle to gain fully functional freedom in the U.S. It did not take long for Jim Crow laws mandating segregation to spread across the land. It became the calling of the black church to lead in this struggle.

On the home front, there was the aftermath of the Civil War in which segregation and discrimination, fostered by Jim Crow laws, caused the plight of many blacks in the U.S. to be worse than it was during slavery. This meant that, being the only institution that African-Americans had under their control, the black church had to lead in the struggle of her people for full citizenship and human rights in the country of their birth. Somewhere in the struggle, the vision for world evangelization that many of the early black Christian leaders had exhibited became blurred. As a result, large scale neglect of the international missions enterprise was experienced among African-Americans. In spite of this, neither the interest nor the sense of responsibility for a lost, dying world was lost.

There have always been those African-Americans who were willing, and even anxious, to serve alongside their white brothers and sisters on the international mission field. Even here, there have been hindrances. During the 19th century, African-American missionaries serving under appointment of white-administered missionary-sending agencies most often had to have white supervisors available before being sent to the field. It was well past the mid-20th century before most white-administered sending agencies (especially those that are denominationally based) would accept African-American candidates. These hindrances no longer exist.

Even before the time of Lott Carey, there were black Christians who felt that God had given them, as a race, the mandate to have primary responsibility for taking the gospel back to Africa. Many of the efforts to start state, regional, and national bodies had this mandate as a driving force. The desire was so strong that a number of leaders sought to have black Baptists join with white Baptists in order to expedite this mission, even though the sting of their mistreatment in white churches during and after slavery was still fresh. Some opponents of these suggested alliances argued that white American Christians had ignored Africa and that if blacks did not chart their own course, the missions efforts of the whites would dilute, and even hinder, the efforts being made by blacks to evangelize Africa.

As the 20th century was born and matured, many of the negatives of the 19th century passed away. In spite of all that has changed for the good, things are still not what they should be. Various walls of separation still exist in some areas. The color of one's skin is still a hindrance in some arenas. Attempts at segregation are still being made by some. However, in spite of these challenges, tremendous strides are being made in world evangelization because the Body of Christ continues to learn to work together as *one*, learning what *unity* really is!

The results of these changes is evident. With even a cursory look at current events, one is left standing in awe at what God is doing with African-Americans in international missions.

Numerous organizations established to mobilize African-Americans toward more participation in international missions have been born over the past three decades. Mainline white denominations and missionary-sending agencies have begun to actively seek and enlist blacks to serve overseas alongside their white missionaries. African-American denominational leaders are being challenged to provide more opportunities for their constituents to participate in international missions in a meaningful way.

God is raising up a new generation of pastors in the African-American church: pastors who are being led to seek out opportunities for their own involvement, and that of their congregations in international missions. International partnerships between black congregations, associations, state conventions and fellowships in the U.S. and overseas entities are developing at an ever increasing rate. The number of African-American Christians participating in short-term international missions opportunities continues to rise. Finally, there is a developing trend toward ever-increasing numbers of African-Americans planting their lives overseas, serving long-term as Christian missionaries.

The African-American church is a sleeping giant in the area of international missions: a giant that is being awakened by her Lord. Only God knows the extent to which His Kingdom will be strengthened as the full potential of this giant in international missions is realized!

Endnotes

1 David Cornelius, *Perspectives on the World Christian Movement*, Pasadena, CA: William Carey Library, 1999, pp. 287-292.

In this article, the term "international missions" is used instead of the more familiar term "foreign missions." While they may be used interchangeably, the writer's preference is "international,"' due primarily to some negative connotations that the word "foreign" has incurred over the years.

2 Leroy Fitts, *A History of Black Baptists*, Nashville, TN: Broadman Press, 1985, p. 109.

3 C. Eric Lincoln, and Lawrence H. Mamiya, *The Black Church in the African American Experience*, Durham, NC: Duke University Press, 1990, p. 90.

4 Ibid., 74-75.

5 While it is clear that the motives of the ACS were racist and self-serving (they wanted to send freed slaves back to Africa so they would not be problematic to the white slave owners in the United States) men like Coker, who accepted their help in getting to Africa, were far more interested in spreading the Gospel among the Africans. The Society even went so far as to negotiate with African leaders for property to be used for colonization by those returning.

6 Fitts, p. 110.

7 Carey's grandmother was one of those influences. After being brought from Africa as a slave, she became a Christian. She longed to see the Gospel preached in her homeland and had said (in young Lott's presence) on several occasions that he might be used of God to do just that.

8 William J. Harvey, III, *Bridges of Faith Across the Seas*, Philadelphia, PA: The Foreign Mission Board of the National Baptist Convention USA, Inc., 1989, p. 16.

9 The Convention was known simply as the Triennial Convention because it met every three years.

10 Carey, along with William Crane and several others, had organized the Providence Baptist Church in Richmond, VA, before they sailed for West Africa. Today, this church continues to have an effective ministry in the city of Monrovia, Liberia.

11 History reports that the explosion was an accident that occurred as he was preparing to defend the colony against an invading tribe. Some (including at least one of Carey's descendants), however, believe that Carey's death was an assassination. Proponents of this theory believe that they have evidence to support their belief.

12 A record of these individuals may be found in the archives of the International Mission Board, located in its home office building in Richmond, VA.

13 Bouey was appointed by the South Carolina Baptist Educational, Missionary and Sunday School Convention. That convention is now known as the Baptist Educational and Missionary Convention of South Carolina.

14 For a list of possible reasons with explanations, along with a more extensive discussion on W. W. Colley's missionary ministry, see Sandy D. Martin, *Black Baptists and African Missions: The Origins of a Movement, 1880-1915*, Macon, GA: Mercer University Press, 1989, pp. 49ff.

15 The National Baptist Convention of the USA, Inc., was organized in Sept. 1895. It resulted from a merger of three smaller conventions: the Baptist Foreign Mission Convention (founded in 1880), the American National Baptist Convention (founded in 1886), and the Baptist National Educational Convention (founded in 1893). The resolution leading to the founding of this convention read, in part, "That there shall be one national organization of American Baptists. Under this, there shall be a Foreign Mission Board, with authority to plan and execute the Foreign Mission work, according to the spirit and purpose set forth by the Foreign Mission Convention of the United States." Stated another way, a major part of the work of the new convention was to be to carry on the foreign mission focus of the Baptist Foreign Mission Convention.

Black Man's Burden

Robert Gordon

Granted, there should be more black missionaries—but where does the problem lie? Not primarily with racist mission boards, said Robert Gordon [in 1973].

Robert C. Gordon, a member of Missionary Aviation Fellowship, is a graduate of Moody Bible Institute, Wheaton College, IL, and Fuller Seminary School of World Mission, CA. He served as a missionary in Zaire (Congo) from 1965-1969.

Originally published in *Evangelical Missions Quarterly*, Fall 1973. Copied by permission from EMQ, P.O. Box 794, Wheaton, IL 60189.

At the InterVarsity Urbana 1970 missionary conference, George Taylor chided missions because "very, very few" black Christians are represented on mission fields.

How many is "very, very few?" William Warfield of the 25-year-old Afro-American Missionary Crusade thinks that "very, very few" is less than 100. But, as I have found, accurate statistics are hard to come by.

If the contemporary scene is hazy, so is the historical picture. For all the facts in books about Negro contributions to American life, the subject of missions is conspicuously absent. Works on black religion and the black church barely, if at all, touch on missions.

What mainstream churches have known for some time is that there are very few qualified black candidates and even fewer black missionaries. Just how many, we set to find out.

My research shows that out of 30,000 U.S. missionaries, there are about 240 blacks serving in 30 foreign nations. This represents .8 of one percent of the total U.S. missionary force. These results, based on a random sample of known U.S. foreign missionary sending agencies, also indicate that 137 of 450 Protestant sending bodies have at least one black on their staffs.

To check the sample results, I queried North America's 25 largest missions, as well as the major missions serving in Africa, but not contacted in the sample. Responses from a total of 56 missions account for 113 blacks or 47 percent of the 240 total suggested by my sample. If these 12.44 percent of all mission agencies have almost half of our estimated total, it is possible my sample errs on the low side. For a conservative working figure, I suggest 250 as the number of U.S. black foreign missionaries.

This is considerably more than the "less than 100" figure offered by William Warfield. But although it is also probably considerably higher than most black critics of missions have in mind, it is still a disappointing drop in the bucket. Negroes constitute roughly 11 percent of our population, and church membership among them is considered to be somewhat higher than among the white population. Even allowing a higher than average drain for home missions and civil rights programs, it is not too much to expect 10 percent (3,000) of the foreign missionaries from the U.S. to be blacks.

Pre-Civil War Roots: 1790-1860

Historically, black missionary involvement began about 1790 when Prince William was reported to have left Florida for work among the slaves in the Bahamas.[1] It has been suggested that the first American woman missionary may have been a New Orleans Negress.[2] But the early black mission effort gained momentum slowly, largely because prior to 1860, the number of free blacks between [the ages of] 24 and 35 never exceeded 86,000.[3]

Between 1820 and 1860, the main structure for black mission efforts was the Samuel Hopkins and Ezra Stiles-inspired American Colonization Society which repatriated American blacks to Liberia. Though the repatriated blacks were expected to remain as colonists, one of the principal aims was missionary. Hopkins had urged blacks to "settle and improve all opportunities to teach the Africans the doctrines and duties of Christianity."[4]

Negro evangelization of Africa was based on the belief that Afro-Americans were obligated to return to redeem Africa because of racial affinity, providential preparation, special adaptation, and divine command.

American black participation seemed particularly crucial as Africa quickly gained the reputation as the "white man's grave." Early white missionaries barely set foot on African soil before they died. Believing the Negro better adapted to tropical climates, American boards began a search for black candidates.

> The early graves of most of the missionaries already sent there, afford affecting evidence that the climate has hitherto been injurious and fatal to the white man. Shall the board therefore encourage white missionaries to go there? Or shall they rest the hopes of Africa as far as sending out as missionaries, colored men, whose constitution is so much better adapted to that climate? Without deciding the first of these questions, they would advert strongly to the second. Surely among the thousands of colored communicants in the Presbyterian Church there must be many who, if properly educated, would make efficient missionaries to the land of their forefathers.[5]

But there was another reason that missions wanted to recruit black *missionaries*: the failure of the colonists to evangelize. If Africa was to be reached, trained missionaries, not colonists, were needed.

Post-Civil War Growth: 1860-1900

The foreign missionary effort of American blacks increased following the Civil War when the number of free blacks between the ages of 24 and 35 jumped from 86,000 to nearly 665,000.[6] By 1868, twelve of the thirteen Presbyterian Church U.S.A. staff in Liberia were blacks.[7] Blacks serving under the Protestant Episcopal Church outnumbered whites in 1876 by twenty-one to five.[8]

Negro churches in the Reconstruction period established work of their own in Barbados, Cuba, Santo Domingo, Trinidad, the Virgin Islands, and British Guyana.

But even with these increases, the supply of black missionaries was never enough. In 1882, Howard University had to reply to a query from the Livingstone Inland Mission (British) by pointing out that American agencies absorbed all available candidates. Particularly acute was the lack of male candidates.

The Presbyterian Church U.S.A (Southern) was among the most successful in recruiting blacks during this period. Between 1890 and 1950, a total of 14 served on the Congo field pioneered by a black, William Sheppard.[9]

Though statistics are sketchy, they are suggestive of far greater participation than the number of American Negroes would seem to warrant.

The contribution of the American black missionary during this period was not merely numerical. Many, like the Rev. Joseph Gomer of the United Brethren in Christ in Sierra Leone, "acquired wide influence among the native African tribes, frequently acting as umpire in their differences and sometimes even settling wars between opposing chiefs."[10] During the first 10 years of Southern Presbyterian work in the Congo, "there were times when almost the whole burden of the work was borne by them."[11]

There were failures, of course, but overall, one gets the impression that the success of black missionaries was largely determined by the same factors that influenced the success of their white colleagues.

In this connection, we must examine two fallacies that both contributed to the initial increase in and the eventual decline in the number of black missionaries.

First, we need to consider the supposed racial adaptation possessed by blacks. It was believed that they were constitutionally better adapted for life in Africa. Was it so?

History gives us the names of men like Thomas Birch Freeman, a mulatto who outlived several white colleagues, the Rev. Joseph Gomer (who served for 21 years), Mrs. James Thompson (for 30 years), and the record-shattering 40-year ministry of James Priest.

But history also records the names of blacks whose overseas ministries were measured in mere months. Wilber Harr, in his dissertation entitled *The Negro as an American Protestant Missionary in Africa* (University of Chicago, 1945), on the basis of Presbyterian mission records, was able to compare the longevity of black and white missionaries. He found that the blacks in his sample averaged 6.7 years to 5.5 for the whites. The 10 blacks with the longest records averaged 20.7 years, while their ten white counterparts averaged 18.8 years. This is hardly an overwhelming advantage for blacks.[12]

It appears, then, that the belief that the black was better able to endure the rigors of the African tropics was something of a myth.

Second, we need to look briefly at the supposed cultural adaptability of American blacks to traditional African cultures.

It was the opinion of George Washington Carver that American blacks "in their language and religion and customs...are American, as much so as the Europeans who have come here from the earliest days to the present time."[13]

Testimonies of recent black missionaries tend to bear this out.

> In my desire to learn Bulu well, I only demonstrated how very "white" I was. Many began to see me as a European.... One day a fellow missionary told me that one of the Africans she was working with wanted to know what 'that black white lady's work' was—referring to me.[14]

Probably most black missionaries have had the experience of Kermit Overton.

> Upon my arrival in this country, the Africans gave me the impression that they expected me to take up their habits, customs, and language without difficulty...After a while they concluded that I was not one of them. The result is that they accepted me as any other missionary.[15]

20th Century Decline

Though it is not yet possible to graph accurately the black involvement in foreign missions, it appears that there was a significant decline shortly after the beginning of the 20th century.

The Protestant Episcopal Church, which had boasted more than four times as many blacks as whites on its Liberia staff in 1876, was all white by 1943.[16] Southern Baptists, who had sent blacks to Nigeria (1855) and to Jamaica, had, in 1949, a policy against appointing blacks.[17] The Presbyterians (U.S.), even though well satisfied with the work of their black missionaries, nonetheless, found American Presbyterian Negro interest lagging. As a result, "the number of Negro missionaries for the Congo declined sharply after 1915."[18]

There were exceptions, of course. Blacks on the Congregationalist staff numbered 10 percent in 1943, and their contribution was so valuable that they were being sent to non-African fields.[19] And the Colored Churches of the Southern States pioneered the Galangue station in Angola in 1922-1923. As late as 1945, it was still manned entirely by blacks.[20] Some American missions, it is true, passed rules excluding black candidates. But by and large, as Harr concludes, "mission boards seemed interested in the role of the American Negro as a Protestant missionary."[21]

Why then the serious decline in black missionaries? We suggest seven reasons.

First, we must note the growth of independent Negro churches following the Civil War. In 1859, there were probably between 26,000 and 30,000 blacks in independent Negro churches.[22] But by 1916, the figure had risen to slightly over 4 million.[23] Initially at least, the membership for the newly formed Negro denominations came from the established white denominations, particularly the Methodists and Baptists. Latourette estimates that within a few years of the close of the Civil War, the Methodist Episcopal Church, South, had lost more than half its 215,000 black members.[24] This represented a period of great vitality for black Christians, but at the same time, it effectively cut off the Negro community from the mainstream of missionary concern in America.

Second, the effect of the Student Volunteer Movement must not be overlooked. This dynamic movement was the crest of American missionary activity in the last 25 years of the 19th century. But recruitment was aimed primarily at the university campuses—precisely where blacks were least likely to be found.

Third, quinine. Africa's reputation as the white man's grave was due in large part to the deadly effect of malaria. Mass production of quinine in the 1890s destroyed the terror of the "African Fever." And once that occurred, one very important reason for Afro-American missionaries vanished. White missionaries could now work and live in Africa.

Fourth, black dollar power never equaled that of the whites. The revivals of the 18th and 19th centuries, backed by the booming American economy, insured a vital missionary outreach for white Protestants. But the loss of federal protection for blacks in the South in 1877 denied blacks a share of the prosperity.

Fifth, paternalism. We must remember that the black missionary was often expected to remain permanently in Africa. He was also frequently placed under white missionaries and in many cases assigned menial tasks. Though many were faithful teachers of the Word and preachers of great power, they were usually sent out as teachers or craftsmen. Then, too, they tended to be educationally inferior to their white colleagues.

Sixth, in some countries in Africa, black missionaries were not welcome. South Africa utilized obstructive tactics and legislation to exclude black missions, which they considered dangerous to the Bantu. In other nations, blacks were excluded for fear they would spread "Garveyism," the subversive [belief in] "Africa for the Africans."

Seventh, growing Negro materialism effectively choked off concern for missions.

Negroes have never really tasted the economic fruits and are not certain that they are within their grasp. Denied so long, the Negro now believes that, economic rewards are the ultimate values which he is psychologically unprepared to forgo.[25]

Black theologian Joseph Washington in his book *Black Religion*, goes on to say, "The socio-economically disinherited and undernourished Negro becomes the most materialistic of religious men."[26]

The result of this materialism, according to Washington, is that:

Negroes are fantastically difficult to recruit in any endeavor which includes sustained sacrifice for the well-being of others...the Peace Corps, the Ecumenical Voluntary Projects...and even Crossroads Africa are each extremely hard-pressed to enlist Negro volunteers. The search of these organizations proves what the mainstream churches have known for a very long time.[27]

Washington sees the low level of black involvement in missions as something far more pervasive than reticence of white boards in accepting black candidates.

Certainly it is true that mainstream organizations eagerly seek out Negroes who are easily accepted, especially in these days of acute sensitivity and increasing guilt. Few missionary organizations or church boards would not welcome a roster of competent Negro men and women to bolster their effectiveness in the mission of extension. It is to be expected that few Negroes will be involved in white missions when even the predominant Negro institutions are near total defection in the realm of missionary endeavor.[28]

The lack of black missionaries, then, is not the result of discrimination in white boards, primarily. The problem is a lack of qualified Negro candidates. Mission boards do not create candidates—churches do. Mission boards do not train candidates—Bible schools, colleges, universities and seminaries do. To place the blame on the white mission boards is to charge the victim. Mission agencies, like the black community, are victims of the system.

Black Missions or Integration

Black evangelicals have been needling mission agencies for their failure to appoint black candidates. In view of the virtual lack of black candidates, this seems unfair. But beyond that, one questions if integrated mission boards are really what blacks want. Beneath the furor for integration, one detects a desire for diversity with equality in the civil rights issues. Integration may very well be a transitional step to separate development.

This separate development has sound sociological, anthropological, and psychological rationale. This is true for missions as well as for the larger society. Mission administrators are faced with a cultural distance between black and white personnel when they integrate their boards. Blacks have a distinct culture, and the distinctiveness may be intensifying. Add to the cultural differences the tension over civil rights, and there is a serious question regarding the advisability of mixing defensive blacks with guilt-laden white missionaries.

Dr. Donald McGavran believes, "Blacks, if they run their own program, could do an outstanding job." But desirable though multi-racial boards would be, now is not the time, he feels. He fears that multi-racial teams will be riddled with "cross-cultural adaptation problems. Until the brotherhood issue is solved in America," he warns, "the separate groups should be kept in separate missions, with their own jurisdictions. Don't," he pleads, "put one black in with 95 whites."[29]

McGavran is not a racist. This position is absolutely consistent with his own mission practice and teaching during the past 40 years. His brand of "pragmatic sociology" stresses the value and effectiveness of working within fully functional homogeneous units. For McGavran, not only race, but economic levels, educational attainments, cultural focus, language, all taken together, put blacks and whites in separate groups.

Dr. Arthur Glasser, former Home Secretary of the Overseas Missionary Fellowship and student of black affairs, is not convinced that multi-racial teams are practical. But he suggests that the greatest contribution white boards can make to black mission efforts would be to accept blacks on an intern basis.

Sensing a weakness in the ability of blacks to run international missions, he would bring blacks into white missions for short training programs. During this time, they would develop necessary skills and experience.[30]

This would be a creative first step in re-establishing black contact with the mainstream of Protestant foreign missions. It avoids the problem of isolating capable blacks in white boards, but sends them back into the black community to organize for missions.

"Organizing for missions" in the context of the contemporary American black community means more than forming black mission societies. Societies without recruits are useless. Somehow, what Washington calls the "death knell of segregation" must be broken. Black leaders and white missions must work to re-establish mission contact with blacks on the congregational level, to establish foreign mission service as a life option for dedicated blacks.

Some black leaders, like the Rev. Joseph Jeter of Philadelphia, PA, have taken on the challenge. Over the past five years, he has placed more than 30 black youths with established mission agencies from Liberia to Nova Scotia for summer assignments. He is also planning to establish a missionary training school geared to the needs of the black community where educationally deficient blacks with a call from God to serve can be assured of adequate training. "It will be the first school to be organized solely to train blacks for missionary service."[31]

Almost, but not quite. A Foreign Mission School for Blacks was founded at Cornwall, CT, in 1825. It closed its doors in 1827 for lack of a single black student.[32] One prays it was a good idea 147 years ahead of its time.

But we can expect little change in the involvement of blacks in missions until their theology reads, "Ye shall be witnesses of me in the slums of Harlem, in the barrios of Latin America, and unto the uttermost parts of the world." Only when black missionaries are free from the accusation of having copped out on their "soul brothers" will the Great Commission break out of the ghetto. Until then, Ghetto will be capitalized and Great Commission will continue to be spelled with a small "g."

Endnotes

1. Vivian Prozan, Master's thesis, Columbia, MD: Columbia Bible College.
2. Ralph Winter, Class lecture, "The Historical Development of the Christian Movement." Fuller School of World Mission, 1971. From R. Pierce Beaver, *All Loves Excelling.*
3. *Historical Statistics of the United States: Colonial Times to 1957*, Washington, DC: U.S. Bureau of Census, 1960, p. 11.
4. Wilbur Harr, *The Negro as an American Protestant Missionary in Africa*, University of Chicago, Ph.D. dissertation, 1945, p. 13.
5. *Board of Foreign Missions of the Presbyterian Church in the United States of America, 1840*, p. 16. Quoted in Harr, p. 29.
6. *Historical Statistics of the United States: Colonial Times to 1957;* op. cit., p.11.
7. Harr, op. cit., p. 31.
8. Ibid., p. 22.
9. Charles Ross, *The Emergence of the Presbyterian Church in the Kasai, Congo,* Pasadena, CA:Fuller School of World Mission, CA, master's thesis, 1967, p. 33.
10. Daniel Burger, *History of the Church of the United Brethren in Christ*, Dayton, OH: Brethren Publishing Co., 1897, p. 442. Quoted in Emmett Cox, *The Church of the United Brethren in Christ in Sierra Leone: Its Program and Development,* Pasadena, CA: Fuller School of World Mission, 1969, master's thesis, p. 60.
11. Ross, op. cit., p. 33.
12. Harr, op cit., pp. 120, 121.
13. From a speech recorded in Arthur T. Pierson, *The Miracles of Missions,* New York: Funk and Wagnalls, 1899, p. 239.
14. Jeanne Davis, "Negro Missionary Reaction to Africa" (Symposium), *Practical Anthropology,* Vol. 11, No. 2 (March-April, 1964), p. 63.
15. Ibid., p. 68.
16. Harr, op. cit., p. 23.
17. Ibid., p. 21.
18. Ross, loc. cit.
19. Harr, op. cit., p. 18.
20. Ibid.
21. Ibid., p. 35.
22. Kenneth Scott Latourette, *A History of the Expansion of Christianity*, Vol. 4, "The Great Century: Europe and the United States," Grand Rapids, MI: Zondervan,1970, p. 342.
23. Ibid., p. 356.
24. Ibid., pp. 341, 354.
25. Joseph R. Washington, Jr., *Black Religion*, Boston: Beacon Press, 1964, p.149.
26. Ibid., pp. 157, 158.
27. Ibid., pp. 151, 153.
28. Ibid., p. 153.
29. Donald McGavran, Personal interview by author, Fuller School of World Mission, Pasadena, CA, 1971.
30. Arthur Glasser, Personal interview by author, Fuller School of World Mission, Pasadena, CA, 1971.
31. Joseph Jeter, Personal interview by author, Port-au-Prince, Haiti, 1972.
32. Clifton J. Phillips, *Protestant America and the Pagan World: The First Half Century of the American Board of Commissioners for Foreign Missions, 1810-1860,* Harvard, CT: Harvard University, Ph.D. dissertation.

Joseph Jeter

Thomas M. Watkins

When Rev. Joseph C. Jeter, Sr., felt called to the mission field 35 years ago, he was determined to get there his own way: God's way.

"We went without deputation or anything like that," recalled Jeter, founder and president of Have Christ Will Travel Ministries (HCWTM) in Philadelphia, PA. "My approach has always been to trust God. God's got the money, and when we've needed it, we've just asked Him for some more."

Joe and Catherine Jeter's faith walk has taken them from the north Philadelphia ghettos where he grew up, to an international faith mission with works in such places as the U.S., Haiti, India, Nova Scotia, Liberia, and Nigeria. Still highly involved and motivated at age 68, Joe is considered one of the patriarchs of world missions mobilization among African-Americans.

Joe was saved in a traditional Baptist church at age 17. While on vacation in 1960, Jeter experienced the call to preach the Gospel of the Lord Jesus Christ. Within 18 months, he was pastoring a small storefront church in north Philadelphia while taking evening classes at Philadelphia College of the Bible.

But it wasn't until about age 28, as a student at Philadelphia College of the Bible, that he became aware of missions. Seeing a steady parade of missionaries come through the school, he wondered why he hadn't seen them before.

At the same time, he came under the influence of Viola Reddish, a career missionary to Liberia, West Africa. On leave from the mission field and teaching at a local elementary school, she asked Jeter one day if she could use his church building to hold a Bible club for the school children who wanted to know about Jesus Christ. What he didn't realize was that it was also the beginning of missionary discipling for him and [his wife,] Catherine.

"She joined our church and for two years taught much about Africa," Jeter wrote in a chapter he contributed to the book *Evangelism & Discipleship in African-American Churches* (Grand Rapids, MI: Zondervan Publishing House, 1999,Lee N. June, Editor). "Then she returned to Liberia, West Africa, where she died in the Lord's service in 1970 at ELWA [Eternal Love Winning Africa] Hospital near Monrovia, Liberia, with her vision fulfilled to disciple my wife, Catherine, and me as missionaries."

Thomas M. Watkins is Director of Donor Services for Trans World Radio, an international Christian radio ministry based in Cary, NC. He has served as a contributing writer and editor of Christian books and periodicals, as well as business trade publications.

Jeter credits Miss Reddish with influencing him, his wife, and daughter Diane to go into missions, as well as four other children, Rhonda, Priscilla, Joseph, and Paul, to serve as short-term missionaries with the Jeters' pioneering work in Novia Scotia in the late 1960s and 1970s. "You have to understand that blacks knew nothing about missions," Jetter said, recalling the early days of his involvement.

> There were officers in the churches who had never heard of missionaries. One of my shared burdens was that no white missions would take black missionaries. I couldn't even talk to a white missionary in my own home. I think we're still seeing the fallout today from those days. I used to say that blacks were about 150 years behind whites when it comes to missions work, but I think it might be 200 years now.

While a number of black Christian leaders have been involved in the reconciliation movement in recent years, Jeter has a different view.

> I've chosen not to get involved in reconciliation; my philosophy is Gospel, Gospel, Gospel. I have some white churches that support me and our ministry evangelizes people of all colors. Without the support of white Christians we would not have gotten off the ground. (Memorial Baptist Church, Huntington Valley, PA, Carol and Elwood Shultz, Marion and Bill Frye, etc.). However, I don't feel that reconciliation of black and white Christians is something I should do. Reconciliation has already occurred between some black and white Christians and God has done that. If more is to happen, God will do that as well. Why would I focus my time on reconciliation, when I can preach salvation? That is what God has called me to do.

In addition to Viola Reddish, the ministries of missionary-evangelist Ernest Wilson and Rev. Montrose Waite of Philadelphia also had a profound impact on Jeter's life. At Wilson's invitation and experiencing God's call, Jeter went on his first mission trip to Uganda in 1965. It was then that the fire for missions began to burn deeply within him. He made his first trip to Liberia the next year. By 1968, through the ministries of Waite, Wilson, and Reddish, Have Christ Will Travel Ministries was born.

In those days, black missionaries, for the most part, came either from the black denominations or represented one of a few independent faith missions like HCWTM. Jeter challenges blacks to break with their tradition of typically not supporting black missionaries—what he characterizes as the "slavery mentality."

> It's the biggest barrier to blacks going into missions. We could not go and now it is in our psyche not to go. Whether it's blacks in home missions or in foreign missions, the churches won't support them. If you tell a church it takes $34,000 to support a missionary, you'd better run for cover. Sometimes you run into situations where if one particular church supports you, another church won't consider you because you are associated with that other church.

Jeter further writes in *Evangelism & Discipleship*:

> The concept of the support of the missionary who will work in evangelism and discipleship is a major determinant of how effective the missionary will be in the church's program. Unfortunately, most will get little support and will spend more time at another ministry or get a job to support themselves. Thus, they will have less time to pray, prepare, and present the program (the Gospel of salvation and edification).

But despite struggles and frustrations through the years, the Jeters have witnessed God's hand of provision in some incredible ways—what Jeter terms as "living daily miracles." It has been true in the provision of the needs of his family as well as his ministry.

When it came time for the Jeters' oldest daughter to go to college, they sent her off to Carver Bible School with $72 and a letter stating that when God gave them the money for tuition, they would send it. Shortly afterward, an Episcopal pastor called Jeter and said his church had just voted to pay his daughter's tuition every other semester. Such began a legacy of God's provision that has resulted in all five of the Jeters' children graduating from college.

In 1985, Jeter felt God's leading to purchase an old mansion in Philadelphia as the headquarters for HCWTM for $125,000. $56,500 was raised by the ministry and a mortgage of $68,500 was obtained to complete the purchase of the property. Shortly afterward, he wrote a letter to Emma Glenn, a schoolteacher in Albany, CA, (a member of North Oakland Missionary Baptist Church in Oakland, CA) who had befriended the ministry, asking if she would be willing to help them raise money to pay off the mortgage. Jeter's concern was that the burden of the mortgage was going to hinder the other things the ministry was committed to do.

> Emma told me later that every time she went to write a letter, the Spirit of God told her, 'You can do it.' One morning, she phoned my office and said that the Holy Ghost had told her that the money we needed to pay off the mortgage would come in between January and Easter. Believing God, she wrote us two checks: one a real check for $1,000 and the other a "faith promise" check of $60,000 that we were of course not to cash at that time. By Good Friday, she had gotten all the money together and had given us a cashier's check of $60,000.

> We were still a couple of thousand dollars short, but I had asked a pastor in Pittsburgh, PA, (Rev. Richard Farmer, Bethany Baptist Church) for a special offering. God provided for our entire need, and on Easter Monday the mortgage was paid off in 13 months and seven days.

Other testimonies to God's faithfulness through the years have included the provision of property in Nova Scotia that was valued at $189,000 but was sold to the ministry for $15,000, and the early payoff of Jeter's home mortgage after he prayed that God would eliminate it.

There were also numerous instances in which God intervened to provide for the Crust of Bread ministry that provided meals to some of the poorest people of Haiti.

> We delivered the meals on a donkey, but one day the donkey died. I told a small church of about 25 people in Los Angeles, CA, about our need, and one of the men wrote us a check for a donkey. We also had a poor woman in Pittsburgh who sent us $1,000 so that we could begin providing hot meals. During the first three years of the Crust of Bread ministry, we only bought bread once.

Today, *Have Christ Will Travel Ministries*, with a staff of some 120, is geared toward assisting mission boards and missionaries on various mission fields of the world, plus the sending of short- and long-term missionaries. Foreign partnerships include Genesis Christian Ministries in Nova Scotia; Genesis Basa Church in Liberia; Children to Christ Ministries and Holy Trinity Bible Institute in India; Faith Christian School and Clinic, Bethel Christian School, and Genesis Bible Clubs in Haiti; Grace Christian School in Corpage Demay; and the Nigeria Missionary Training Institute. Home missions involvements include Bethlehem School of the Bible and Missionary Training Institute and HQ Bible Club in Philadelphia, "The Ambassador Hour" radio broadcast, and short-term service in rural America.

Jeter clearly credits prayer as the one factor that has made the biggest difference in his ministry. He wrote the following in "Prayer in Leadership," a chapter he authored in the book, *Called to Lead—Wisdom for the Next Generation of African American Leaders* (Chicago: Moody Press, 1995, Eugene Seals and Matthew Parker, Editors).

> Prayer anchors me to the Master and to His purpose, whether it be establishing and maintaining a work in Africa, building a church in America, teaching a Bible club in India, or caring for my family's needs. A leader must know His Master's will without a doubt, or his efforts will be empowered only by his own ability and charisma. This works very well for some people some of the time. But more than one ministry has come to a crisis of funds, spirituality, or impact because of prayerlessness on the part of the leader, the board, or the supporters.

He goes on to talk about some of the inherent difficulties of mission work:

> The work is often tough. Let me dispel any illusions that it is all fun and games to be on the road and in the air 150 days out of the year--much of the time with my wife, a lot of the time without her. Over the past 30-something years, I have ridden on roads with potholes so deep it made you wonder how any transport vehicle could make it

through even one way, let alone come back to get you two weeks later. Some of the transports were so old and sagging it is truly amazing they could take large numbers of people where they needed to go. I have spent many a scorching day broken down by the side of a remote road in interior Africa, Haiti, or India waiting until another truck would come by and provide some assistance. Although the local people are accustomed to such interruptions in their schedules, we Americans sometimes find ourselves praying in such circumstances that the Lord will grant us patience and that He will do it quickly.

Jeter laments what he feels has been a loss of adventure when it comes to missions.

Short-term missions has now become the end instead of the beginning. Unfortunately, a lot of our younger people in particular have gotten swallowed up in materialism. They don't want to go; they have to live too high. It's become so high that God can't honor it. Everybody wants the $30,000 car—people want it for style. That's missionary support money that's going into personal wealth, and all they've got is bills. You can't minister to needy people if you're living too high."

In order for things to change, Jeter believes that the whole concept of God has to change in the thinking of evangelicals today.

It really doesn't require any kind of extraordinary faith to be a missionary like a lot of people think. It just takes normal faith, and a normal Christian life that's surrendered to Him and willing to keep taking the next step He reveals to you.

In conclusion, Jeter writes in *Evangelism & Discipleship*:

Missionaries in the African-American church must assist the church in evangelism and discipleship, must be empowered by the Holy Spirit with a vision for evangelism, must implement a program of discipleship, and must reap that harvest. Missionaries must remember what Jesus did in Matthew 9:36-38—that is, He looked with compassion, saw the people and the harvest, and instructed His disciples to pray for laborers.

Churches in the African-American community must likewise assist the missionary in his or her attempts to spread the Gospel," he continued. "The financial and spiritual support of the churches would greatly enhance their effectiveness in building the kingdom of God.

An Interview with Elder Donald Canty

Wendell Robinson

In 1968, Elder Donald and Mrs. Charlotte Canty were the first couple to go on the mission field as missionaries for Carver Foreign Missions, Inc. Mrs. Canty had seen her first missionary in elementary school. She was shown some of the things the missionary was doing in Ethiopia. "Even unsaved, I wanted to be like that lady," said Mrs. Canty. Saved in junior high school, she desired from then on to be a missionary.[1]

Donald Canty grew up in north Philadelphia, PA. He was called into the ministry in 1960; as a result he attended Philadelphia College of the Bible. He met his first missionary at this college during a missionary conference and was called to world missions in 1961.

These two servants met at the college in 1962 and were married in 1965. Soon after, a friend, Joe Jeter, saw the work Carver was doing in Liberia and told them about it. Mrs. Canty had a burden for teaching elementary education and Elder Canty had a burden for teaching the Bible; Carver had both. They arrived in Liberia in 1967. Both used their teaching gifts in many areas. While Mrs. Canty taught in Monrovia Bible Institute (MBI), the Carver Mission Academy, Elder Canty taught in MBI as well as in some of Monrovia's high schools. He also taught death row prisoners. "I saw four of my students hung while there," he said. "They were all saved before passing on." During his second term Elder Canty served in radio broadcasting and some telecasting, and also as Carver's field supervisor.

DONALD CANTY'S TESTIMONY

Philadelphia and God My Provider

I grew up in Philadelphia, a major sending city for African-Americans. It was the missions capital and had the National Baptist headquarters there under Dr. C. C. Adams, followed by Dr. Harvey. The Afro-American Missionary Crusade was also headquartered there under Rev. William Jackson. Some other African-American missionaries who came from Philadelphia were Montrose Waite, Dr. James E. East, Gladys East (daughter of Dr. East), Viola Reddish, Dorothy Evans, Virginia Antrom, Reginald and Clara Shipley, Andrew and Marie Trusty, Ken and Jean Thorpe, Martha Thompson and Dr. Foster. I refer to Philadelphia as being the

Wendell Robinson served as an Associate Pastor for six years at Mt. Olivet Baptist Church in Portland, OR. He is presently preparing to serve overseas with Ambassadors Fellowship.

mission capital of the world for missions as far as African-Americans are concerned.

But, there were some problems. There were no evangelical schools open to black Americans except on a quota basis. Most of the major mission-sending schools had no African-American enrollment policy. This really stunted the vision of mission for African-Americans. I went to Philadelphia School of the Bible to get training. It was one of the only schools willing to train African-Americans. This period of my life was a great motivation to pursue vocational ministry on the mission field. I had offers from many white mission organizations to do mission work in the states, what we would call home missions. However, the same mission organizations who would pay me to be a home missionary would not give me five cents to go to the foreign mission field. I knew God had called me to serve as a missionary in Africa. Finances were a factor for a number of African-Americans because they could not raise the support needed to get to the mission field. It took me two years to raise $600 of monthly support. The money came from the African-American church. I thought, "If God can't take care of me in Philadelphia, don't look for me in Africa." But He did take care of me and I quit my job in order to raise support to go. God prepared me and helped me to look to Him as my Provider.

Trusting God Along the Way

I spent 12 years in missions. I went to Africa in 1968 and returned in 1980. I feel that I learned more on the mission field than I actually taught. People today don't really believe in supernatural things. God would wake me up in the night and teach me things. I was a city boy and one night God woke me up and taught me how to fix a well. I didn't know anything about wells. Another time I was on my way to Liberia from the Ivory Coast. We were having car trouble. Most roads in Africa were two narrow lanes. A gasoline truck was coming at us head on and a collision was imminent. I recall God lifting the truck up into the air and putting it back on the road. Some kind of way it completely missed our car! Miraculously, we avoided certain death by God's hand. When we returned to the mission station, we found out that the staff had been praying for us at that precise moment.

We warmly remember the building of the church in King Gray. Women in the community sold food by the road daily, and if they made $1 per day, a good wage. The people there were responsible for building the church. The chief's wife gave her whole-hearted support by saving about $15 to purchase a window for the church. That really spoke to us more than anything else because there was someone who had nothing and was willing to give all that she had. We hold dear the hospitality and undying love of the Liberian people. Some of the sacrifices they made because of their commitment to Christ literally put us to shame here in America. I remember how the students were willing to give their lives for us. They literally placed themselves in front of us to let the people with the weapons know that we were their missionaries. They didn't want anything to happen to us.[3]

As an African-American I have been to places where no one of any other race could have gone. I have been places where white missionaries would have lost their lives seeing what I saw. I walked out of various tribal encounters having seen tribal secrets where no white missionary could have walked out alive.

We went to Liberia with one child, Deborah, and had our second child, Lydia, while there. Both the third and fourth daughters, Tamar and Vashti, were born in the U.S. while we were on furlough. Once back in Liberia with all four children, we considered coming home for the sake of the children's education because school was more expensive in Liberia. This concern changed into a definite decision when the military coup occurred in 1980. It was time to go home.[4]

From Liberia to Atlanta

In 1981 I became the deputation secretary for Carver Foreign Missions. As deputation secretary I traveled for Carver until 1987. In 1987 I was asked to become the director of Carver and served in that position until 1996. In 1990 , I had moved from Philadelphia to Atlanta, GA, while still serving as director.

Once in Atlanta, we discovered that the Lord had a new assignment for us. By accident we found New Birth Missionary Baptist Church, pastored by Bishop Eddie L. Long, and felt that was the place the Lord wanted us to stay. We began counseling one couple and the Lord worked through our counseling to restore this couple's marriage. Bishop Long asked if we would do more counseling. We obliged, realizing that the Lord was taking us back to the pastoral gifts He had given us. Thus, in 1991, we began serving as biblical counselors for New Birth. When we came to the church, our basic purpose was to introduce New Birth to missions. Today, New Birth has done some tremendous things for missions, and Bishop Long has allowed us to do whatever we need to do concerning missions work. We now serve full-time on the New Birth staff, directing the counseling ministry. This eventually led to serving full-time as missions director.

Increasing Mission Involvement

I feel exposure to missions for the African-American church is essential. I began to take African-American pastors on short term exploratory trips to Africa. I found very few pastors who went and came back with the same commitment to missions. One pastor had served on a mission board and had never been on the mission field. When I took him to the mission field, his church increased its mission support the following year more than 200 percent. When pastors are taken to the field, it literally changes the way they perceive missions, and their support follows. Most African-American pastors have never been exposed to missions. The African-American church experience with missions has been primarily within and around the four walls of the church.

When we came on staff at New Birth Missionary Baptist Church, there was no budget for world missions. After exposing the senior pastor and leadership to global missions, their vision and support has gone through the roof. In year 2000, they sent seven adults to the mission field for at least one year, all as a result of the senior pastor going to Kenya last year. Since then, everything changed as it pertains to global missions.

I have witnessed this type of transformation over and over. I recommend strongly that larger churches that are able, whether black, white or other, help underwrite the sending of some African-American pastors to the mission fields. The return is always greater than the investment.

One of the down sides of white mission organizations is that they want to expose the African-American church to the point of getting them involved in their particular organization, but not to the point of considering them as candidates to go to the mission fields. I do acknowledge that there is a push now to encourage African-Americans to join the white organizations, but this is new. Many white organizations wanted to send African-Americans to the mission fields, but they were afraid of losing their support. I believe that in order to help mobilize African-Americans towards missions, the major white evangelical churches should allot a portion of their budget to sending African-American missionaries.

The African-American missionary is needed. There definitely are places we can go and things we can say that those who are not African-American could not. Many African-American missionaries who desire and feel called to serve abroad face tremendous challenges in raising financial support in the African-American churches. There still is a lack of understanding when it comes to supporting missions and missionary candidates on a monthly basis. A lot of it comes from not realizing that a missionary cannot work [full-time outside jobs], for the most part, in foreign countries. Many African-American pastors today are still bi-vocational, the church being their supplemental income. Their assumption is that missionaries can and should do the same thing.

For those called to missions, we would like to leave this advice. First of all, know that God has called you. Then, keep your eyes on Him and realize that His grace is sufficient. If you desire to be married, you also need a mate who is open to becoming a missionary. You also need to be debt-free (or close to it). You must be willing to adapt to different circumstances and be able to live a simple life-style. [Most important, you must] have a real personal relationship with the Lord.

Endnotes

1. Vanessa Turner (now Burke), ed., "Part II: Carver's Pioneer Missionaries," *Kingdom Vision*, A publication of Carver Foreign Missions, Inc., Philadelphia, PA, (Winter 1998), pp.1,3.
2. Ibid.
3. Ibid.
4. Ibid.
5. Ibid.
6. Ibid.
7. Ibid.

Virgil Amos

Virgil Amos, Edited by Jean Voss Sorokin

Virgil Lee Amos was born in Oakland, CA, near San Francisco, in 1942 and was reared in the heartland of central CA with a love for the Lord Jesus Christ. In 1961, he boldy entered Moody Bible Institute in Chicago, IL, to major in missions and pastoral studies. In 1962, he enthusiastically became involved in foreign missions with Operation Mobilization (OM). He is the founder and General Director of Ambassadors Fellowship, a missions training and sending agency, which works in Mexico, Spain, Kenya, Nigeria, North Africa, U.S., and various other countries. He is a frequent speaker in churches, on college and university campuses, and in mission conferences. He also lectures in various cities with the *Perspectives on the World Christian Movement* course.

Edited by Jean Voss Sorokin. She is Projects Manager for the Southeast Regional Office, USCWM. She has served administratively in mission work with ISI, ELIC, CMI and USCWM.

While attending Moody, Virgil Amos went on four short mission trips, and one summer crusade to Mexico with Operation Mobilization (OM). He began to realize that living life and relating to people of different cultures would help him in evaluating his own faith and developing his own life, and worldview. The short trips, usually during the Christmas holidays, were powerful evangelistic outreaches, and were the places where his vision for reaching out into the world with the Gospel of Jesus was greatly expanded in his mind.

Mexico 1962—God Will Direct Your Way

That first year with OM, Virgil was asked on short notice to chaperone a small group of young ladies from a college in Indiana to an OM Mexico City crusade. Virgil consented. Upon entering Mexico, he inquired of the young ladies the address and directions for their stay in Mexico City. To his stressful surprise, no one had the address! "Imagine," he said, "going to the largest city in the world without an address or directions to get to where you are going!" After getting over being angry, he realized that he was facing a faith challenge— how to find your way in a large, strange, foreign city when you have no address or directions. Such a situation demanded serious faith and earnest prayer. God spoke to his mind saying, "Follow that Grey Rabbit Bus." This he did for over 100 miles. Then the Lord said, "Stop." When he pulled over to ask where they were, he was surprised to find that they were only two short blocks from their destination. Pray without ceasing. "Challenges like these deepen faith and make the Lord seem more real."

Marriage, Family, and Ministry—God's Choice

That same year, 1962, he added an additional joy to his life—his wife, Martha. How does a missionary choose a spouse? Virgil married Martha at the age of 20. Even though this may seem an early age to some, he knew she was what God had in mind for a helpmeet suitable for missions work. They both were aware that missions work was what they were called to do. For the unmarried, he suggests, "Seek the Lord first, get involved wholeheartedly in serving Him, and let the spouse be one that God adds to you."

Virgil and Martha began a family and after finishing at Moody Bible Institute, they willingly served as missionaries with OM for 10 years in various countries of Europe, Southern Asia, and Western Asia.

What should be done with children when you are sent overseas? When the Amoses went to the mission field for their first extended time of four years, their two daughters, Norma Ellen and Lou Ellen, were close by their sides. The children were never a hindrance to ministry and they opened up many opportunities to minister in a variety of ways to other families. He shares, "In many countries children give the parents the social status to be heard."

Spain 1965—God Has a Plan

During the summer of 1965 Pastor Amos was privileged to lead a summer team with his family in Spain. They worked in the provinces of Albecete, Leon, and Oviedo, distributing Christian literature in all the towns and villages. At that time, Spain was closed to the Gospel and it was illegal to evangelize and distribute Protestant literature. The team had two major challenges: take the Gospel literature to the people, and keep from being stopped by the police. The Lord showed Himself very strong during that summer. As he prayed each morning over the map for outreach strategy, God would reveal which places to go, and even the order. While this may sound unbelievable, the team followed the Lord's direction and evaded all of the schemes and roadblocks the police set up to catch them.

In Bilbao, a portion of the team did get arrested when one member began to preach on the street. A crowd of about 500 Spaniards quickly gathered around the foreigners. A news reporter happened to be in the area and he wrote down the testimonies of the team members and took copies of their materials before the police escorted them away. The newspaper published the team members' testimonies and tracts on the front page of the nationwide news! Evangelical leaders had tried to communicate the Gospel using public media without success. It had been forbidden by the Catholic regime. The Lord accomplished it free of charge!

India 1966—People Are Lost without Christ

India is best described using the word "many": many people, many living in poverty, many religions, many idols, many languages, etc..

Pastor Amos worked near the city of Bombay as an evangelism team leader and trainer for Indian believers from the south of India. He distributed literature in nine major languages on the street sidewalks in downtown Bombay. There he saw in a deep way that men were lost, not because they didn't have sufficient information about life through Jesus Christ, but because of the deep spiritual blindness of their hearts. Individuals would easily discuss the various religions, but their countenance would change when the discussion centered on Jesus Christ. They would usually want to change the subject.

Although some mission outreaches may seem to have no fruit we must sometimes plow up the hard ground for the seed of the Word of God to be planted in the future. Even in the darkest part of India, people are coming to know the Savior.

Iran 1967—God Desires Man to Be Saved

Ministering for eight years in Iran was a challenge that seemed to increase daily. In the late 1960s and 1970s during the reign of the Shah, religious freedom and expression existed, especially on paper documents. However, since at least 85 percent of the population was Islamic, freedom to minister the Gospel was greatly restricted to what the leaders of a village, town, or city would tolerate, especially outside of the six main cities.

During his first year in Iran, he was part of a team that went to one of Iran's southernmost cities. The team knew that the police chief staunchly opposed any Christian activity into his area. They dispersed themselves throughout the city while Virgil Amos went to the police station to register. Soon the entire team was in the police station. Each member had been picked up one by one. The police deported the team from that city after some lengthy delays and interrogation. Before the whole team had been rounded up, a baker received a tract. He later read it and wrote in for more information. He also enrolled in a correspondence course and studied the Gospel of John. Soon he accepted Jesus as his Savior and recruited 12 friends to studying with him about Jesus through the correspondence course. When this new believer wanted to be baptized, he willing went, because he had to, 400 miles to the nearest church.

Study to Show Yourself Approved

In 1976, Virgil decided to stay in the U.S. and enroll in Biola University to finish his bachelor's degree in social science/missions. He went on to complete his master's degree in missions at Talbot Seminary in 1979.

But what about the cross cultural adjustment missionary children have to make if and when they return to the U.S.? Even though the Amoses' two daughters traveled extensively while they were very young, and studied in five different schools between kindergarten and the fifth grade, they turned out well in their growing years. Both accepted Christ as their Savior while they were very young. They developed strong personal identities from their strong family relationship. They studied hard and developed an enlarged worldview by being abroad. The youngest daughter scored in the top 2% of the nation on the Scholastic Aptitude Test in her junior year of high school. Pastor Amos encourages families considering missions by saying, "One needs not worry about taking his children to other nations. Children are an asset to ministry."

Forward in Faith—God's Leading

Virgil Amos' love for missions and mission work continues to be sparked with zeal from the Holy Spirit. At the time of this writing he is the founder and General Director of Ambassadors Fellowship, a missions training and sending agency, which works in Mexico, Spain, Kenya, Nigeria, North Africa, U.S., and various other countries. He is a frequent speaker in churches, on college and university campuses, and in mission conferences. He also lectures in various cities with the *Perspectives on the World Christian Movement* course.

Focusing on the completing the task of evangelizing the world, Pastor Amos also is currently recruiting churches in the West to participate in the Adopt-a-People project to plant churches among 1739[1] unreached people groups of the world. An unreached people group is "a people group within which there is no indigenous community of believing Christians able to evangelize their group."[2]

With over 37 years of mission ministry experience in various parts of the world he offers quality insights and inspiration to his leadership.

And his family, how have they made this transition? His daughter Lou Ellen and her husband, Art Garcia, are veteran missionaries from Spain now living north of Denver, CO. The Amoses live in the Black Forest area of Colorado Springs, CO, close to their ministry base.

Pastor Amos' Closing Thoughts

Pastor Amos reminds Christians that, "There are individuals ripe to receive the Lord in the most resistant and hostile situations. We must take the Gospel to them.

God is raising up a growing interest and involvement in missions among African-American believers across the U.S. It is our time to do our part in the extending of the Kingdom of God to the regions where the Gospel has not yet reached. It is time for us to rise to the challenge by taking the Gospel to every creature. God is faithful. He doesn't send us alone. He goes with us each step of the way as we move out in faith.

There are things you will have to give up when going to a distant land for an extended period of time. What you gain by leaving friends, family, home, and comforts is more than what you lose in staying with them. God has given us a mission to take the Gospel throughout the world. Our faithfulness to the Great Commission has eternal rewards for us and eternal consequences for those who hear the message"

Endnotes

1. AD 2000 & Beyond Movement, Colorado Springs, CO, [www.ad2000.org], (March 1998 and April 2000), Source: *Joshua Project List*.

2. Ralph Winter, and Bruce Koch, "Finishing the Task," *Perspectives on the World Christian Movement*, Steve Hawthorne and Ralph Winter, eds., Pasadena, CA.: William Carey Library, 1999, p. 514.

Dr. Ben Johnson An Intellectual Force In Black Missions Movement

Thomas M. Watkins

• Christ Baptist Church, a 100-member black church in Philadelphia, PA, sends out 13 home and foreign missionaries between 1955 and 1968.
• A church of only 60 members gives $6,000 annually to missions.
• Hundreds of students at Moody Bible Institute in Chicago and Manna Bible Institute in Philadelphia develop a new appreciation and burden for missions.
• Malcolm X is personally confronted with the Gospel of Jesus Christ and is intellectually challenged to consider the claims of Christ.

The one common thread in each of these significant events in the African-American missions movement is Dr. Benjamin W. Johnson Sr., a prominent longtime National Baptist Convention, U.S.A., pastor, missionary, educator, and scholar. For more than 40 years, Dr. Johnson has been a well-known, effective, and intellectual voice motivating three generations of black Americans to respond to God's call to missions. From founding and pastoring missions-minded churches, to lecturing and preaching at conferences, schools, and churches, to visiting and encouraging missionaries at home and abroad, he has influenced countless lives for missions in his 76 years.

Dr. Johnson is a study in contrasts, a self-described cynic and agnostic philosopher before he accepted Christ. Early in his life he showed exceptional musical talents and had set his sights on attending the prestigious Juilliard School of Music before God called him into the ministry.

"Growing up, I always thought I had to be perfect," recalled Dr. Johnson. "I would read the Bible and talk to Christians, but they couldn't get through to me. I went into the U.S. Navy, and one night I was on a French ship unloading 100-gallon drums when one fell and just missed me. I had this awareness of someone lifting me up by the collar so that my life would be spared.

"The Lord kept waking me up at night after that, and I started going to church. Then on the fourth Sunday of April 1944, I was baptized at Second Baptist Church in Los Angeles, CA. I read the Bible every day and began witnessing. One day I was reading the Bible and it all became clear to me: the reference to 'the Word became flesh' was Jesus. For about six hours, I said over and over, 'It's Jesus!'"

Thomas M. Watkins is Director of Donor Services for Trans World Radio, an international Christian radio ministry based in Cary, NC. He has served as a contributing writer and editor of Christian books and periodicals, as well as business trade publications.

After he got out of the service, he was still planning to attend Juilliard. He was by himself on a trolley one day headed to north Philadelphia, but found that he couldn't get off. God was speaking to him about giving up his musical aspirations and becoming a minister, but Dr. Johnson initially resisted. Finally, he submitted his will to the Lord's.

"I saw Christianity as a scale balancing sin versus good works, when God showed me that I was guaranteed to go to Heaven forever. He got me when I realized it was a guarantee." The year was 1949, and Dr. Johnson was 25 when he totally committed his life to Christ.

Dr. Johnson is quick to give credit to those who influenced his life for missions:

>*Dr. William J. Harvey, III.* Perhaps the earliest influence, Dr. Johnson met Dr. Harvey in 1947 when he was pastor of Pinn Memorial Church in Philadelphia. "He allowed me to preach and sing during the Baptist Training Union meeting at the church," Dr. Johnson recalled. "Dr. Harvey has become one of my role models as he is a man deeply committed to the concerns of foreign missions. It was 50 years before I met him again, and it was a blessing for me to listen to him and see for myself that he still had the same passion for missions that he had demonstrated throughout the years."

>*Dr. C.C. Adams and Dr. Daniel S. Malekebu.* Also in 1947, before Dr. Johnson was fully committed to Christ, Dr. Adams challenged him to consider becoming a missionary. Dr. Malekebu spent time with Dr. Johnson and shared his concern for young black men and how important it was for them to go to Africa. "Dr. Malekebu stressed the great need especially for missionaries in Malawi. Seeds were planted in me that would eventually sprout and mature into a lifetime commitment to foreign missions. How many times have I thanked God for the challenge that was given to me!"

>*Virginia Antrom and Gladys East.* Missions came down to an even more personal level for Dr. Johnson when Virginia Antrom, his classmate at Philadelphia College of Bible, shared with him that she was going to be a missionary, and he promised her that he would visit her. "She told me that she was supporting a missionary by the name of Gladys East, and I told her that I would support Ms. East financially. Three years later, during the Keystone Baptist Association assembly, my wife and I sat beside a lady--it was Gladys East! What a joy it was to finally meet the missionary that we were encouraging. This started a longtime friendship."

It was not long before Dr. Johnson transitioned into the role of influencing, encouraging, and mentoring others in missions, rising to prominence within the National Baptist Convention, U.S.A..

In April 1955, Dr. Johnson founded Christ Baptist Church in Philadelphia, pastoring there until June 1968. It was during that time that the church sent out 13 adult missionaries to home and foreign missions fields. Better known among the workers were Daisie Whaley to the Ivory Coast and Reginald, Clara, and Marcia Shipley to Liberia.

Another turning point occurred in 1957, when the Afro American Mission Board invited Dr. Johnson to become a board member. "It was an opportunity for me to be involved in foreign missions and to visit missionaries throughout the world," he observed. "The board had a mission station called Bopolu among the Kpelle tribe in Liberia. In 1963 it was my privilege to go there for three months and gather a report for the board. During my stay in Liberia, I was invited by Mother May Davis to have a Bible conference for a week. It was a wonderful experience for me to spend a week at Suehn and to be with my former classmate, Virginia Antrom."

From 1968 to 1973, Dr. Johnson served as a home missionary with the American Missionary Fellowship, formerly the American Sunday School Union. His tenure with that group gave him the opportunity to visit mission fields in South Africa, Canada, Losotho, Botswana, Spain, and Haiti as a conference and Bible teacher.

Dr. Johnson has also had a distinguished career in academia. He taught missions for 18 years at Manna Bible Institute in Philadelphia. His influence extended from Philadelphia to Chicago, IL, when he relocated there in 1972 to begin teaching at Moody Bible Institute in the departments of missions, Bible, and evangelism. He served as a full-time faculty member from 1972 to 1982, and then as an adjunct professor from 1982 to 1994. Desiring to also be active in the African-American community, he pastored two Chicago area churches during that time and founded a third one, Christ Community Church.

"This church also sent out missionaries, seven to Kenya in 1991, and some of the members visited mission fields in Nova Scotia," noted Dr. Johnson. "While I was in Chicago I was asked to be a board member of the Ambassadors Fellowship. We visited Liberia, Nigeria, and Kenya on behalf of missions, and took groups to Mexico every Thanksgiving. In 1990 I received an invitation to visit Israel, Jordan, and Gaza and visited missionaries while journeying in that part of the world."

Although Dr. Johnson has never had the opportunity to serve long-term in foreign missions overseas, the fire that has always burned brightly in his heart for missions continues today.

"God confirmed to me that I was to stay here. He said I should be still, pray, write and mentor. I pray for missionaries about five hours per day, whether I'm at home or riding along. I started praying for missionaries in 1951. When I'm not with people I am in intercession."

Among the unique doors of ministry that God has opened up to Dr. Johnson was the opportunity to discuss spiritual matters with Malcolm X.

"I love to argue," he conceded. "When I'm debating someone, I ask them to define Christianity, and then I deal with the foundational premise of their worldview. I take a person's statement of faith and go from there. Muslims, however, can't define this. They learn by rote and the average Muslim doesn't know what his statement of faith is."

Dr. Johnson believes that Malcolm X was a Christian at some point early in his life, but strayed from that faith.

"I asked Malcolm who he was condemning, the church, people, or behavior. Malcolm was a believer, but he was not taught. You must understand a person's ethnic-cultural conflict. Malcolm's father was killed by white men, and that was part of the root of his characterization of the white man as the

'blue-eyed devil.' But when he went to Mecca and saw white men bowing down to Allah, he no longer called them that.

"He went to jail because he was accused of going with a white woman. In prison he met highly-skilled teachers who taught black history and culture. That's one of the reasons Islam has been effective in converting blacks. It gives the black man self acceptance and self-esteem. When a man knows who he is, that's a tough man."

One of Dr. Johnson's unique strengths has been his intellectual defense of Christianity rooted in his many years in the academic world and his lifelong pursuit of learning. He was 59 years old when he received his master's degree from Wheaton Graduate School. At age 72, he was awarded a conferred doctorate degree from Great Commission Theological Seminary in Bowling Green, KY.

Recognizing science in the Bible and teaching it is one of his passions. "It's generally a no-no to teach science in Bible schools. So I took the Book of Genesis and taught 17 different sciences out of it. Psalm 104 alludes to 35 different sciences. Through the years, I have led at least five professors to Christ through this approach, along with Jews and Roman Catholics. You have to help someone study the Bible using their own background."

Since retiring from Moody and from his church in Chicago in 1995, Dr. Johnson has resided in the Nashville, TN, area. He has been partly responsible for the founding of Franklin Bible Institute in nearby Franklin and does a lot of lecturing, conferences, seminars, and speaking on missions, spiritual warfare, and prayer. Dr. Johnson also teaches and speaks on urban evangelism and how to minister in multiethnic, multicultural societies. He has published a number of works, recorded audio and video series, and is currently writing a manuscript titled, "*What God Taught Me Through My Wife*."

Dr. Johnson's gifts in intercessory prayer and as a worship and music leader have been and continue to be used by the Lord in many ways as well. He has traveled on occasion with Christian performers Michael Card and Steve Green, led congregational singing at concerts, done narration for special events such as Christmas presentations, and mentors pastors in missions and intercessory prayer. One of his callings is to also help churches have missions conferences--he is currently assisting four different churches desiring to hold their first conferences. Among those churches he has assisted has been his own, Greater Pleasant View Baptist Church.

Wherever Dr. Johnson travels, his rallying cry is for African-Americans and their pastors to be sold out to missions, but he is sobered about the many obstacles.

"God is moving. People want to go, but sometimes it is the pastors who stop them," he lamented. "A lot of it goes back to how poorly we have often supported our own churches and pastors. I know pastors of churches with 400-500 members who have to work full-time outside the church to make a living. One pastor told me his best givers were two families who were considering leaving for the missions field. In another church, five people gave almost half of the church's income. These are the kinds of situations we are up against when people feel called to missions.'"

Even at his age, Dr. Johnson acknowledges that "the fire (for missions) has not gone out. I can't go but I can send." He took the opportunity to issue a final challenge.

"Few folks, black or white, really follow Christ. Salvation is free, but service is costly."

African-Americans Crossing Cultures

Wanted: Black Missionaries, But How?

Leslie Pelt

Leslie Pelt has served with SIM International in Nigeria since 1984 in Christian education curriculum development. From Chicago, she holds degrees from Moody Bible Institute and Wheaton College Graduate School.

Originally published in Evangelical Missions Quarterly, *January, 1989. Copied by permission from EMQ, P.O. Box 794, Wheaton, IL 60189.*

In Nigeria, I've been surprised at the number of people who have said to me, "You are the first black missionary we've ever seen. Aren't black people in America Christians?" Or, "Please tell more black missionaries to come."

The fact that there are so few black American missionaries serving cross-culturally is disheartening. Historically, blacks have been deeply involved in missions all over the world. But in this century the vision seemed to die and the missionary force dwindled. In the average black church today, the missions committee focuses on nursing home visitation and food distribution. Very few blacks are going across cultures with the Gospel.

But there are signs that the black church is beginning to awaken to Christ's command to spread the Gospel throughout the world. The Destiny '87 Conference proved this. Approximately 1,600 black Americans gathered in Atlanta, GA, for a conference on the significant contribution we can make in reaching the world for Christ. Testimonies from some of the few black Americans who are serving as missionaries, as well as challenges from national church leaders, inspired conference participants to take Acts 1:8 seriously.

Representatives from a number of well-known mission-sending agencies attended. Sensitive to the scarcity of blacks in their organizations, they came with their displays and application forms, seeking out those who sensed God's call. As I observed the mission representatives interacting with the conference participants, I thought of the many challenges these predominantly white mission organizations will face in their attempts to recruit and retain black missionaries.

I wish I'd had the opportunity to ask each mission agency represented why they want to bring blacks into their organization. A respectable motivation is fundamental. It sometimes seems that mission boards are spurred to action by current missiological trends: unreached groups, Muslims, "world-class" cities. A current trend now seems to be minorities in missions, and mission organizations are endeavoring to bring blacks, as well as other minorities, under their umbrellas.

But in their efforts, I hope that the motivation isn't merely to keep up with the times. If it is, that is painfully near to the tokenism that we experienced 20 years ago when blacks were given a few conspicuous jobs to make the employer look good.

I remember when someone from my mission said, "I'm glad you joined the mission because we need more blacks." This person meant well, but I would rather have heard, "I'm glad you joined the mission because I think you'll make a valuable contribution." Blacks should not be recruited because mission agencies feel they need to have black missionaries, but because their gifts can be used to expand and strengthen the ministry.

Unique Challenge for Blacks

As mission agencies strive to bring in more blacks, they need to realize the unique challenges we as black Americans face as we awaken to our global responsibilities.

A principal reason why so few blacks serve as missionaries is because all too often we still consider ourselves to be a mission field. "Come over to the inner-city and help us" many black churches have called for a good part of this century, and for valid reasons. Between 1910 and 1930 close to a million blacks from the South migrated to northern cities in search of jobs and in hopes of escaping poverty, lynchings, and discrimination. They soon discovered that the North held few solutions to these problems and most were forced to live in crowded, run-down slums. The black church began to focus on developing the black community and dealing with the poverty, crime, unemployment, and despair that were destroying our race. Assistance from outside the community was generally welcomed, and the inner-city became a mission field.

Today many blacks still live in inner-city communities, urban problems are as prevalent and corrosive as ever, and people are still going to the inner city as missionaries. But urban squalor no longer describes the situation that the majority of black Americans find themselves in. Millions of them have moved into the mainstream of American life. Good jobs, quality education, nice homes, and strong, stable churches are all part of the scenario.

Although many of our communities no longer need outside help, we haven't totally left behind the mission field mentality that we had in the ghetto. I asked the pastor of a large, wealthy black church in California if they sent out or supported missionaries. He responded, "Why should we? We are looking for missionaries to come to California and work with us."

This church was meeting the needs of its Jerusalem in exciting ways, but it was also teeming with talented, well-educated Christians who could make an impact on the world, yet lacked the vision. Far too many black churches have this limited perspective, but fortunately not all.

I put black churches into four basic categories related to their response to the Great Commission. Many are unable to get involved in missions outside of the community because their own needs are so great. Many are unwilling to get involved in missions outside of the community because they still consider themselves a mission field. Many are unaware of the role they could have in missions outside of the community and have yet to discover their potential. And many would love to get involved in missions outside of the community, but they don't know what they can do or where they are needed. These churches need mission agencies, and mission agencies will find such congregations enthusiastic and responsive. The secret is discovering these churches.

Mission Boards Unknown

During my furlough I spoke in a number of black churches that wanted to get involved in missions. In these churches I found that almost no one had ever heard of my mission board, even though it is very well known in all the white churches in which I spoke. Few black churches are familiar with any mission boards.

I've also observed that most blacks serving under nondenominational mission agencies come from predominantly white churches. People learn about mission organizations through missionaries, but because very few missionaries are in contact with black congregations, mission organizations are virtually unknown. As a result, hundreds of potential missionaries have no idea about what to do to get to the mission field.

Unfortunately, there are no simple solutions to this problem. Mission boards and black churches won't come together naturally, primarily because there is a polarization between the black and the white church in America. I'm not saying this as a criticism. Black worship reflects black culture. Proponents of the homogeneous unit principle would say that this division is ideal for church growth. But we must find ways to bridge this chasm if we want to work together to reach the world for Christ.

Mission organizations can take the first bold step by encouraging culturally sensitive representatives to make contact with black churches and build bridges. As the churches learn of the ministries of the mission, many will be interested in having missionaries come and speak, as well as national church leaders when they are in the country. Young people could be encouraged to participate in short-term projects, thus giving the church an initial taste of what it's like to send out a missionary as well as an inside perspective into what the mission field is like. As trust and understanding are built, more blacks will join these mission organizations.

Financial Support

Another major challenge in getting blacks to the mission field is financial support. Imagine that a black congregation has a burden for missions, is familiar with a sending agency, and a family from the church senses God's call to Papua New Guinea. The church will be thrilled until they learn that the yearly support for a family of five could be over $40,000. For a church that has never supported a missionary, this figure is astronomical. The shock might be enough to extinguish their missions vision.

I know a family of four from a black church who have been raising support for almost two years and are still painfully short. Mission organizations will lose a lot of candidates at this point, unless they are aware that support raising is a foreign concept in many black churches.

But if mission boards are willing to strategize with black appointees, and help them to network with other churches, they will be more successful in getting these new missionaries to the field. For example, if mission agencies are aware of churches that have financial resources, have the desire to support missionaries, and perhaps have no prospective missionaries of their own, they can bring these churches together with black churches that are overwhelmed by the responsibility of supporting their first missionaries. This could produce an exciting partnership that could break down racial barriers, to the benefit of all the members of both congregations.

Perplexing Field Situations

This is just a sampling of the many issues mission sending agencies will need to work through as they recruit blacks for missionary service. But the challenges don't end here. Once black missionaries are on the field, they face another series of perplexing situations that may initially be difficult and discouraging, but if handled properly will strengthen the mission organizations.

When I arrived in Nigeria, I was immediately welcomed and warmly embraced in a way that most missionaries are not. It was a great feeling and my initial conclusion was that it is definitely advantageous to be a black missionary in Africa. But I soon noticed that people seemed to have higher expectations of me than of my white counterparts. I sensed that the Nigerians thought, "Because she looks like us, and because her forefathers probably came from this area, she should learn our language faster, have an inherent understanding of our culture, and not have any of the white man's peculiar habits."

As time passed, I realized that when I made cultural mistakes, and when I displayed some of the white man's peculiarities, their disappointment was much greater than if I had been white because their expectations were so much higher. Fortunately, I loved the culture and I adjusted quickly. Later I concluded that being black could also be a disadvantage. Because of the Nigerians' expectations, if a black missionary is a cultural imperialist and has little appreciation of the national way of life, he or she will be ostracized more rapidly and much more severely than a white person who behaves the same way.

I've talked to black Americans who have visited Africa and said they were in shock when after a few days the Africans began to call them "white men." I'm sure this was because they were expected to be more understanding and accepting of African ways, but when they proved to be typical American tourists, their skin color was no longer visible, and the Africans made it a point to let them know.

If a black missionary doesn't live up to the higher expectations, if he or she is culturally insensitive or arrogant, and thus made to feel unwelcome in the host country, they probably will leave the ministry. Instead of seeing their mistakes, they will believe the old myth that Africans don't want to see black Americans anyway.

But I found that if a black missionary is sensitive to culture, many extraordinary avenues of ministry will open that don't ordinarily present themselves to missionaries. So, mission organizations should be prepared to deal with cultural issues before the black missionary is sent to the field, to reduce the chances of failure and promote unique ministry possibilities.

The black experience in America will give the black missionary a unique perspective on a variety of situations. A common practice that black missionaries might be particularly offended by is exclusivism among missionaries. Fortunately, in many parts of the world the days of hospitals, schools, and compounds being restricted to missionary personnel are over. Nonetheless, shadows of this era still linger. As I talk to missionaries serving on various fields, I learn that the missionary subculture still excludes national Christians from many activities and conveniences in many subtle ways.

To black Americans, this is reminiscent of the old Jim Crow laws in the South, or apartheid in South Africa. The black experience in America has made our race sensitive to issues, attitudes, and practices that offend nonwestern people. While missionaries often must be told that something is offensive, the black missionary may already have an innate awareness of this. Because of this, an integrated missions force can help mission organizations better perceive subtle acts of discrimination that can hinder the Gospel.

The black missionary might also find himself in an uncomfortable position during times of church-mission tension. Once again, the black experience will affect the black missionary's perspective. When national church leaders voice such complaints as, "Missionaries underestimate us. They dictate what ministries are most important and try to exercise too much control over church government," the black missionary may immediately remember the years of feeling dominated and powerless in America, and find himself much more sympathetic to the national church than the mission. Caught in the middle, the black missionary could act as a bridge to help resolve these recurring issues. But such problems could also result in division if Satan is allowed to get the upper hand. However, if these situations are dealt with in patience and love, the mission organization can only be strengthened.

Numerous unique challenges and hurdles confront blacks as they move into the mainstream of evangelical missions, but the benefits will be immeasurable. Many black churches are ready to connect with mission agencies. I'm convinced that God will use this new partnership in ways beyond imagination to reach the world with the Gospel of Jesus Christ. A multiethnic mission society is a testimony to the unity we have in Christ, and, as Francis Schaeffer used to say, that is our best apologetic.

Bibliography

Banks, William L., *The Black Church in the U.S. Chicago*, IL, Moody Press, 1972.

Beaver, R. Pierce, *All Loves Excelling*. Grand Rapids, MI: William Eerdmans, Pub. Co., 1968.

Gordon, Robert, "Black Man's Burden." *Evangelical Missions Quarterly*, Fall, 1973.

Jacobs, Sylvia M. Black, *Americans and the Missionary Movement in Africa*, Westport, CT: Greenwood Press, 1982.

Jones, Howard O., *Shall We Overcome?*, Westwood, NJ: Fleming H. Revell Co., 1966.

Prozan, Virginia M., "A Religious Survey of the Bahama Islands, British West Indies." M.A. Thesis, Columbia Graduate School, 1961.

Trulson, Reid. "The Black Missionaries." HIS magazine, June, 1973, 37:9.

Tucker, Ruth A., *From Jerusalem to Irian Jaya.*, Grand Rapids, MI: Zondervan Pub, 1983.

Williams, Walter L., *Black Americans and the Evangelization of Africa*, 1977-1900.   Madison, WI: U. of Wisconsin Press, 1982.

A CHRONOLOGY OF BLACK MISSIONS

Prior to 1800

1770s. John Marrant, a free black from New York City, was already ministering cross-culturally, preaching to the Indians. By 1775 he had carried the Gospel to the Cherokee, Creek, Catawar, and Housaw Indians.

1782. George Liele, former pastor of First Africa Church of Savannah, GA, upon hearing that the British were declaring peace with the colonies, indentured himself to a British officer in order not to be re-enslaved by his former master's heirs. He and his family moved to Kingston, Jamaica. After two years he had paid back his indenture and was able to devote all of his energy to preaching. With four other former American slaves, he formed the First African Baptist Church of Kingston. In 10 years the church grew to over 500. He is considered to be the first American missionary.

David George, of the Silver Bluff, SC, Baptist Church—the first black Baptist church in America—went to Nova Scotia and ministered to exiled blacks there. In 1792, he traveled with 12,000 black settlers to Sierra Leone, West Africa.

Brother Amos, from the Savannah church, sailed for the Bahamas and settled in New Providence, where he planted a church that grew to 850 members by 1812.

1783. Moses Baker and George Gibbions, both former slaves, left America to become missionaries in the West Indies.

1790. Prince Williams, a freed slave from SC, went to Nassau, Bahamas, where he started Bethel Meeting House. In 1801, he and other blacks organized the Society of Anabaptists. At age 70, Williams erected St. John's Baptist Church and pastored there until he died at age 104. Subsequently, 164 Baptist churches were planted in the Bahamas.

Black Missions in the 1800s

1815. Lott Carey, America's first missionary to Africa, was born a slave in VA. He became pastor of the 800 member African Baptist Church in Richmond, VA, and in 1815 led in the formation of the Richmond African Baptist Missionary Society. After collecting $700, Carey and his wife, together with Colin Teague and his wife and son, sailed for Sierra Leone. After establishing a mission among the Mandingoes, Carey moved to Liberia. By 1826, he had formed a missionary society in connection with his church in Monrovia.

1818. John Stewart, a free-born black from VA, was converted at a camp meeting. He went to the Wyandot Indian reservation in OH, where he met Jonathan Pointer, a black who had been taken prisoner in his youth by the Wyandots. Pointer knew their language, so he interpreted for Stewart. In 1818, his successful ministry came to the attention of Ohio Methodists, who licensed him to preach. Even though the Methodist Episcopal Church officially formed its missionary society in 1819, John Stewart's ministry among the Indians is considered to be the actual beginning of Methodist missions.

1820 to 1860. The primary sending group was the American Colonization Society, which repatriated American blacks to Liberia.

1821. Daniel Coker went to West Africa with the first group sent out by the American Colonization Society.

1823. Betsy Stockton applied to the American Board of Missions and went to Hawaii. She is recognized as the first single woman missionary in the history of modern missions. She served as a domestic assistant and conducted a school. Prior to going to Hawaii, she had lived in the household of the president of Princeton College and while there had read extensively in his library. She was well qualified to teach.

1827. Scipio Beanes sailed for Haiti.

1836. The Providence Missionary Baptist District Association was formed, one of at least six national organizations among Negro Baptists whose sole objective was African missions.

1849. Robert Hill was sent to Liberia by the Southern Baptist Convention.

1860 to 1877. General missionary activity increased after the Civil War, as the number of free blacks increased from 68,000 to over 665,000. The gains made in education, politics, and civil rights began to manifest themselves on the mission field. By 1868, 12 of the 13 Presbyterian USA staff in Liberia were blacks. Blacks serving under the Protestant Episcopal Church outnumbered Whites by 21 to 5 in 1876.

1883. William Colley and five others left VA for Liberia.

1890. William Henry Shepherd went 900 miles inland in the Congo. Liked by the Africans, he became skilled in their language. He was a teacher and preacher who offered medical aid when he could. He also helped to ransom slaves.

1894. Mary Tearing was 56 years old when she left America for the Congo. Because of her age, she was not accepted for support, so she sold her house, collected her savings, and raised $100 per month support from local church women and went to the Congo. She was instrumental in starting homes for girls and young women. Her work was so exceptional that within two years she was receiving full support from her board.

Black Missions in the 20th Century

The 20th century saw a decline in black missions, in part for the following reasons:

1. The membership growth of independent black churches from 30,000 in the late 1800s to over four million by 1916. This cut off the blacks from the mainline sending denominations. More blacks interested in the ministry stayed at home to serve this growth.

2. The Student Volunteer Movement, the chief recruiter of missionaries, worked primarily at colleges and universities where blacks were least likely to be found.

3. The development of quinine to fight malaria reduced the fears of whites about going to Africa, thus reducing the needs on one of the primary fields that blacks were recruited to serve.

4. Lack of money caused a drop in the ability of many black churches to support missions.

5. Paternalism of the blacks by the whites on the mission field caused less interest by blacks in working under white missionaries.

6. Some American blacks were not welcomed in some countries for political reasons.

7. Growing black materialism choked off concern for missions. "If we expect to see an increase of black missionaries on the foreign fields, the black churches of America must awaken to their own financial obligation to their missionaries" (Howard Jones).

(Based on a paper, "The History of American Black Missionaries," by Larry Filbert, Robert Mosely, Richard Smith, and Frans Van der Heever, courtesy of Ken Mulholland, dean of Columbia (SC) Biblical Seminary and Graduate School of Missions.)

Back to Africa

Harold R. Isaacs

Harold Robert Isaacs, born in 1910, in New York, NY, received a B.A. at Columbia College in 1930. He was a member of the Academy of Arts and Sciences (fellow). Isaacs was known as a political scientist, educator, editor, journalist, and author. He traved to and became an expert on China and Southeast Asia. He wrote for numerous entities such as: China Press, Havas News Agency, Columbia Broadcasting System, Newsweek, Harvard University, Cambridge, New School for Social Research, and MIT. His writings reflect his heart for people suffering under oppressive rule.

Taken from *Practical Anthropology*, Volume 10, 1963 (now: *Missiology: An International Review*), 616 Walnut Ave. Scottdale, PA 15683. Used by permission.

This article was originally published in *The New Yorker Magazine*, May 13, 1961.

*A*frica has a special appeal to many an American Negro who wants to be a missionary, and the American Negro missionary often plays a very important role for Christ in Africa. However, the sense of romantic identification which he often feels in the U.S. is frequently shattered quite drastically when he arrives in Africa, and a new identification based on the reality that his culture is miles apart from African cultures has to be built up slowly over time. In this [1961] article Mr. Isaacs is not discussing missionaries, but he is discussing the strains and contradictions in American Negro life in Africa. These social forces are part of the contemporary scene, and need to be in the thinking of Negroes and Caucasians alike.

It fell to me last summer to travel across West Africa to observe, among other things, some of the interaction between world politics and race relations, a matter on which I have been making a special inquiry for Massachusetts Institute of Technology's Center for International Studies. This interaction is a pretty lively affair in West Africa just now and since. My travels took me from Nigeria to Ghana and then to Guinea and Liberia, and I saw and heard quite a bit of it taking place. One aspect of it in particular acquired new dimensions for me as I began to meet American Negroes and talk with them about their experiences in Africa. The matters of which we talked were impersonal, in the large, but were also intensely personal, and, for that reason, in my account of these conversations I will use no names and will blur places while I try not to blur what these individuals had to say.

One of the first American Negroes I met was a young but highly qualified professional who had come out on a three-year contract to teach in his special field. I asked him why he had taken this job, and he said, "I came to Africa because I was looking for a place to be comfortable. I thought I might feel easier here, feel more free, just settle down and do a job and be myself." He shook his head at my unasked question. "No," he said, "I haven't."

Practically all the American Negroes I met in West Africa had come to the ancestral continent with some form of the same idea in their minds. They had come looking for freedom from racism and prejudice, or at least for a racial situation that counted them "in" instead of "out"—that provided solace and a sense of identity in a world where everyone was black. They had also looked for a chance to share in the new pride of achievement stemming from the black man's reassertion of himself and his "African personality." In West Africa, in a small way and for a short time, the Negro pilgrim can find some of this. But it does not last long—hardly past the first flush of the sensation of being in a place where the white man is not master. Almost invariably, the Negro pilgrim in Africa soon finds himself not free at all, more than ever without solace and a sense of identity, fighting new patterns of prejudice, and suffering the pangs of a new kind of outsider-ness. He had thought that he was alien in America, but he discovers that he is much more alien in Africa. Whether he likes it or not, he is American, and in Africa he becomes an American in exile.

The outburst by some Negroes in the gallery of the United Nations Security Council in New York during the Lumumba demonstrations in February at least served to make more people aware that American Negroes are experiencing their own kind of confusion over the events in emergent Africa. It is a peculiar and painful confusion, cutting to the core of what Negroes think about themselves and about their place in American society and in the world. Everything is changing in their universe, too—those winds blow not only across Africa—forcing upon them all kinds of new conceptions and self–conceptions, and among these are new ideas and emotions about Africa itself, the hitherto remote and rejected ancestral homeland. The gallery demonstrators were merely an extremist handful, but at some point these new stirrings touch all kinds of people in every part of the American Negro community.

The idea of going "back to Africa" has a long history among American Negroes. It has always been one ultimate option for those who felt despair over the prospect of achieving their full rights as human beings in the life of America. Such was the despair that in the years after the First World War led hundreds of thousands to line up with their money for Marcus Garvey's Black Star Line.

Today there is certain despair among many Negroes over the slow pace of change in America; the faster some changes come, the more intolerable become the persisting survivals of the past. But despairing Negroes now can feel what Negroes could not feel in Garvey's time—astonishment and exhilaration over the swift pace of change in Africa, offering them for the first time the basis for a proud association with the continent of their remote origins. Hence the whole new stir of impulses among American Negroes. Hence the fact that if you go to Africa now, you meet American Negroes, working, traveling, and questing.

Most of the Negroes you meet in West Africa nowadays are travelers, come, like everyone else, to have a look at the boiling and bubbling turmoil of the African emergence. Some of these are notables—guests at the frequent celebrations, delegates to the innumerable conferences, members of advisory commissions—and others are more ordinary folk, such as a fast-moving, exuberant Chicago, IL, schoolteacher I met who was spending her savings on a swift tour of the continent, all by herself, just to have a look, "so I can tell the children in my classes what it is really like." A much smaller number of the Negroes have come out on particular jobs—scholars, teachers, technical specialists on contract for one, three, or five years to various African institutions. Then, there are the Negroes scattered through the official American establishments: an ambassador, regular embassy staff members, cultural attachés, information officers, members of technical-aid missions—perhaps a dozen in all. Besides these short-term expatriates, there is a smaller group of longer-term, or even permanent, expatriates, who have come to try to make new lives for themselves in Africa. Leaving aside the Negroes who live in Liberia, with its history of special links with America and American Negroes, this is now a small number of individuals, varying greatly in activity and outlook. A few of the expatriates are businessmen who have come, scored, and stayed. These are people who live as American and European expatriate businessmen, have usually lived abroad, sending their children home to school and getting back themselves once in a while for a visit. But there are at least two kinds of expatriates who have made rather more permanent commitments. The first consists of young women who have married Africans, usually as a result of campus romances in

America, and have come to Africa to live. These may number up to several dozen in West Africa now. Finally, in the smallest numbers of all—I met only two and heard of only two or three others – there are migrants who left America because they were no longer willing or able to bear life here as Negroes, and who are committed to seeking some kind of new life for themselves in their new setting. One of the two I met was a young woman who had become a Liberian through naturalization and then a Ghanaian by marriage. She was, incidentally, the only American Negro I met in West Africa who had given up her American citizenship.

Here and there in the several countries I visited, I met individuals in each of these situations, and I listened long and hard to some of them. The forms of their experience and the details varied greatly, but with only one or two exceptions they were all moving toward the same conclusion. It was perhaps best put by a young man who had come to Africa to see if there was any relief there from the anger he carried in his heart against America and the whole world of white men: "I came to Africa feeling like a brother, but there I was, I was not a brother. I was not Senegalese or Nigerian or Ghanaian, I was American, an American Negro from Anglo-Saxon culture, or as much of it as filtered down to me determining what I am, what I think, what I feel. I could come back, and color might not be a problem, but I would always be an outsider coming in. It would be true of any outsider, and true of me. It's the way anybody looks at a stranger."

The young professional who had come out to teach because he was "looking for a place to be comfortable" had been very successful at home, a man who was among the first in his field and in his particular job. But he was weary of "being special," weary of always fighting, always being vigilant. In his college days he had met some Nigerian students who impressed him by their air of dedication to something larger than themselves. So when the chance came to him to teach in his field in Africa for a few years he took it up. "I was greeted with, 'Welcome, brother, you've been through a hard time'—that sort of feeling," he told me. "I did not like being patron-

ized this way. I also found that the air of dedication was deceiving. It is the old rat race here that it is everywhere else." He also found that being an American did not mean, if you were a Negro, only that you were a victim of discrimination. It also meant that you were used to telephone conversations that worked, too; that is, appointments that were kept, promises that were carried out, or decisions that were remembered the next day. "It's ridiculous, but I had never before realized how much of my life had nothing to do with the race problem at all,"' he said. "I mean just the way you do everything you do, what you mean when you say something, and how you understand what the other fellow means. I simply cannot function the way they do here. I like things put straight and got out of the way. Nothing is done that way here. Nothing is fixed. Do you realize what it means to have to bargain about the price of the bread you buy every day?"

But there was a sharper and deeper edge to his feelings than mere impatience with slow or inefficient African ways. When he invited me to his home that evening to take potluck with him and his wife, I discovered that they were servant-less, having fired their "steward" only the day before. In their long recital of their experience with him, it became clear that they had fired him not only because he was incompetent, dishonest, and unresponsive, and not because the unfamiliar sensation of having a servant made them uncomfortable or uncertain. The breaking point came when, after one of their final expostulations with him, he argued back that he was held in contempt by his friends and fellow-stewards because he was working for them and they were not white. This was the real reason they threw him out.

The subject of relations with servants came up quite often in these encounters. Indeed, one of the more ironic experiences that an old Shanghai resident, which I happen to be, can have in West Africa these days is to listen to members of a new generation of American expatriates talking about their servants—the humor and irritations of dealing with them, and what there was to learn from them about African mores, habits, and character. There was also an echo of old China days when I dined one evening in the home of a white American who had been raised in China. "There is just no comparison," my hostess sighed. "No comparison at all between these African servants and those wonderful Chinese servants we had!" Thus the ironies in all the talk about servants cut several ways and made a crisscrossing design of their own among the swiftly changing relationships of our time. It was not only that these were Americans, white or Negro, who would probably not have servants at home; this was largely true in the old days, too. Nor was it that they were likely to have ideas of equality and dignity that did not fit with the master-servant relationship; this was also true of some in the past. But in the past it was possible for many expatriates to be drawn quite easily into conformity with the established order of things—the colonial system was one big master-servant relationship, after all—and even to begin taking to the habit of mastery with increasing relish. Today, as everyone now knows except the Portuguese, colonialism is dead or dying. Some of its behavior patterns survive among the older expatriate hands and are still seized upon by a few of the uglier newcomers. But, generally speaking, everyone nowadays is called upon to be as democratic and equal as possible, and Americans are more self-conscious about this than any other people, including the Russians. Hence it comes as an embarrassing shock—especially to the American determined not to be ugly—that the "'new" democracy is for him to practice, while his hosts, the upper crust of the newly emancipated people, treat their own servants, and all other inferior orders, with remarkable contempt. In West Africa, as in most of Asia, there are few things uglier than an upper bureaucrat's bearing toward a middle bureaucrat, or a middle bureaucrat's bearing toward a lower, or the bearing of any of them toward any menials in their service. "They treat them horribly!" exclaimed a dismayed young woman, a Negro traveler who had enjoyed all of her journey until she stayed for a few days in the home of some African friends. "'The servants need force, they tell you, and even say they are not human and you don't have to worry about them. They

feed them scraps from the table, they yell at them and call them names. I would try to be nice to the servants, but my hosts never liked this." This behavior on the part of Africans is peculiarly shocking to anyone who has idealized the African struggle for freedom, or who has thought that only whites treated blacks with disrespect, and it is especially painful to Negroes, for until just the day before yesterday almost the only place open to them in society was that of menial or servant. "I run into this quite a bit," observed an American Negro who is now a permanent resident in Africa. "In the attitude of the policemen toward the people, for example, and the customs officers at the border. There is the attitude toward servants and also the attitude of the steward toward the 'small boy,' of the cook toward the steward. The same attitude exists in the government bureaucracy—obsequious to the higher, nasty to the lower. This does not exist among us. My mother, at home in America, is a domestic—she still is, because she likes to work. But she likes the people she works for. She is never made to feel anything like this; she is an individual. But here, unfortunately, it is very common; you get it right through the society."

There is an even more mordant aspect to the matter as well. Hardly any scorn is more justified than that felt by Negroes for whites in America who say they "know" Negroes because they have had them for servants or work hands all their lives. Yet I met Negroes in West Africa who "knew" all sorts of things about Africans—things they had gleaned almost exclusively from their servants.

The experience of American girls who have married Africans and gone to Africa to live is a subject impatiently awaiting its author. It is hard to know just how many such marriages there are now; I was told last summer that in the city of Accra alone there were then about a dozen. As more and more African students come to the U.S., there will be more and more of them. In the eyes of the African, the educated American Negro girl is a great prize. By marrying such a girl he is often making a major bid to complete his passage from his own traditional culture to the new world of modernism and change. American girls are attracted to these romances for different reasons—Lorraine Hansberry showed us one of them in *A Raisin in the Sun* —but one of the most poignant is the groping of the dark Negro girl for the regard and acceptance that are still so largely withheld from her in American Negro society. Wherever these marriages begin, however, they soon run into rough going, or so I was told. The American wives of Ghanaians in Accra were described to me by other Negro residents and by two of their own number as a group of unhappy and frustrated women who spend much of their time sharing their complaints and trying to console each other.

The complaints vary, but living conditions are large among them. While some of the husbands manage to do well with the professions they acquired abroad, most of them have to be satisfied with jobs that give them a standard of living miles above that of the lowly African laborer but still not so high for a girl raised in modest, or even poor, circumstances in Harlem or on Chicago's South Side. Even where there is not actual poverty, or what seems to be poverty, there are the hurdles of differences in habit, taste, and diet, there are the complexities of marketing and bargaining, and there are the deeply engrossing problems of ordinary sanitation. Although these are not necessarily great things, they are not easy to adjust to, either. But much more painful, it appears, are the problems of American girls married to husbands who often have rather un-American ideas about the status of women. "In Africa," one of these wives told me, "even when they are Christians, they do not understand that a wife can talk up to her husband and that she has a right to be heard by her husband. They just don't understand this!" There was also some discussion of the peculiarly nettling combination of male jealousy, resulting in strict control of the behavior of the wife, and a freewheeling view of the permissible behavior of the husband. This is not uniquely African, but in the African setting it is often bound up with some profoundly different customs and attitudes. In certain groups, for example, child-spacing is achieved by an imposed continence until well after the child is weaned—sometimes a matter of two years,

or even more. In this period, the wife is restricted and the husband definitely is not. This may lead, as anyone can readily see, to serious problems in an American girl's marriage.

What these girls have to cope with is the familiar but always difficult pattern of contradictions and ambivalences in the ways of a human being in motion between two cultures. Only very rarely does such a person succeed in shedding all the old ways and adopting all the new. However far he does go in one direction, he is still tied by a thousand bonds of upbringing, habit, and family to the customs and practices of the culture in which he was raised. These conflicts can sometimes be gracefully reconciled, but usually they are not—especially not in an inter-cultural marriage involving an American girl, with her ideas of her own rights and dignity. African cultures have not assigned many rights or much dignity to women. They are the hewers and the drawers of the society; in fact, to put it quite bluntly, they appear to do all the great volume of work that the men have been able to avoid doing. African traditional culture is also still quite largely polygamous, and this is an issue about which emergent African men are going to hear more and more from emergent African women. I was not told of any American girl who was confronted with another wife to share her husband and her home. One assumes—or hopes—that this is one issue that is settled before marriage, and that an African taking an American wife knows he is committing himself to a one-and-only. In any case, there are other problems, and they are quite formidable enough. Often much worse than the matter of the husband's relations with other women is the matter of the wife's relations with her husband's family.

On first arriving almost anywhere in West Africa now, an America Negro visitor feels a tingling thrill to see black men everywhere, black men doing all the jobs, lowly and high, right up to the black men who now sit in the seats of power, occupy the palaces, and whiz through town in their limousines. It is like a dream he never thought could come true. He feels a great relieving pleasure wash over him at the loss of conspicuousness in a black crowd. "It gave me a sort of joy," said a young man from the Midwest. "On the streets, the billboards with black faces, and, most of all, that great sea of black faces the day I went to the stadium." Yet almost at once this young man's sensation became mixed. He did not want to get that lost, and, more particularly, he did not want anybody to mistake him for an African.

"I will confess that sometimes I resented the fact that I was mistaken for an African," he told me. "Like going into a bank and not getting received there like an American—I mean sometimes getting attention. This would just come as a flash in the mind. When you were mistaken for an African, you did not get that kind of service, even from Africans. Walking the street as a black man, I was just part of the crowd. But never once did I want to be an African. Why was this? I would ask myself. It was a pleasure to me not to stand out in a place, the way you do whenever you walk into a room full of white people. You don't want that kind of special attention drawn to you. In Africa I enjoyed not having this special place. But I didn't want to be mistaken for an African. When I walked into that bank, I wanted special service as an American. I put on a robe once, and sandals, but I really wanted to be seen not as an African but as an American wearing this apparel. I wanted to be understood to be an American. I can't explain this contradiction. As a Negro, you are always pushing so many things away. Maybe I have never really faced up to it. In Africa, I wanted to get lost in that black sea as a black man, but I did not want to get lost as an American in an African culture. In America the Negro is conspicuous but also is not seen as an individual. I am not *me*; I'm some kind of Negro. In Africa I was not conspicuous, and could be taken more as an individual, but I wanted to be taken as an American individual, not an African."

There was another reaction some of the Negro visitors had as they moved among these busy masses of black men so newly free of their white masters. It was a certain stab: here were these Africans, who one had always thought were so far behind, now running so far ahead. Thereafter, the reactions would divide; some of the visitors would go

on feeling left behind by the Africans, and would bow their heads lower and lower as they ran into African views on this subject; others would begin to discover virtues in their own American identity that they had never suspected were there. After a while, some actually would come to the point of saying, as one man said to me, "Please don't misunderstand, but I find myself thinking: Thank God for slavery! It got me out of this and made me what I am instead!"

In most places, the Negro visitor is still likely to get a hearty first greeting: "Welcome, brother! When will *all* our brothers come home?" There is a lot of this, but the subject of that original departure remains oddly guarded. I was told that Africans do not much like to talk about it. Few Negroes seem to have given much thought to the fact that black Africans had a good deal to do with the capture and sale of the slaves. Eight years ago, when the late Richard Wright first came to that coast, he bridled at the first African he met, selling him as the great-great-great-grandson of that so-and-so who sold his great-great-great grandfather into slavery. The Negro pilgrim today can visit some of the places where such sales were made. Until recently, Kwame Nkrumah [prime minister and president of Ghana] occupied one of them as his official residence—Christiansborg Castle, right on the sea at Accra. But the old slave dungeons and passages here have long since been sealed off. When I visited it—Nkrumah having just moved out to take over the governor-general's residence in town—I came by accident on a room, now a workshop, through whose walls some workmen were tunneling in an effort to find those dark corners of the past. Ninety miles up the Ghanaian coast, at Elmina Castle, there is more to see. To be sure, the descriptive leaflet they hand you there studiously omits any mention of the castle's role as an entrepôt in the slave trade. You are given its dates, an account of its successive Portuguese, Dutch, and British occupants, and a description of its present use as a police-training barracks. But here you can walk into the dungeons and crouch your way through the passages, look through the slits where the chiefs watched their "catch" sold to the white traders, and follow the stone path to the slithering rocks from which the slaves were run out to the ships beyond the breakers. The pilgrim looks out over the water and into the dimness of that past and thinks his thoughts. The African policeman who acts as guide gives no sign of appreciating the emotions involved. He even seems to think the visitor has come to see the police barracks, and not a place that his ancestors may have passed through as naked slaves so long ago. I must confess that when I stood at that spot, bleakly pondering the problem of faith in the spirit of man, I had the small but faintly consoling thought that my ancestors, whatever other sins they might have been committing at the time, were sequestered in some Eastern European ghetto, and could not have been among the slavers who waited out there on those ships. The Negro pilgrim who stands here, on the other hand, can think with pride and wonder of the strength and resilience that his ancestors must have had to survive their ordeal, and the great power to endure, to sorrow, and to win that [which] has been handed down to him. I have one friend who stood here and felt the great burden of shame for her slave past finally lift from her shoulders. She realized that it was to her black ancestors that she owed her powerful instinct to fight for life against all adversities, and with this she at least put to rest the obscure shame she had felt all her life in the belief that as a descendant of slaves she was somehow less than other people.

Now, in any case, the returning Negro pilgrim is greeted like a long-lost brother. Sometimes—usually in the remoter areas or among the less sophisticated people—this is a genuine, open-hearted welcome full of admiring wonderment at the strange brother who has been far away and has become something remarkably different, educated, successful, and, like all Americans, rich. Among the more sophisticated Africans and in the main centers, the Negro pilgrim also finds a welcome, up to a certain point. A good part of his feeling of welcome has simply to do with the fact that he finds himself at last in a place where he can go anywhere, anywhere at all, and feel blessedly free of that everlasting fear of humiliation, restriction, and exclusion.

This is no small thing, and the enjoyment of the sensation can last a long, long time. Some visitors never get beyond it, and they cherish the experience. ("Two whole months," said one. "For the first time in my life, two whole months without incidents or insults.") On occasion, the welcome is more active. Kwame Nkrumah and other African politicians are willing to exploit whatever capital there may be in the link with a politically important American minority, and both in Accra and in the U.S., whenever he has come here, Nkrumah has made much of the relationship. On his first return to the U.S. as Ghana's Prime Minister, Nkrumah shook a crowd at the armory in Harlem with a passionate appeal to race brotherhood and kinship. He hails successful Negro athletes and performers. Negro notables who come to Accra can be sure of high-level hospitality on the cocktail-and-dinner-party circuit.

But it does not take long for the Negro pilgrim who stays on for a little and gets past the first friendly greetings to discover that he is much more of a stranger than he is a brother. As Richard Wright learned on his journey in 1953, the stranger among Africans finds his path studded with difficulty, pain, and sometimes even danger. Wright was accused of blundering, of not knowing how to appreciate and get along with Africans, of probing too hard in the wrong places. It is certainly true that some Negro Americans have managed to get along better in West Africa than Wright did, but it is also true that they have done this by settling for much less than he was ready to settle for, and by not asking the questions he insistently asked. The truth is that the Negro American in West Africa today is much more like Wright's stranger than like Nkrumah's brother. He finds this out in a host of ways—some that barely pierce the surface of his feelings, some that cut deep.

It is painful for a black American to be rejected by black Africans, but it is both painful and unbearably ironic for him to be rejected, along with white Americans, by black Europeans. Among the new men of power in West Africa are a great many black Africans who are more British than the British, more French than the French. Indeed, long before they dreamed of becoming free Africans—which happened only recently—many of these men aspired mainly to become black Englishmen or black Frenchmen. They took from their masters not only their language but also their systems of thought, their views of history, and their ways of buying, selling, worshipping, running schools, and operating a bureaucracy. They also took all their little and big snobbisms. Mixed with their hate of the British and French colonialists was (and is) an intense desire to be as [much] like them as possible—a familiar phenomenon in the endless complexities of the struggle between higher and lower orders—so when they moved on at last to the greater joys of sovereignty, they carried their legacy from their ex-masters with them into the places of power. Hence the American who goes to Africa still not uncommonly meets in Africans a kind of low-grade copy of a variety of low-grade prejudice he used to meet in certain types of Englishmen and Frenchmen. According to this view, "Americans" are brash, loud, pushy, vulgar, materialistic, without culture or sophistication, wit, or knowledge. The West African who is so disposed applies this prejudice to all Americans, without regard to race creed, or color. No matter how alienated he may feel from his own society at home, the Negro American in Africa usually finds it no easier than the white American to keep his hackles down when this sort of thing comes up.

A well-known Negro social scientist in a visiting post at a West African University was not invited to the home of a single one of his African colleagues during his first nine months there, and in two years he was invited out in this circle only two or three times. When I saw him, near the end of his stay, he was still pondering the matter in some perplexity, unable to decide what kind of snobbism had been at work—British, academic, conservative, or plain African. Another Negro, serving on the staff of a U.S. embassy, recalled with some retrospective amusement how, on his first contacts with local government officials, he had had to face down remarks like "You gross Americans..." A young Negro in Senegal spent a whole summer finding his way through the personal, political, racial, and cultural haze of his relations with some Senegalese students.

"At bottom, I think they felt I was a barbarian because I wasn't French," he told me. "It was a schizophrenic sort of thing. They were African Frenchmen looking down on me, an American, just as they looked down on any English-speaking African. They were always talking about culture, and I finally realized that by culture they meant French culture!"

Besides being amusing, or annoying, this snobbism is sometimes damaging. Entrenched British and French attitudes about American education still govern much of West Africa—attitudes that were built up in the past partly out of real (if deluded) convictions held by the Europeans, partly out of the wish to keep young Africans from being infected by American ideas. Until quite recently, Africans who managed to get to America and earn degrees, even as medical doctors, had a hard time getting posts from African superiors trained by the British or the French. Americans have met with the same kind of rebuff. An American Negro girl who is a trained nurse was not accepted at a hospital in Accra and is still working in the city as a secretary. Another Negro, a man who has left America for good, was refused a teaching job because the local authorities would not recognize his degree. This pattern is breaking down, of course. Nkrumah himself was educated in America; thousands of African students are flocking to American colleges, or trying to, much to the dismay of some of the older group of European-trained officials; and American teachers and other specialists are making it hard for the old prejudices to survive. But meanwhile, the Negro American is not likely to be overcome with warmth toward those of his African kin who throw European aspersions on his hard-won American education. It is often an odd sensation for him to feel defensively American.

Negroes come questing to Africa for something they call "acceptance." What they seek may not be findable by anyone anywhere; certainly they do not find it in Africa. "The Negro who comes here has to have the right attitude," said one of the older hands among the American Negroes in West Africa. "He has to know he is not going to be able to run for President here, either. He won't get into the political arena, or even into the educational arena, until they shake off the British heritage, while in business it will depend on how he operates." In other words, in Africa, as in certain other parts of the world that Negroes are acquainted with, they can get along all right if they know their place. As for business, it is true that there were a few Negro sharpshooters who came to Africa to make a killing among the brothers. Some of the people who knew Nkrumah when he was a student in America came rushing over, and one or two of them had to be rushed out. Africans—some of whom are becoming pretty good sharpshooters themselves—keep saying they will welcome Negro entrepreneurs and specialists, and a few of those who have come have made places for themselves, but the way is not open or easy or free to all comers. "They have no intention of seeing people with better backgrounds and education come in here and take over," said a young man who regards himself as a "permanent settler" in Africa. "They don't want to let any outsider get ahead faster than Africans do." But it is not often as aspiring politicians or ambitious moneymakers that the pilgrims come; the "acceptance" they want is acceptance as human beings—something to do with full freedom, to be what they are and become what they can. Here, among those who come to Africa seeking this, we begin to encounter the more truly wounding discoveries of their strangerhood.

For a first thing, Africans scornfully reject the term "Negro." The great confusion among American Negroes about who and what they are has long been illustrated by the angers and controversies that have arisen over the elementary matter of a name to go by. At one time or another, the names in use have included "black," "African," "colored,"' "Negro," "Afro-American," and "mulatto" and its various subdivisions based on quarterings of color. On each of these hangs a complicated history of color caste, group prejudices, irrationalities, and complexes. By now the term "Negro" is most widely accepted, although there is a large faction of conservative or older people who still insist on "'colored"' and a much smaller group, younger or more chauvinistic, who self-consciously champion "Afro-American." Visitors to Africa, if they are of the latter group, may suffer an even worse confusion of identity, because, while they may be glad that Africans do not accept "Negro" either, this attitude does not bring them any closer to defining what they are. If they are Negroes content to be called Negro, it is not a happy thing to find that Africans want no part of the term, think of it as representing something lowly or unworthy, and worst of all, associate it with the history of America and with slavery—that in Africa a "Negro" is someone with a stigma. African rejection of the term "Negro" is part of the assertion of African superiority over Negroes. A person who only yesterday still thought himself superior to Africans, and whose ego is fragile at best, does not take this blow lightly.

Another blow is hidden in still another kind of terminological confusion. Langston Hughes, in *The Big Sea*, was probably the first American Negro writer to report the startling experience of being called "white" by Africans. That happened nearly 40 years ago, and Hughes said he was told that the designation was based not so much on color as on identification, in dress, language, and background, with the European. In the Twi Language, for example, the word *obouroni* apparently is used for both "stranger" and "white," and even my scrumptiously black friend, whose marriage experience I described earlier, was, to her bewilderment, called "white lady" by the market women. It sounds simple enough, but there is a confusion here that, followed far enough, can take us into some of deepest inwardnesses of this encounter. When an American Negro, of whatever color, hears himself called "white," it not only startles him but stirs up anew all the mixed ingredients of his sense of himself. I will mention only three of these, which indicates how critical they are: his feeling about *blackness* and being *black* ; his own mixture of ancestries (black, white, American, or whatever); and his share of the *yearning* to be *white*, the cancer that has been eating away for so long at the Negro's ability to accept himself. These are matters that cannot be wrapped up in a word or two. Let the details suggest themselves in a few glimpses:

The light-skinned Negroes who had trouble convincing Africans that they were Negroes. One young man, nearly desperate, said he wanted to hang a sign around his neck proclaiming his identity.

The tan American girl in Guinea who found that Guineans believe in race purity, that you have to be black to belong to the accepted group, and that "some hold the mulatto to be inferior, lower than the black."

The dark-skinned American, who was asked, "Are all American Negroes light as you?" This "shocked me very much, because I've always thought of myself as fairly dark."

The very dark American girl, who found that for a summer, Africa was "one place I could be accepted without conditions." As she explained it, "American Negroes never think of themselves as black, [but] always think of themselves [in] terms of white people – this or that what is most 'white' about me, my features or color or whatever. Now I think of myself as *black*. It's given me more respect for myself."

"Why do you Negroes want to be *white*?" demanded a group of Senegalese students as they bore down on two young American Negroes. "But we don't," the Negroes replied. "Then why do Negroes put grease on their hair? Why do they sell skin bleaching?" The young Negroes tried to explain—to tell who did this sort of thing and who didn't, and how it came about—but it was hard; it was hard to explain the whole business of being a Negro in America.

There is a deep pool of mutual prejudice between Africans and American Negroes and it is easily stirred up. Some of these stirrings come from a long way down. Until the day before yesterday, American Negroes generally considered themselves superior to Africans. They rejected the thought of their kinship with Africans, wanted no association with them, even used the word "'African" an expletive to suggest wild or barbarous or ignorant or wicked ways. The sources of this feeling lay in the great, obscure tangle of the Negro's struggle for acceptance in America, his lack of footing in any non-American past, his racial mixture, his effort to escape the lowliness universally associated in the dominant white world with blackness, Negroidness—with, in short, being African. Thus, Negroes usually saw Africans only as benighted and backward creatures who had never been able to come out of the jungle. Some Negro missionaries went to Africa to "save" them, but efforts made by benevolent or malevolent whites for more than a hundred years to send American Negroes back to Africa as Colonists had little success. All but a few Negroes scornfully rejected the idea. Those who did go back and founded the Republic of Liberia did not exactly make a record calculated to arouse pride and a feeling of association among many Negroes in America. The small sprinkling of Africans who began to come to American schools—especially American Negro schools—were looked upon either as barbarians or as ex-barbarians who had become snobbish Europeans. At Negro schools, they were made to feel this prejudice most explicitly and painfully: they were isolated, made the butt of harsh jokes, and generally left to huddle among themselves and nurse their counter-contempt and counter-prejudice against their American "brothers." They found that, as foreigners enjoying different accents and British passports (no Africans came from French territories until quite recently), they could often gain admission to places where Negroes were forbidden to go—movies, restaurants, and the like, even in the South—and they often did so, sneering back at the Negro for his lack of status in his own country. Some of Africa's new leaders went through this American experience—Nkrumah; Nnamdi Azikiwe, now Governor-General of Nigeria; and others, less well known. It is against a background of such memories that they now proffer their "Welcome, brother!" and obviously their enthusiasm must have its limits. Once the American Negro in Africa gets past the surface amenities, he is often made to feel the back of an African hand.

This is happening even in Liberia, the one country in Africa where American Negroes have had certain ties—where they have been looked upon as more successful older cousins, and where, as helpers and supporters, and as doers of good works, they have enjoyed status and prestige. The descendants of the Negro colonists from America, who founded Liberia in 1822, held fast to their American connections. Since they faced hostile tribes in the interior, rapacious Europeans on their borders, and indifferent whites in America, American Negroes were through almost all their history their only friends anywhere—and, indeed, there were not too many of them. Only a very few Negroes in America appreciated either the regard or the dependence of the Liberians, the rest being generally embarrassed by the Liberian performance. Nevertheless, those Negroes, mainly in the churches, who did interest themselves in Liberia's problems maintained the thin bonds through the years, helping to establish and staff churches and schools. The Americo-Liberians sent their sons and daughters to American Negro schools and, whenever they could, married them to Americans. An American Negro whom I met in Monrovia described the position in these words: "Psychologically, they feel here that they are a part of the American Negro group. They use the word 'home' in this way. One speaks of a ship coming from 'home.' They have always looked for their American brothers to join them here. The churches are all closely connected to fellow-churches in the U.S.. In this society, girls born and raised in the U.S. are the highest prestige group, higher on the marriage scale than Liberian women are. Girls born here of parents who came from the U.S. are the second-best group as marriage partners. No president of Liberia has been the son of two parents born in Africa; at least one has always been American-born."

This is almost enough in itself—without going into the complex history of Negro–Liberian relationships—to suggest the simmering jealousies and the rancors of dependence that must lie deep in the Liberians' feelings about American Negroes. Now, suddenly, great events are conspiring to free them of this dependence. Africa is waking up. White America wants African friends, and is beginning to spend money in Liberia—real money, not the dribble of dimes and quarters that could come from earnest but poor American Negro churchgoers. And

beyond white America lies white Russia, which might be interested in helping Liberia, too, if America should not move fast enough. There is now, indeed, a faction of growing power in the Liberian government that wants to open negotiations with Moscow and begin to derive the advantage to be gained by "neutrality" in a world of contending benefactors. There is no place in this big time for the small-time American Negro benefactor who has been around all these years to serve as the Liberian's only rich uncle. "Now there has been a reaction of feeling against Negroes," said the Negro observer in Monrovia whom I have already quoted. "People here feel that Liberia has been in the backwash of Africa, and some of them think this is because they have allowed the U.S. to be represented here all this time by American Negroes. Now they want roads and harbors, they want what the other countries are getting, and they think the answer is to get American whites and Europeans in here."

This change in the Liberian climate was signaled by the rumors that flew about in mid-1959, when the post of American Ambassador to Liberia was filled for the first time by a white diplomat. Traditionally, this had been the one post in the world reserved for some politically deserving or otherwise distinguished Negro. But now, it was reported, the Liberians were seeing this as a sign of their second-classness, and had demanded that Monrovia be graced by a representative of the U.S. who was white. These reports were denied by Liberians, but a white ambassador, a regular Foreign Service officer, was duly named to the post.

(This matter of diplomatic appointments for Negroes in Africa is disputed from various points of view. Nkrumah was widely reported in 1957 to have intimated to Washington that he preferred a white to a Negro as the American ambassador to Ghana. Some 10 years earlier, in a similar situation, Premier U Nu, of the new state of Burma, was said to have told the American government, "When you have sent Negroes to London, Paris, and Rome, then send them to us." Nkrumah was credited with similar sentiments; it was said that he wanted Ghana to have first-class recognition, which had to come in a white skin.

Many Negroes had differing and mixed feelings on the matter. They partly agree that Negroes should of course, be appointed to more of the available jobs, wherever they may be but they are also nettled by the clear African implication of Negro second-classness. President Eisenhower did appoint a Negro to be ambassador to Guinea, but he has since been replaced by a white. President Kennedy has appointed Clifton Wharton, the only high-ranking Negro in the Foreign Service, to be ambassador to Norway. Other top Negro appointments are being urged on the President, while at the other end of the scale more young Negroes are entering the Foreign Service and starting up the ladder, appearing in more and more junior posts in various parts of the world. Here, as in many other areas of discrimination, it is a matter of a little more time—time that seems so short to whites who do not know how late it is, and so unconscionably long to Negroes.)

The most direct assault on the American Negro pilgrim in Africa, however, hits him where right now he often feels weakest—in his sense of himself and of his place and his future in American society. The African nationalist, in his new freedom from white control, now feels himself to be his own man in his own land, and is full of self-pride. The American Negro, on the other hand, is still struggling to achieve equality of status within a plural but white-dominated society, and that struggle goes slowly and painfully, is punctuated by Little Rock, AR, and snarling New Orleans, LA, women, by unpunished murders, and is held up by seemingly immovable white supremacists in the South and by smugly self-deceiving whites in the North. In this situation, the Negro is an embattled man, and the African, swelling with self-congratulation and enjoying certain malice, drives his point home. Examples:

"Why don't you American Negroes stop singing spirituals and playing banjos, and get out into the streets and fight for your rights?"

"You Negroes are fools, imitating the white Americans. Isn't it high time you set out to be what you are—*black men, Africans*?"

"Why don't you Negroes stand up and fight for your freedom, *the way we did?*"

The American Negro who gets sneering questions like these thrown at him usually feels vulnerable—that most of the time he bows his head and takes it. He is often too oppressed by anger, despair, and self-hatred to give full, self-respecting value to his heritage of struggle in America. The truth is that his heritage of struggle is by far the longer, and is filled with more men who suffered and fought, and is adorned by a vastly greater number of remarkable leaders, tribunes, and fighters, than one can easily discover in the short histories of the West African movements now so suddenly crowned with power. He so underrates himself that only seldom does it occur to him to ask his jeering tormentor, "Tell me, my friend, about *your* struggle to be free." No question could be more unwelcome to all but a few West African nationalists, because the fact is that the great bulk of the new West African politics came into being to *receive* power and not to *struggle* for it. This is neither a popular nor a widely acknowledged truth among Africans nowadays. They are much too busy building up new mythologies that will forever hide it from their *view*. So they bound angrily away from any such threat of exposure. The result of all this on both sides of the exchange is rarely relaxing or clarifying.

On the African side, what goes on is a reinforcement of the established pattern of prejudice. This is how a young American woman describes the views of her Ghanaian husband and his friends:

"The Ghanaians feel that Negroes in America are stupid to keep on begging for something, while if they had the right frame of mind, they would come back here and really try to work for Africa. But no, they think the Negroes would rather go on begging favors from the white man through the N.A.A.C.P. and that sort of thing. That's what my husband says. He has no sympathy for American Negroes and doesn't want them to come here. I won't say he looks down on them. He just feels they're stupid. Well, yes, I guess that is looking down on them, isn't it? All I can say is that if a Negro comes over here who believes in this fighting for civil rights to become part of white America, he just won't be accepted here, that's all."

But even if you are a Negro who has abandoned that struggle, even if you have come to Africa to make a fresh start among your African brothers, it seems that you are not accepted very warmly, either. As yet, there are not many such individuals. Most Negroes, however alienated they may feel, still come to Africa in a much more tentative, seeking way. But in Ghana, I did meet one young man who had left America for good, he said, some eight years ago and had been struggling ever since to get a feeling of being "inside" with the Africans. He had not succeeded in doing so.

"When I first came, I couldn't get my college degree accepted. It almost made a patriot out of me, I was so mad. An American college degree is actually much better than any degree from Oxford or Cambridge in the things that people need here. But I couldn't get into the educational system or the civil service here. I married an African girl and that helped, it made some difference. As far as jobs went, I certainly remained outside. But I have begun to get a certain superficial warm welcome in many circles. I'm invited around, though I don't have a very busy social live. When I first arrived here an old lady said to me, 'What took you so long to come back?' Ordinarily Ghanaians do often have a sentimental attachment to American Negroes. But upper-class people immediately add to this, 'Watch out, we don't want outsiders coming in and taking over.' Still, I will stay in Africa. I left the U.S. both rejected and rejecting. On the whole, I think it may be more satisfactory here for me, since I grew up on a fence, partially accepted, partially rejected, and I know this is the way an exile feels anywhere. It was the same in the U.S. It is the same here."

But most of the Negroes I met in West Africa during the summer were not ready to give up their fight against second-classness in America simply to accept second-classness in Africa. Not was this only a matter of being a Negro, an American, or an outsider much of West Africa these days, it takes no profound discernment to see however sweet it may be to be relieved of the power of the white man, the power of the black man does not yet smell much like freedom—certainly

like the freedom to which the American has learned to aspire. So, stung by African's scorn and rejection, by his stubborn refusal to accept the American Negro's *bona fides,* many a visitor finds himself cast in an exasperating role: an alienated Negro American passionately defending segregationist America against the attacks of a national-chauvinist African. This was the summer odyssey of one young American who, like so many others, had come to find out whether in Africa he might have the chance he felt he would never get at home. His story:

"As hard as I could ever push it, I could never really think of myself as an American, not ever. When I was in Japan and Korea with the Army, I always thought of myself just as Negro, not even as hyphenated Negro-American, just Negro. But what I have found is that you might get rid of the color problem, but you get into something else. You know, in the beginning I had exactly the same experience Richard Wright had in Indonesia. I got called up in front of a line of Europeans and got waited on first. This was discrimination in reverse, and I have to say I enjoyed the sensation, even though I began to feel guilty about enjoying it. By the end of the summer, I'd thought a lot about it, and I just wanted to get away from there. I had to see that I could never become Nigerian, or any other kind of African, never really become part of it. I could not run away. Maybe the truth is that as an American Negro I have no place to go at all. Maybe that is the situation.

"When the African students talked about American Negroes' wanting to be white, I had to agree this was true. They also said we hadn't done enough to push for equality, that we should get guns, if necessary, and go out onto the streets. But they hadn't done this, either, I reminded them. I tried to trace for them the development of what had been done."

"There was one fellow, a most articulate Marxist type. He kept attacking American Negroes, how American Negroes weren't doing any of the things Africans were doing in Africa. We finally had a real run-in one day, when we were tired and irritated. He said something, and I found myself defending America, the whole thing, in a way I could never have imagined myself doing. I said yes, there was Little Rock on one side, and a lot of things on the other side, people pushing and fighting; all sorts of things can happen and do happen. As I was talking, I found myself being pinned against the wall. They kept coming back at me with 'You try to be white!' And that is true. I realized I was defending something I wasn't even sure I wanted to be defending. But I think at that moment I began to understand. Here I was defending this thing. But it was because I knew there were other sides to it. As big a racist as I am—and I am a racist—I could see that they would only hear of Little Rock and New Orleans, and would never hear of the lunch counters integrated in Nashville, TN. They wouldn't hear it even if you told them about it! I said to myself, 'All right, but I'm going to see that they hear all sides, hear *our* side.' I don't know if they ever believed anything I tried to tell them."

Negro Missionary Reaction to Africa Symposium

Jeanne Davis, Yenwith and Muriel Whitney,

Kermit and Irene Overton, and William D. Reyburn

Aside from Reyburn, the writers in this symposium were all fraternal workers of the Eglise Presbyterienne Camerounaise [the Presbyterian Church of Cameroon].

Jeanne Davis is a graduate of Drexel Institute of Technology, Philadelphia, and taught home economics in Pennsylvania before entering missionary service. She was an instructor in the Ecole d'Enseignenent Général de Jeunes Filles in Elat, Cameroon.

Yenwith Whitney received the B.S. degree from M.I.T. and the M.A. from Columbia University, New York. He worked as an aviation engineer for Republic Aviation before going to Cameroon, where he taught mathematics and physics in Libamba College. His wife, Muriel Whitney, is a graduate of Hunter College and has worked as a social investigator in New York City.

Kermit Overton graduated from Rutgers University in sociology. He is also a graduate of Lincoln Seminary and pursued graduate studies at Union Seminary in New York City. Irene Overton holds a B.A. degree from Pennsylvania State College and taught in Puerto Rico before her marriage

Taken from Practical Anthropology, *Volume 11, 1964 (now:* Missiology: An International Review*), 616 Walnut Ave. Scottdale, PA 15683. Used by permission.*

After Harold R. Isaacs' article, "Back to Africa," describing the problems of American Negroes in Africa, was reprinted in Practical Anthropology *[in 1963], several American Negro missionaries were asked to read it and then to give their own impressions in the light of their experiences in Africa. In addition to having been raised and educated in America and now serving as missionaries in Africa, these people all had experience in Europe. Some of them had already read Isaacs' article when it first appeared in the* New Yorker *Magazine and had discussed it with friends in America. William D. Reyburn provided an editorial summary of the 1964 symposium at the end.*

It's the Interpretation of One's Problem That Counts

Jeanne Davis

Like many unsuspecting hopefuls I arrived in France for language study with many preconceived ideas concerning French society. Included in these impressions were my thoughts on the Frenchman's attitude toward Negroes. Some of my friends who had been in France told me that the color problem didn't exist there. I could go into any public place—hotel, restaurant, or theater—without the slightest question as to whether I should be there or not. Eagerly I looked forward to France and the sense of "real" freedom.

When I first arrived I was separated from my American friends. I was obliged to fend for myself at the hotel and order my meals at a nearby restaurant. It was true people made me feel at ease. At least my problems didn't arise from any color difficulties. I was accepted as a customer and that was that.

After a week we left Paris for a small French town. Things began to be different. After a day or two I noticed that people were always staring at me and my appearance seemed to provoke conversation. When it continued I became provoked and disgruntled at how impolite these people were. By this time language study was well on its way with its many new frustrations. This staring made me uncomfortable. I didn't know how to cope with it. I became very aware of myself and people's reactions to me. They began asking questions. Some wanted to know if I was from a certain part of India. Others wondered if there were other Negroes like me in the U.S.. They remarked about my color. They wanted to discuss Little Rock, AR, "sit-ins," the South, and Jim Crow.

People didn't treat me like an ordinary person. I was always being singled out. I began to realize that what I wanted was to be treated like an ordinary white. I felt caged. I got that same old stateside feeling that I must succeed for the sake of my color. I must show them that Negroes are not inferior. I wanted to advance quickly in my ability to learn French. I was very careful how I walked, talked, acted, and dressed. If they were going to continue to stare at me I wanted to give them as little opportunity to criticize as possible.

Gradually I began to see that in fact I did feel inferior. My language learning did not progress as I wanted it to. My feelings of inferiority grew. Even worse, I was angry, torn, and bitter at myself because of my surprising discovery. Outwardly I appeared sullen and discontented; inwardly I was burning up. Since childhood I had been taught that in spite of public opinion I was just as good as the next person. I had believed I was. Now I had come to France only to discover that I didn't feel this way at all. This was a shock! Was I merely a victim of the color problem? Was this the "real" me? I began to fight back, first by mistrusting my American friends. I couldn't believe that they didn't have prejudiced feelings. Life was miserable for them, and for me, for quite some time.

Curiosity, Not Prejudice

We began discussing this staring and how they, too, felt people were staring at them. They noted people's reactions to me and compared our cases. They helped me to see that this curiosity was based on the fact that we were foreigners. My sickness was deep-seated. I began to see I was my own worst enemy. Somehow I had to stop trying to prove myself and learn to relax in the situation. This came about as I began to understand my problem. I realized that to be treated as if my skin were white does not mean equality. I am different. My skin is black. People having no acquaintance with

Negroes are curious. This inquisitiveness does not spell out prejudice, discrimination, or the color problem.

My time in France was in many ways preparing me for my work in Africa. The fact that I was a Negro would seem to help the situation, not hinder it. I came to Africa expecting to find an opportunity for a unique witness because of my Negro heritage. I thought that here I would not be different. I'd fit into place. Here my being a Negro would pay off. At first, reactions from the Africans were as I expected and even more so. They welcomed me as a long lost sister. They wanted to know why I hadn't come sooner. Of course, I was overwhelmed. I felt at home. One man told me I looked just like a girl from his village. Some compared my coming to Africa with the story of Joseph in Genesis: as one who was sold into slavery and whose conditions improved so much that when met by his family he had riches to offer them.

Again, [came] language study, this time, Bulu. The Africans became aware of my differences. In my desire to learn Bulu well, I only demonstrated how very "white" I was. Many began to see me as a European. Somehow my mannerisms were not African. One day a fellow missionary told me that one of the Africans she was working with wanted to know what "that black white lady's" work was—referring to me. In a conversation with a young African woman, I mentioned that I could easily mistake her for an American if I saw her in the U.S.. She smiled unbelievingly, saying she could never mistake me for an African. My appearance, my way of walking, and especially my figure were just not African.

I began to search for similarities, noticing how many inflections and intonations of the Bulu language—a manner of slurring the voice and sliding into certain expressions—recalled a certain type of Negro speech habit. The Negro-spiritual type of hymn singing and musical improvising, the natural swing that accompanied the Bulu singing seemed to tell me that we, in fact, did have a kinship. I began to feel a relationship beyond that which I can adequately describe. Yet I knew that the Africans saw me as mostly "white."

I've been thinking a great deal about this, wondering how I can come to be seen as one of them. The Africans have a right to look at me. They should, so to speak, size me up. If I want to know them, I must let them get to know me. The advantage of being black was that they accepted me right away. The disadvantage was that they expected much more of me than of a white person. At first, they thought I should understand them better. In some cases I think I do, not because of color but because of similar desires and handicaps. My job is to open myself honestly to them, to accept the African and meet him where he is through the love of Christ, to become part of his society. I'll never be accepted because I am a Negro—only as I become identified, person to person.

Turning Disadvantage into an Advantage

Yenwith K. Whitney

When I was 11 years old I can remember vividly my first real awareness that Africa was a continent with which I was somehow connected. It was in 1935 that [Italian dictaor, Benito] Mussolini invaded Ethiopia with his modern army and crushed the spear-and-shield warriors of Haile Selassie's pitiful army. At that time I lived in an all-white neighborhood where I had been born. The neighborhood kids, seeing me come out of the house, would yell, "Ethiopia!," cry like Tarzan, and dance about waving make-believe spears in the air. I was both angry and ashamed of my heritage, a discontinuous heritage which had been cleaved into two diverging branches: one which had been forced upon us in slavery, and the other which had left us in an almost prehistoric civilization. From that day onward for many years my interest in Africa was on one side a normal curiosity but on the other side something to be ignored and left alone.

It wasn't until after the Second World War that a vague interest began to stir within me. It was an interest which was born of an increasing consciousness of the great changes beginning to take place not only in the U.S.

but also in Africa. We Negroes began to have cause to hold up our heads, to do more than just feel sorry for ourselves. The war had revealed not only to the white man but also to ourselves that we were not insufficient and subhuman, but could rise to any occasion necessary. I had become a fighter pilot and had flown with the famed *Red Tails* of General Davis' 332nd fighter group. This, coupled with the fact that I was now a qualified engineer, gave me the self-confidence and self-assurance, which permitted me to come out of my own shell and begin to look around in the world.

I first came into closer contact with Africa through the speeches of Rev. James Robinson and through contact with African students who were studying in America. I must admit that I was, until this time, a bit cautious in forming acquaintanceships with Africans. My relationships with them were not very profound and no really strong attachments or understanding developed. Through a series of circumstances with which Jim Robinson had no small part, I became more and more interested in Africa. My wife, Muriel, and I finally decided to come and teach in Africa. The impetus of this decision came not only from a spiritual development but also because we were convinced of the real need for our particular training and talents in Africa. I was convinced that this was the unique opportunity of my life to turn to an advantage what had always been a disadvantage in my life: my color.

I don't think that I had hoped to become assimilated into Africa. I had found no basis for this in the contacts that I had had in America. I was not leaving America because I was not comfortable there or because I was looking for more comfort in Africa. I had misgivings as to whether I would even like Africans or whether they would like me. Jim Robinson said that they would. I had great expectations for Africa, "the budding continent." I hoped that I would have a hand in shaping its destiny. I often asked myself how many geniuses had been lost to mankind in the African jungles. What would have been the course of Africa and the world if these people had come into a full fruition of their gifts?

Brothers in Color

Our reception in Africa by the Africans was one of the warmest experiences of our lives. We were welcomed [in Cameroon] like the proverbial Prodigal Son. The women of the local village turned out and danced for us and brought us gifts of food. They told us how glad they were we had come. Now this treatment is by no means unique since missionaries very often receive this warm welcome. However, we were called brothers because of our color. One of my earliest encounters was on a trip into Makak, the local government post. I went up to the church, and after the service a group of the teachers approached me and asked me if I wouldn't come and talk to them. I was the first American Negro that they had seen. They pressed me with all sorts of questions about the Negro in America. They had heard all sorts of fantastic stories about the situation in the U.S. and they wanted to hear what an American Negro himself had to say about it. They had heard what the white missionaries had said and now they wanted to see if what I said coincided with the other stories. They were woefully ignorant of the history of slavery and the origin of the present problems. One of the reasons for this, I believe, is that the white missionaries, who were ashamed of the situation in the U.S., talked very little about the Negro, both through lack of first-hand knowledge and through embarrassment. We had a long conversation in which I answered the questions they threw at me. I never avoided a question or pulled any punches. I told them frankly what I liked and what I didn't like about my country. At the end they thanked me again for coming and asked me to help them as much as I could.

Also early in our first term my wife had an interesting experience. I was preaching in a village not far from the school and after the service an old lady came up and threw her arms around my wife and said, "I had heard that there were black men in America, but now I believe it. Now I'll believe them when they tell me that some day I'll see Jesus."

In our second year here we were studying the Basa language at another of our mission stations. I was asked to preach in a local chapel. The question of translation came up and I suggested that a missionary do the translation. They were immediately wary and said that they would prefer that he didn't since they wanted to hear exactly what I had to say. I had to assure them that this man would translate faithfully whatever I said. Quite reluctantly, they accepted. I talked about the bus boycott in Montgomery, telling how the Negroes had resisted in a peaceful way to obtain their rights. After the sermon, once again, they cornered me and threw all sorts of questions at me. One of the questions was: "Why don't all of the Negroes leave America where they are mistreated and come back home to Africa?"

Early in our first term I had an interesting incident happen to me. Because of a new regulation at the school, the students decided to go on strike and not come to class. However, my class came and they were quite careful to explain to me that they came only because of me. I had not known them very long so the only conclusion I could draw at the time was that they considered me a brother and wanted to show this to me. As I recall, they also went on strike in the African teachers' classes.

I should explain that we were the first American Negro family that most of the Africans in this region had ever seen. There had been another family in Cameroon in 1928, but the younger generation had not known them. Some had seen Robinson when he came, and others had seen the Rev. Mr. Galamison of Brooklyn, who came out for a couple months, but by and large we were new to them.

White Man and Black Man

As the students got to know us and began to talk more freely, we discovered some interesting things. Did they consider us white men or black men? We found that we were considered both. At times we were white and at times we were black depending upon the situation. Normally, because of our way of living, our way of acting, we were thought of as white. We commanded the respect that was given the white man. Sometimes when they were angry with us we were *vous les blancs* ["you whites"]. However, we were able to "cross over" when the occasion demanded it. We could speak to the students as one black man to another and get across some telling points. Very often they let us overhear remarks about the Europeans since we were not considered completely European. I distinctly remember one such occasion when a class of students was grumbling about some decision which had been made affecting the hour of a certain class. They said that the white man was imposing himself on them. I made it clear that I was talking to them now as a black man and I showed them my hair to prove it. I then dressed them down for confusing *racism* with simple discipline, and their failure to distinguish between those who were here to help them and those who were not. I was able to put the situation into its proper perspective and I believe they understood.

This, then, is one of my most important functions as a Negro, to act as an interpreter. I can put on my "black man" hat as the situation demands. The African can deny my culture but he cannot deny my color.

The second important function that we have as Negroes is interpreting the Negro problem in the U.S. Especially in these troubled days with the riots and bombings in MS and AL. We need to explain what is really happening behind the headlines, the metamorphosis of which the violence is only a surface symptom. We explain that what is really happening is an evolution, which is unique in the history of sociology. A group of people is struggling to gain recognition and equality. We explain also that many whites as well as the Negroes are working together to attain this goal.

What does all of this mean? What are our impressions now as compared to our original ones? In general, of course, our impressions have had to change as we got to know the country, the people, their customs, and their way of thinking. We have come to know them and to admire and respect many. We have good friends. We are no longer shocked by different ways of thinking and acting, and we try not to judge actions always by our own standards. We do insist, though, that because Africa is emerging into a Western world they must conform in certain areas if they want to compete in it. We see our corner of Africa consisting of people with strengths and weaknesses. We see a good future if the right leaders gain control.

As far as our personal relationships are concerned, we are happy, happy that we are what we are. Most of the time we are considered as Europeans, outsiders, but that does not hinder our work or handicap us in any way. We did not come here with the idea of finding a place where we could be accepted exactly equally as members of the family. How could we? We are foreigners with completely foreign ideas and customs. But we came to do a job and we are happy to be able to do it—effectively, we hope. We are happy that we are Negroes and that we can cross over occasionally. For the most part we forget our color and simply do our job.

We feel that in our neck of the woods a Negro has an initial advantage, but this can mean something or nothing depending upon the individual person. In the long run what really counts is not what color you are, but what is under your skin.

Color or Culture, Which Is Skin Deep?

Kermit Overton

As a Negro born in the U.S., I used to raise issue over the label Americans gave to us. The label "American Negro"' somehow implied that we were Negroes first and Americans second. This suggested second-class citizenship to me, wherein the label "Negro American" implies for me that we are Americans first with a different racial background. In reading Mr. Isaacs' article, I realize that both are correct, depending on the setting.

In my experience in a former French colony in Africa [Cameroon], I have been accepted as a Negro or a person of African descent but there is also the neon sign, which reads to the African: "American." As a missionary I have perhaps had a certain advantage in my relationship with our African brothers, which probably has not been experienced by my fellow Negro compatriots in government service. Being a missionary puts me in a sphere where I am respected. This, of course, follows a missionary tradition.

I must qualify my statement about respect. In the villages and small towns, I am considered their pastor: one who teaches them and their children and one who administers the sacraments to them. Because of this they have accepted me. I am identified in the Christian community as a brother. In the larger cities I am identified as non-African, and this is my fault because I, too, am like my compatriot of whom Mr. Isaacs writes. I do not want to be identified as an African. I understand this feeling about myself better than my compatriot does. I do not boast of any pure motives, but I had wanted Africans to know that I was an American who felt a real kinship and concern and a desire to identify in their struggles, to give of myself and also to receive their insights. This seemed possible to me because I had experienced this with an African in the U.S. who was and still is one of my dearest friends. I must confess that there is a certain amount of superiority in my attitude, thinking deeply that I had more to offer than to receive. Here I am a victim of my American culture.

The question presents itself, "Why was I not accepted as someone with sincere concerns for the African?" The question is too complex to attempt a simple answer. However, in my opinion, one factor is that the African sees black or white. He does not see the shades in between. I have had several experiences, which have brought this home to me. I mention one of them here. There was a question of a certain vacant missionary house on a station, which an African pastor wanted to occupy. There were procedures to be followed, agreed upon by the African and the U.S. churches, in obtaining the house. I knew that these conditions had not been met and I explained the simple formality. I held the key to the house. He was unwilling to accept these conditions and held me personally responsible for his inability to enter the house. He terminated his tirade by accusing me of being a racist. What a blow! In this case and others in which I did not support them on their own terms (which were non-Christian), they felt I did not have sincere concerns for them.

Such things highlight the fact that we are very far apart in our points of view and our ways of thinking. Yet I believe that the Negro American is sympathetic to the African's situation in terms of the background of superstition and fear which he has yet to overcome, and in terms of a social ethic which he has yet to develop in order to interact with other nations with justice. The African feels, perhaps, that we have lost our identity as black men. He feels that we have nothing unique to contribute to life and we are being absorbed into the white man's civilization. In my opinion, the African meets this with intolerance. The question of Negro contributions to American society is, of course, another subject.

Upon my arrival in this country, the Africans gave me the impression that they expected me to take up their habits, customs, and language without difficulty. For them, this seemed the most natural thing for me to do. After a while they concluded that I was not one of them. The result is that they accepted me as any other missionary.

There is another factor which I feel influences relationship between the Negro American and the African in this country. It is that the African here knows very little about the life of the Negro in the U.S. They know that we were slaves and are now victims of discrimination. For this reason, those who have had some schooling tend to regard us as inferiors. Under the French system of education, they have received very little information about the U.S., except for geography.

I conclude by saying that, as a Negro, I cannot content myself with the racial situation in the U.S. Yet I, too, find myself defending the only country I know and would claim as my own. I can be sympathetic to the African position and I am happy to work in Africa, but I cannot be African.

A Wife's Observations
Irene Overton

Not only have we found that we are not accepted by Africans in a spirit of kinship, we have found that different tribes do not accept each other. Anyone outside his own tribal region is considered a stranger. It is natural that we are considered likewise. It is evident that our way of thinking sets us farther apart.

I have never been one to want to "go back to Africa," but I had felt a real kinship to Africa and a desire to serve there. However, many Africans that I have met think their way of doing things is the best or at least the best for them. If it's a practice that they don't want to give up they present all kinds of reasons to justify it.

We have met a feeling on the part of some Africans that Negro Americans are second-class Americans. When I attempted to teach Negro spirituals to one of my English classes, they refused to learn because "they talk about slavery and black people and we want to forget that." They don't know American Negro history at all. They know about Little Rock, but not about George Washington Carver. They tell us how we must sit in the back of the buses in the South, but they have never heard of Martin Luther King.

Summary Comments

William D. Reyburn

There are two major points, which may be summarized from these articles. The first has to do with the learning of culture; the second concerns color in communication.

The learning of one's culture is a process of interaction with many people, which takes place over a period of formative years in life. A child learns to respond in expected ways to countless signals which he receives from his equals and superiors. He learns in turn how, where, and to whom he can signal for response from others. These signals, which are primarily linguistic also, concern a vast area of behavior, which is nonlinguistic. They are extremely subtle. They may be at times unpredictable, but they are normally intelligible and to some degree acceptable. To say that one has acquired American or French culture is to say that a person has learned to respond to signals from fellow Americans or Frenchmen in such a way that the sender of the signals feels the responses are not foreign to his expectations.

Knowing a culture means functioning as a communicator in interaction with other members of that system. Acquiring one's culture, then, is learning the rules of communication and interaction in the broad sense. What makes it an extremely subtle affair is the fact that the rules are not rules in the ordinary sense of the word but are markers, which can be moved about as the game proceeds. They are normally not fixed and their limits are to a degree determined by the nature of the immediate situation. Moreover, situations are determined by the individuals involved and the purposes which lie behind the immediate circumstances. In brief, as one learns a communication role, one learns a sensitivity to situations, which guides his behavior and enables him to proceed in the business of living with other people.

Lying behind the signaling which goes on between people are many presuppositions about status, rank, distance, time, position, and even color. One of these assumptions in American life, which has been much preached, is that of egalitarianism. It is the belief that anybody can become president. It is a log cabin psychology of social and economic improvement. This acceptance of egalitarianism is one of the "rules of the game" in American life. However, this rule is apparently one-sided since it developed when white persons were scrambling over each other to subdue the wild west and reduce the Indians. The Indians were apparently not too aware that they were being shot and scattered because all men (white men) were created equal. Again, when the Negro population in America learned that egalitarianism was one of the rules of the game, they were told that it did not apply to them. Special rules had to be concocted for them. However, the minorities in American society cannot play the game and attain the highly touted rewards of a business culture unless all can gamble with the same rules.

Egalitarianism is only one of the many values that characterizes American life and provides an expected basis for interaction. It seldom occurs to us how we learned when to laugh and when not to laugh, when to smile and when not to smile. We did it simply because the group we grew up among also did it. We learned that certain situations and remarks are a signal for a smile or a laugh. This is an expected response.

Is it possible to be truly bicultural? Perhaps it is where no two systems are completely in contrast. The greater the disparity between cultural systems, the more likely there are points of strong contrast. It is hard to imagine a person who in one culture is moved with compassion at the sight of another's misfortune and whom at the same time in another culture responds with amused laughter.

American, Not Black

The writers above all express their vivid awareness of being American when they are confronted by Africans. They realize that they have learned to function in an American system of values, to receive and send signals according to American rules of the game. They did not learn to be black. They learned to be Americans. This takes us to the second point, color in communications.

It appears that Africans, like some Americans, assume that color is deeper than culture. They expect more from the Negro. In the educated Negro they tend to see a person who has achieved a status which they aspire to and because of color they are able more easily to enjoy that status through identification with the Negro. This applies to the lower-class Africans and students who are still aiming beyond their present status. It is not in the least true of the highly educated and sophisticated African today. The village African feels in his bones that there is a bond between him and a person sharing his skin color. Negroes are outsiders and in our cases here are accepted in the missionary role. This means that they are missionaries plus. The plus is the possibility of accessibility as an object for identification.

This emotional identification based on color moves the African to open himself more to the Negro than to the white missionary. However, here is precisely the point where

the balance may be swung either way. This identification may be harmful for both the Negro missionary and for the African or it may be directed into wholesome channels for good. On the one hand it is a temptation to paternalism, or again it may create a feeling of disgust toward the African who, instead of struggling to get ahead as the Negro missionary has done, appears to be sitting back and showing little initiative. Still again it may mean the giving of deep-felt confidence on the part of the African who is driven by his cultural background to humanize and personalize his Christian experience.

In Africa the Negro missionary discovers that the culture, which he has learned and the only one he knows, is the very culture which has hounded him for his skin color. The African seizes upon color as evidence of brotherhood and perceives shortly that color does not serve to bridge the cultural chasm. In the American society skin color punishes the Negro for being "black." In Africa his color accuses him for being "white."

The problems for the Negro missionary are by no means small. Until the Negro has full equality with whites in the U.S., he will be forced to explain and interpret the life of the American Negro to his African colleagues. He may continue for a long time to be snubbed as inferior by the upper-class Africans. His skin will be a deceptive signal to the simple villager who will expect far more of the Negro than of the white missionary. The class on the way up will tend to identify itself with the Negro missionaries' success.

Their task is not easy, but the very people who wrote these articles would not be in Africa today were they not accustomed to a struggle. The Christian message can receive new insights coming from a people that know existentially that "this world is not my home." Christ's forgiveness can be made alive and real only by those who have truly forgiven others.

Is Anyone Safe Around Here?

Michael Johnson

I sit here [in Kenya] watching a movie about white lynch mobs in America. All good Bible-believing white folks. Confederate-flag-waving, cross-burning, sheet-wearing, gun-toting, and conservative white folk, chasing down black folks like hunting deer and killing roaches. They do it in God's name. Saving America for the good Christian white folks. Saving America from the bogeyman, the nigger.

What is worse than a white mob searching for a black man on a dark road in rural America? I'll tell you. A black mob searching for another black man in rural Africa, especially when they can't distinguish you from the people for whom they search. That's right. Lynching in Kenya is as commonplace today as barbecues and cookouts in America. In fact, fire and burning flesh are an important part of this tradition too.

I remember seeing it in pictures in America, with black men hanging from trees or [burned] on bonfires for somehow insulting the white race. These pictures scared me from ever wanting to go into any part of white America; I thought their version of burning flesh on an open pit was not the kind of holiday I could enjoy. So here I am in Africa, "safe" from lynch mobs!

Fortunately for Kay and me, white missionaries were among us on this dark night. There have been a few occasions where we have been warned not to leave the compound unless accompanied by a white missionary. As I said before and will say again, it is good to be with white people in Africa, sometimes.

It was rather eerie. We heard the yells and screams of a dozen or so Kipsigis men hiding in the trees. They had already made at least one assault on the hospital compound. They were intent on murdering the Ogutas, a family of four. Domatilla, was a nurse on the hospital surgical wards and her husband, John, worked in accounting with Kay. Their two children hid with their mother in one room as their father and a friend were trying to hold the front door as men with axes and machetes tried to break it down.

Domatilla looked out the keyhole and saw John struggling to save their lives. She heard the anger of the lynch mob. She heard their cursing and drunken oaths recited in the darkness of that night. She heard the splintering of the door and felt a sure doom. She could in her mind, no doubt,

Michael Johnson and wife, Kay, sold their home and cars, closed a busy and prosperous surgical practice, and moved to Kenya with their four children in 1990. The Johnsons have since been involved in a variety of ministries in Kenya. Most of the ministries have revolved around hospital administration, surgical care for the extremely impoverished people of Kenya, work with street children providing health care to more than 30,000 children of Nairobi, and the training of Kenyan physicians.

see the bodies of her family with blood splattered around the house. But then she opened her eyes even wider she saw the hand of God reach out and hold back the door, just as the crowd outside heard her yelling, "Jesus, Jesus, Jesus." Their response was, "It's only women and children. Let's leave them alone."

We missionary men ran to the scene after being alerted of the danger by one of the hospital staff. We were in a missionary station meeting. We were praying about the tribal conflict brewing on the compound and how it was necessary for us to carry out our assigned duties in orderly missionary-like fashion. Little did we know that at that very moment, the lives of men and women were being threatened. The call came over the mission compound phones. We rushed to the scene. We arrived just in time to see the men regrouping for a renewed attack on the Oguta home.

We ran the quarter mile up to the hospital compound entranceway. We placed ourselves between the gateway leading to the house and the group of men who were yelping like animals and screaming from high up in trees and behind bushes along the road. We stood there, led by Dr. Ernie Steury. Dr. Steury was the first physician to come to Tenwek hospital full-time, and for the first 10 years was the only physician.

Dr. Steury had over the past 25 plus years served as obstetrician, pediatrician, pastor, medical doctor, hospital administrator, hospital executive officer, church counselor, preacher, teacher, undertaker, mortician, and, on many occasions, burial crew. Many among the Kipsigis refuse to bury their own dead. They didn't mind this white man doing it. Except for Clark Kent, Ernie Steury is the only Superwhiteman I have ever known.

Dr. Steury had been in the Tenwek community for a long time. Everyone knows and respects Dr. Steury—everyone except the man wielding the machete in Dr. Steury's face. He and about eight or 10 other men stood there in the middle of the night, waving their weapons at us and most threateningly at Dr. Steury. We were all scared. I was very scared because [I am black.] At least

they were white [men]. Killing a white man is still frowned upon in Kenya.

White people seem to have such a great deal of protection. Its only because they are white of course, but because they represent a power from beyond the shores which can actually change the balance of power in a given region of the country. Historically in Kenya, you don't kill a white man unless you want trouble.

For the past several years since our arrival in Kenya, the news headlines have been filled with the murder of Julie Ward, a young British woman who was killed while camping in a game reserve. There have been numerous investigations by the feared Kenya Criminal Investigation Division and even Scotland Yard. There have been Kenyan police, politicians and game reserve guards investigated, probed, questioned, harassed, accused and even sometimes jailed with little resolution over the exact circumstances of her death.

At the same time, hundreds of Kenyan school children have died in bus accidents, drownings, epidemics, and disasters. I can't name even one of these young black Kenyans. However, the name of Julie Ward has, to quote American rap artist Kool Moe Dee, left a "stain on the brain" of Kenyans. This kind of stain reminds them that their lives are of little note when compared to the life of a white person. "Don't kill a white man in Kenya. You will be in trouble."

It is pretty much the same in America, of course. Black people don't kill white people because justice is not color blind. Now killing a black missionary would be a mistake to be sure, but by the time they discovered you were only a black man pretending to be white, it would be too late and "Oops!" does not look good on a headstone. It would be easy to kill a black man like me and get away with it. Just like those white conservatives in America got away with it in "the good old days." Killing a white missionary would get Kenyans in trouble. But for me it meant I was in trouble, as much trouble as the Ogutas. I found it even more dangerous as time went on.

We must have been surrounded by angels. Dr. Steury talked slowly to the men and convinced them that killing was not in the best interest of the hospital or the community. The man raised his machete and swung it in Dr. Steury's face and stated "Just because you are a white man doesn't mean you won't bleed." He lowered the knife and bit his own arm and started to cry. He could not bring himself to cut this white man. The man convinced his coconspirators to cease and desist. We then secretly moved the Oguta family and several other staff members who had been threatened to a safer location in the hospital, behind steel bars and cement walls, where the money is kept.

We had tried calling the Bomet police. We told them we were in danger of being overrun by the community thugs and schoolboys who wanted every out-of-tribe staff member put out at once. The police informed us that they could not get through since the roads were blocked by the schoolboys and they did not have a police car. They would come to our aid, however, if we could pick them up in one of our cars.

It was obvious "the Cavalry" could not help us. I would have even welcomed John Wayne. We were on our own. We stayed in the office with the staff for a long time and as the night became colder and darker, we became more scared. Some of us men took shifts and stayed with them [Ogutas] for several hours. We didn't know *if* or *when* the attackers would breech the walls of the compound. We were afraid for their lives and ours.

The night passed. No one was injured except the young painter who had been taken by force from his home and marched around the compound with a knife to his throat. He was told he must give the names of any people of his tribe and their location or be killed. They made a small laceration on his cheek to show they were serious. They let him go and he later joined us in our hiding place. We didn't know what to do from there. Dr. Steury bade all the missionaries to go home and rest. We did, and he went on to make arrangements for a plane to fly the endangered staff out of Tenwek the next morning. It was a long night but we survived.

The next morning the front of the hospital was filled with angry community members. They were not angry with the perpetrators or instigators. They were angry that the hospital had harbored these evil elements of non-Kipsigis tribe members. Literally hundreds of people lined the roads, crowded the hospital entrance, and hung around waiting for something to happen. We looked for who was going to make it happen.

They were mad at all of us for hiding the out-of-towners. We surrounded these out-of-towners like a human shield as they loaded themselves into the car and made their way to the airstrip in Bomet about five miles away. As the caravan of cars carrying missionaries, the Oguta family, the painter, and our Swahili teacher made its way out of the compound, I was reminded of all the fears I felt being chased by angry white mobs in Chicago, IL, just for crossing the tracks or sitting on their part of the beach.

There were at least two other occasions when I felt this [kind of intense] fear while in Kenya. I have yet to understand the deep and bitter hatred, which drives people to kill because of a difference in tribe and custom. I have heard Kenyan church leaders justify the hate and prejudice they feel for one another. I have come to understand that the most dangerous thing one can do in this situation is to open one's mouth in defense of someone. No one is safe in this [type of] situation. We were only kept by God's grace.

Rosa Parks, Please Come To Bomet

First of all, "Lord, why did you send this city boy who was born and raised in Chicago, had spent the last 10 years of his life in Philadelphia, PA, to this place that is not even a speck of dust on the map? What did I do wrong, Lord?"

Bomet is where we found ourselves permanently stationed in 1990. I almost want to say "condemned," but that would be a bit too depressing. If you were to visit there, however, you might think otherwise. As you walk the "streets" of Bomet, the most striking thing is how much it resembles a town from the early 1700s in America. The only sense of order in the town planning is that the buildings are in straight lines.

A variety of buildings line these streets. The surface of the streets is nothing more than gravel and dirt. Deep ruts caused by the heavy rains have unearthed stones as the mud is washed downstream. A visit to the bank in Bomet during our early days there was best made on a sunny day. It was nearly impossible to count the money if the sky was overcast because there was no electricity and only kerosene lanterns were used in the bank.

Walking down the streets you'd see people gathered in groups discussing a variety of topics. Town gossip, politics, and, of course, farming issues are very important. Too much rain, too little rain. Too much sun, too little sun. Why did the government sell us bad seed? Why does the government buy crops so cheaply from us and sell them so high on the open market? Cows and other livestock also congregate. You must be careful where you step in the streets or you might be gored by a cow or jostled by a herd of sheep and goats.

Boys and girls run up and down the roads. Most are clad in ragged, dirty clothing but some have shoes. They play just like kids all over the world. They laugh and smile at us. They kick old empty cans and homemade soccer balls made of old plastic bags and strings.

There are bars and restaurants and a myriad of general stores. You can go into these stores and buy the much-needed necessities: seeds, fertilizer, barbed wire, dish soap, and even spaghetti. No spaghetti sauce is available, but you can buy spaghetti.

We had to learn Swahili. It was a good thing to do. (If you are going to communicate with people, knowing their language sure makes it easier.) We took advantage of this, not because we really wanted to, but our mission demanded it. We complied and actually enjoyed learning a new language.

It was necessary to make one trip to Bomet in order to practice our language skills. "This should be fun," we thought. "Well, at least it will be a challenge." We walked to Bomet because it is only five miles away and we needed the exercise. It was a sunny day and this provided a break from Swahili classes.

Kay and I and our friend Denise walked together. We looked like the missionary version of the Oreo cookie, with Denise being the white filling. Upon our arrival in Bomet,

we set about our task conversing with the locals and buying things in the store to practice our Swahili. We had to get the storekeeper to understand that we wanted new matches and not a blue mattress. We managed to buy some things needed in the average African-American home, such as a hoe, a pick axe, chicken feed, and some spaghetti. We knew how to make our own sauce.

It was now time to go home, but it began to rain. "So what do we do now?" We decided we would ride the local matatu bus (read "Matatu Hell" for more understanding of this). We knew how these matatus moved. We were aware that many of these vehicles had no brakes. This really didn't matter as they couldn't go too fast because the ruts in the road were too big. Besides, a sudden stop always could be managed by hitting a cow or running into one of the rocks on the side of the road.

The only real problem was there was only room for one more person in the front cab and there were three of us. The turnboy (conductor) looked at our "Oreo" cookie. He had a real problem now—how to take these foreigners and treat them appropriately? He solved his problem by segregating us! There were three people in the front cab, including the driver, but one more person could be held in place if the rope was tightened on the passenger door handle and the driver leaned the right half of his body outside of the car. Now, who would ride up front? Well, our friend Denise was white, like the filling of the cookie! This was a "no brainer" in the conductor's eyes.

Denise was invited up front and Kay and I were directed to the back of the matatu. We were fortunate to be given places beneath the tarpaulin instead of having to hang on the outside. They did treat us a bit better since we were obviously foreigners. I couldn't believe it! This had never happened to me at home. I'd come all the way to the "mother land" to be treated as the alien child. Fortunately, Denise had more of Christ in her than to be segregated like that, so she sat in the back with us.

Worship services at Tenwek reflected this same attitude. I won't even speculate who was at fault. There was obviously a precedent set here and I am not sure if even Rosa Parks could have stopped it as she did at in Birmingham, AL, in 1955, by refusing to give her seat to a white person. On any Sunday morning you could see the continuation of this segregation. Kenyans who arrived at 10:20 a.m. for the 10:30 a.m. worship service almost exclusively took seats in the back of the meeting room. Missionaries who arrived at 10:25 a.m. for the same service would sat anywhere they wanted, but most frequently in the front and middle sections.

I observed this for all of the years I was at Tenwek. I asked the Kenyan in our men's Bible study about this one day. "Why do you guys sit in the back?" I asked, "Even when you come early, you sit in the back. What is the purpose of this?"

They laughed at me in an uncomfortable way, covering their mouths and snickering. It was not an easy question to answer. No one readily volunteered. I looked to a doctor friend of mine in the meeting and he looked away shyly. His face can't turn red. I remembered that these were some of the same guys who told me that they were born to pick the white man's tea on the plantations.

"What if I and the missionaries came to the meeting room first and sat in the back? Where would you sit then?"

A strained silence cames over the room. No one had ever thought of this before. This could have presented a real problem. Then my doctor friend spoke up boldly, with a chuckle, "I guess we'd have to sit outside!"

Carter G. Woodson, the father of black history in America and author of *The Miseducation of the American Negro* said, "If you teach a man to use the back door long enough, when he comes to a place that has no back door, he will make a back door." I was seeing that back-door mentality. Someone had obviously set this precedent either intentionally or by neglect. There was no question that this hampered their growth in Christ. Somehow the possibility of being an equal person in the eyes of God had never been adequately and effectively transmitted or captured.

Many Kenyans have received the Gospel as it had been given to them, without fully considering the implications of their accepting all of its trappings. I would venture to say that most white missionaries are completely unaware of these trappings, which come with being from a culture which is arrogant and aggressive.

Again this is no fault of their own. When you grow up in America as a white person, you are bound to think of yourself and your kind as superior. It is part of the system.

We need to help release people from the back-door mentality. We need to help people be free to think. We cannot give them the freedom to think. When we give them this freedom, it is not theirs. We must remove our culture from our Christianity. We must do as Moses did and claim that God has sent us to "Let My people go" or rephrased, "Let My people think."

I am always amazed at the number of Johns, Josephs, Ezekiels, and Elijahs in Kenya. It seemed the names of the Bible were so much more common there than here in the U.S. I asked men from our Bible study, "Why do Kenyan men have such names and the women as well, Sara and Zipporah and Leah? Why are these names so common?"

They replied, "Those are the 'Christian' names they get when they are baptized." I did not understand why they didn't use Kenyan names as Christian names. I met many a Stanley and Cynthia, names I have not found in the Bible. It appears that a Western name is equivalent to a Christian name and an African name cannot be so. We have encouraged people to disassociate from their names of their ancestry, advising them that such names are completely devoid of Christianity and to take names associated with the West, which are automatically "Christian."

Among the people we worked with, people were named in a variety of ways. The male child would take the father's last name as his first name and then would have another name indicating the time or situation at the time of birth. Others had names from their father or mother and then in order of succession in birth, were named for grandparents and great-grandparents. There is rhyme and reason to this.

When the name is for situation or time of birth, it may be recorded as "when the cows come home," or "time of getting water," or "an important guest has arrived." Such names have meaning and significance to the family. But it appeared that one must have a Christian name. I was told that the name must be a biblical name, which I know doesn't mean much because Beelzebub and Jezebel are in the Bible and no one gives their child such names.

If people can think, they can see themselves as a reflection of Christ and not a reflection of the missionary who taught them about Christ. This will allow our Kenyan brothers to sit anywhere they want in the church building, worship, and fear God rather than the people who taught them about God.

My Experience as a West African Missionary

Daisie Whaley

I was raised and groomed to be ecstatic about missions. As a member of Christ Baptist Church [Philadelphia, PA] under the leadership of its founder and then pastor, Rev. Benjamin Johnson [*see separate article on Dr. Ben Johnson*], I was encouraged to be mission-minded. I was just graduating from Manna Bible Institute. This equipped me to ultimately become part of the place where God led me. Therefore, I've got a different perspective on blacks and their place in missions.

I finished my 30-year experience in Ivory Coast in 1999. In retrospect, I came home realizing the tremendous change that had occurred since 1969. I will begin with that change, my calling, our commission and our commitment.

As I reminisce over my 30 years in Africa, I remember my first encounter with an African. All of my missionary co-workers were Caucasians from Australia, New Zealand, England, and France. At that point, even though it wasn't in style, I'd gone back to wearing my hair natural. My Caucasian coworkers advised me to this since Africans didn't have straight hair. They didn't perm or use a straightening comb on their hair, so it was suggested that I take on a very natural form. I was more than willing to do this to win souls for Christ.

I was driven up-country, arriving in the Ivory Coast on January 1, 1969. I was taken from house to house to visit with the elders and meet the prominent people in the church and from town. The African residents stared at me. This was their first time seeing an African-American person. They touched their nose, then touched my nose. They touched their hair, then touched my hair. They touched their hand, then touched my hand. They said, "She looks just like us. I wonder if she will love us." In all my 30 years as a missionary, I have never ever forgotten this.

On the way to the Ivory Coast, coming over on the ship as I left New York Harbor, I became acquainted with two ladies who became my Liberian mothers. As I was leaving my mother, father, sisters, and brothers in America, their advice to me was, "Love the people. And if you have a problem, go into your secret closet." This reference was used by both cultures. I used it to ask Christ to fill me with love for the people I would be helping. This was December 1968. It was already in my heart that if I did not go in love, I would not have any reason to minister. At my young age, I did not

Daisie M. Whaley graduated from Manna Bible Institute and spent 30 years of full time mission work with WEC International in the Ivory Coast, West Africa. Upon retirement from the field she now is a full-time missions mobilizer in African-American churches. She also helps take short-term teams from USA to various mission fields.

Lezlie B. McCoy contributed to this article.

Edited by Shannon Newlin and Jean Voss Sorokin of the Southeast Regional Office of the USCWM.

have much to share of my life, so I had get involved. I went with preconceived ideas.

I read everything about Africa as a young person. Not many books in those days were written by Africans that I could put my hands on. However, as I arrived in Africa, stopping in Liberia and visiting Ghana, I would go to university bookshops to buy up African writer series so that I could read about the African child before I arrived. I got my hands on every piece of material written by Africans so I would have a different perspective of life. I did not compare how I lived in America or what we did in America. My idea was to cleanse my mind of my education and my background. I needed to be reborn in the African culture. That was very good for me.

I met African students. I was particularly challenged by a young man named David. I knew Africans needed to see blacks from America. I knew I had to go to minister to the total man by establishing a holistic ministry.

How was I going to do this, coming out of America's turbulent 1960s, from a white mission board? Back in the U.S., we blacks were fighting for our equal rights in America and for the birth of a new nation. I addition to this, the Ivory Coast had just received its independence in 1965. Here I was going to a new nation, a new birth. Was I willing to take on this new birth as I went?

As I read the article written by my brethren who went in the early 1960s, I know I arrived in Africa under totally different circumstances. The black uprising in America, the surging of Dr. Martin Luther King, Jr., and other occurrences during the civil rights movement, although not a militant or radical, these incidents deeply sensitized me. Being in the African-American language study when Martin Luther King was assassinated, not one of my fellow Caucasian classmates from America spoke a word about the situation. It was as though nothing had ever happened, that Dr. King had not been assassinated. I had been deeply touched by these events. I knew they were going to shape my life for the future. I was also going with a mission that had never had a black missionary before. This was my calling.

As I integrated into life in the Ivory Coast, I was asked to remove my jewelry, which was an offense to me at the time. However, I decided to accept this so I could be better integrated into the life and culture of the Gouro people. I was called to them by a white couple who had come home on furlough and they had such love for the people that it transcended the color of their skin. They were extremely involved with these people. I saw this and knew I wanted to be a part of this couple's life. Not only did I want to be a part of them, but to be involved in their work.

I got there and my first thought was, "I belong to them." I was probably one of the first Americans to put on African garb. The Gouro came and said, "Here is our black-white woman." I was black like them, but I lived like the whites in a house with the whites. "Black-White Woman" was my name for a long time until they began to learn, understand, and embrace me as their lost sister.

In West Africa where I worked, if a child had not been home for a long time, or if the child had been away on a visit, the grandma would get the child and remove her load, put the child on her back and say, "Welcome back." This is the reception I received. Everywhere I'd go, they'd say, "Oh my goodness, she looks like us. Get on my back." It was an enlightening time of knowing, "Hey, this is where I came from!"

I experienced an opportunity of seeing the similarities to life in America. Things my ancestors had not dropped, little things, like putting your hand on your head when you're sad. I can remember my grandmother saying to me, "Get your hands off your head like a motherless child." That's something we've kept down through the ages. Putting your hands across your head meant sadness. If you have seen anyone in Africa with sadness, then you would know that. Just the idea of our grandmothers and our great-grandmothers eating with their fingers and having certain foods that you eat with your fingers. I remembered that [from when I] was a child. Then I saw that when I came to Africa. I was being educated. My eyes were being opened. This is where I came from.

There was also the importance of having funerals and taking the bodies back to the mothers in the village. We as African-Americans would always take the body back to where we were raised in the South when we were growing up. All these similarities really connected me. It was great for me to be released by my family, going back to the Motherland and being accepted by this ancestral land. It was good that I was not fair in complexion. I was dark like them.

Though now I'm in America, I still feel very African because I was integrated right into the culture. Another thing that helped my integration was being in a rural village where I learned the language. We made sort of a pact that we wouldn't speak any other language. For a time, the only outreach I had to our Western world was the BBC on my little transistor radio. I didn't speak French. I learned the language on a grassroots level. I lived with the people. I went to the pond to wash my clothes. I went to the plantation. I went to the farm. I laid my clothes out on the grass and bushes to dry. While I did sleep under my mosquito net and drink filtered water, I ate their food and sat around the fire. I lived by a lap [valley] out in the village on my little camping bed. Maybe that's where the difference came. I was really initiated into the life and to the people.

Being from the Philadelphia area, as a young person I can remember having about 20 African-American people, couples and singles from the PA/NJ area working in Liberia. I was raised in a church where missions was the lifeline. Our pastor, Ben Johnson, who now resides in Nashville, TN, introduced us to missions. We were raised in an urban center, but we knew missionaries. We took part in mission outreaches. We evangelized in the streets. We trusted God to have our own radio broadcast. We were a group of young African-Americans who went out and evangelized every Sunday afternoon, converting different areas and starting Bible clubs and home Bible study groups. This is why I have this perspective. My desire as a young person was to see Sunday every day of the week, 365 days a year. This is where I received my calling.

We were young people moving from one degree [level] to another. From going out into our baseball stadium to evangelizing at a

Jehovah's Witness convention, my need for going to Bible school was realized. During my second year at Bible school, I was challenged to missions. I went back to the university and felt that I didn't fit in there. The Lord was calling me to full-time service. Also, in my second year, a young pastor named David was studying here in the U.S. from Kenya. David said that more African-Americans from the U.S. needed to come. We were hindered for ages because of language barriers and finances.

Here I was, a young woman challenged to go on to Africa in the early 1960s. God was able, but what mission did I know about? I did know one not far from Philadelphia called Worldwide Evangelization for Christ, started by C. T. Studd, a cricket player from England who threw everything overboard for Christ.

This was the prime of my life. I could have been married. I could have been doing other things. But this was the call upon my life. I moved forward and God blessed. The calling was very much there. I came from a Bible-believing church and a Bible believing youth group from the city of Philadelphia. I was inundated with missions all around me. My mentor, Dorothy Evans, had gone to the mission field when I was a young girl of 12. Her fiance had passed away and here she was doing the will of the Lord in Liberia. There were other young women and young couples I knew who were throwing everything overboard to go. The Cantys were going to Liberia, the Thorpes and Viola Reddish went to Bopolo, Liberia. Martha Thompson went to Liberia. So many were trusting the Lord to go out and to share the good news in the English-speaking countries of West Africa. Then God called me.

I went into missionary work in the midst of the African-American rioting in the U.S. of 1965. I said, "I want to join your mission because of God's call upon my life." It was a turbulent time, but God was good and faithful.

There was a couple that came to the U.S. and talked about missions. John and Grace Reeder talked about the need for missionaries. They said there was not a missionary national pastor to take up the slack in Africa.

Also, the Bible was in its first draft of the of the New Testament, and two women were dedicating their lives to completing it.

A church was going forward and reaching out. Different ethnic groups were helping out. I was completely fascinated by all this. Step by step, the Lord led me to do my studies in Canada, where I was the only black [in my class]. I was a young person who had already done things for Christ in the 1960s. I was around people who were proud of their blackness. The black revolutionary movement in the midst [of this time] may have influenced my life.

My mom taught me that, "God had a flower garden. He loved flowers, but He didn't make all the flowers the same. Some were buff, some were small, some were yellow, and some were green. The flowers were different because God wanted a beautiful flower garden. That's what humanity is all about. God made us different. In your difference, you can do anything you want to do. You can go anywhere you want to go." I never knew that I was poor. Everyone around me was poor and we never talked about poverty. We just always said, "We will see what we can do." That was the mentality that I grew up with. You weren't any better than me because you had blonde hair, blue eyes, a thin nose and thin lips. I had brown eyes and black hair and a flat nose and thick lips. I was pleased with the way God made me. I was one of the flowers in his garden. I love that garden concept.

God commissioned me. All around me my counterparts were getting married, but I knew that for me it was missions. I took anthropology courses. I went forward. Everybody was saying to me, "Why don't you get married to a pastor and stay here." Or they'd say, "you're too young to go." Even my family said, "Why can't you work for Jesus here, there's lots of work to be done." But I saw the big picture and moved forward.

As mentioned earlier, I came into Africa in 1967, stopping in Liberia during Christmas. I stayed a week in Liberia, again being influenced by all the great black mission boards such as the Church of God in Christ, Pentecostal, Afro, and Carver. They were there. There were working and my eyes were

opened that I would not be the only one. These were my folk from Philly.

I got there and was readily accepted. Was it my color? Was it my attitude? I don't really know. I saw a [group of] people, masses of children. "Why, I could minister to these children!" I thought I couldn't minister to the women because I was a young, single woman. I thought, "Maybe in time I can win their confidence."

The most important thing to me was to learn the language. The concept the senior missionaries gave me during my first two years was to learn. [That meant] you didn't say much. You just looked and took everything in. You immersed yourself with the language. You taught in the government schools. You interacted with the government's teachers. You were invited out by the midwives in town and by the elite. You learned what they learned. You had the opportunity of sharing another language. In addition, I wanted to conquer the Gouro language because they were talking about me. They spoke about my hair, my shape, my legs, etc., and I wanted to know everything they were saying. So I worked very hard to master the language of these people. This was my commission. I yearned to be able to reach out to the young people and schoolchildren involved in camps.

I set my feet on Ivory Coast soil on January 1. I felt that I had arrived. From that, point on I just moved forward. This was God's plan. I wouldn't stay in the capital. I would go up with the rank and file, up to grassroots levels. I would get it [the language] from the ground up. I met the schoolteachers. I was chauffeured all around. I was learning all the different cultural things such as how to greet people, how to go to their houses, and how to learn their language.

I prayed, cried, and wondered if I would ever get the hang of the language. "Would I become one with them?" They said to me, "Well, you look like us. You've got a nose like ours. You should get this language in two weeks." It was so funny. They'd call me the "black one" or "Mademoiselle Ms. Tizan" while all my other coworkers were called "Fuzan." I was black like them. I was moving among them, learning the culture. As I learned the language, I learned the culture. Again, I could relate their culture back to certain things in my culture.

In this culture, men ate together, women ate together, and children ate together, according to their sexes. Dinnertime was a big linking outside event. I said to my parents that Africa was like going to a Girl Scout or Bible camp and never going home--outside toilets, no running water, washing outside with a plunger, filtering your water, sleeping under a mosquito net, burned by your oil lamp if you touched it too closely. At first, it was a learning process. I thank God for the many things that I learned.

The commission was there. Next, the question [to answer] was what language would I learn? I already knew that before I went, so it was in my heart that I was going to learn the [Guoro] language. As I was hobnobbing with the elite, some of them refused to believe that I was an American, which was a very good thing. Many times, I had to display my passport to show that I was really an American. The town got to know me. Many times I'd walk down the street and hear, "Here comes the black American."

I began Bible clubs and children's clubs all around the town. Just meeting the people, seeing the similarities between them and us, was a part of the call. I was commissioned to learn language to be able to help the young people. I also wanted to be able to minister life to them. I was able to share [my] life with them. Of course, I would have to go over everything step by step because I was the first African-American the missionaries had ever seen. "How was I going to be seen [perceived]? How was I going to fit in?" Africans just said to me, "Here comes our long-lost baby that went away in slavery, that has now come back to the country." That was the Africans' attitude towards me. I was black like them and had been in a foreign land and now had come back home. Every place I'd go, I went through a ritual of being put on the back of people, I was the lost one [returned home]. I would have people that spoke the [Guoro] language say to me, "What village is your father from?" This was good and bad. It was so sad to be unable to report that I came from the Bete group or the Garry group, etc.,

[because] I didn't know. They wanted to know but I could not tell them. Still I kept moving forward.

I continued being integrated with the people that I had come to minister to. In my first term of four years I was learning about what I was seeing. The next four years was, "Oh, is that what I saw last term?" By this time, I was beginning to connect. I was accepted because I was "a lost [one] coming back to Africa." "Would I have to deal with my [African] brethren as the black sister that had come back from America with lots of money?" I don't think that ever entered into it because I was like them and they were poor. The money was not an issue until later in my missionary career. They never asked me for anything because they knew I didn't have anything because I was black like them. The logistics of the whole thing was totally different for me. I was not in a big center. I was there in the village working along with the people.

I began to spread my wings away from coworkers, explaining what I wanted to do with [the people and] to pull myself away from them. I wasn't pulling away in a sense of being different from my white counterpart, but I was finally flapping my wings. Here I was that little sheltered baby [bird], but now I was out of the nest, flapping my wings. I now had eyes that saw differently and I could speak the language of the people. I saw [that] the needs of the children in the village had to be ministered to.

The Lord blessed me with a car. I was working with a woman from England, and then the Lord divided that up, and I worked with someone from France. Suddenly the Lord pushed her in another direction. So, there I was in a sense going on a course by myself. That was never heard of in our mission. I was living by myself, with my own house, with my own car and ministry, but within the context of a national church. They [church and mission] couldn't have a young black woman going out in a car by herself. There were restrictions put upon me by the church and the mission for my own protection when I could go out and do Bible clubs. The Bible clubs were very fulfilling to me, using the languages in the different villages, driving on very difficult roads, but only when there were other market[s] there. Everybody in the town knew me and looked out for me. If I had to change a flat tire, there would always be someone there to stop and help me.

I was commissioned to reach children for Christ in the Ivory Coast within the language group and I worked with in the government schools. I knew my goals were fixed. I learned to train. I was committed to the Guoro people, 300,000 strong. There was a team that was doing [Bible] translation. There was a team going out evangelizing. I was taking up the slack with the women. I saw how the women and children were pushed to the back. Any given moment you could go to the village and find the men sitting in the front reading. I had a commitment to the women and the children--the children that were not in the government school. At that point in my career, only a little of the population were school age and actually in school. I devised a way to get out into the villages and teach. I'd have a Bible class for the children. I'd make sure they came to my class with clothes on and they would learn. I would compliment them. This took place from village to village. It was very exciting. This was one stepping stone to exactly where the Lord wanted me to go.

Working with the women was so rewarding. Again, in reference to my friends who have written papers in the past, my experience was different. I was the only one. I was in the village. I sat where they sat. I walked in their shoes. I sat down and listened to their problems. If they were in the village shelling peanuts, I sat down and started shelling peanuts. If they were sorting coffee or rice, I would sit and help them sort, working along with them. Whatever they were doing, I'd do it. That's the way I associated with the women. More and more they pulled me in.

Was it good? Yes. But in the end, sometimes I tried to do too much. My life was surrounded by these people day in and day out, but then God opened doors. Sunday School teacher's training was put on me. I ordered the literature and made sure it was reproduced. Once a missionary left, all those jobs became one of the various hats I had to wear.

Having the Africans in my home, I knew that I was African-American. I knew that the Africans lived differently. I had seen African-American missionaries trying to make the Africans into little Philadelphians or little New Yorkers. I didn't want to do that. My eyes were opened and I wanted to help the young people that I mentored and ministered to keep in their own context. When I left Africa, I wanted them to still belong in their own village setup. They could still go on the farm and work [even if educated].

I was committed to training young people and encouraging them. I saw so many changes in the 30 years I was there. I also had to keep moving with that change. I stepped back and let the nationals take their place, because to me missions means that you are sent for a period of training people, then you move back. These were wonderful times.

There would be three or four girls that started out not being in school, but their parents wanted them to learn how to read Gouro. They had the New Testament and soon after, in 1979, they had the complete Bible in their language. We didn't want these young ladies to get married without reading the Bible and knowing what type of Christian wives they needed to become.

They didn't have an education. We had short-term Bible schools and camps to minister to young Christian girls and really challenge them to live for Christ. The results were beautiful. We had an ongoing program for helping them. The parents would say, "Well, take her, you can have her." There were about 50 girls I was able to minister to in my last 10-15 years on the field. They are now married to leaders in the church. They were given to me as young girls to learn to read the Bible. Once they learned to read the Bible in their own language, I said "Let's get on with the French." And after learning to read French, I'd say to them, "Let's get on and do a trade. There's a trade school in town that teaches home economics." "Go to this school for young women."

Was I ostracized by my coworkers? Yes, I was. [Was I] ostracized by missionaries and national pastors? Yes, but I had a commitment to these young women. It was crucial that the next generation of Christians coming up in the church would be different. They should not be put down. They could read and write. They could expound on the Word of God. Then I started sending them off to Bible school--Change!

As we move into the new millennium, we must establish change. Our young women cannot sit back. I am not a feminist, but I am one for improvement, for training, and [for] seeing the big picture. These young people needed to be trained to take over the things I did, so they could reproduce it even better than I.

These young women were given to me. With all of these girls in my care, I asked the church for permission to build facilities to house them. Bunk beds were built for them. [This meant] they went from sleeping on floors to mattresses. They put windows where screens had been so mosquitoes and malaria would not be so prevalent. I was bringing them up. There would be shelves for everyone to keep their things. I was not going to make them little Americans with the chest of drawers, but they [each] had a shelf. They had to keep their things clean. They had coat hangers and hooks to hang their clothes. Each girl had her own bath bucket instead of a community bucket. They had towels and their own place to keep soap to curtail diseases. I couldn't touch communal eating, because that's a part of their culture-- their own context of living. They could cook on their own outside kitchen.

But, I wasn't going to make them little Whaleys. They were my little daughters for 10-15 years. They stayed with me until they got married. I loved that ministry, but I wasn't taking them out of their culture. I introduced them to keeping their Sunday clothes aside. They were introduced to things that would improve their lifestyle and health. I'm no longer there, but they can now do it for other young people. They know how to cook on a gas stove and keep their kitchens clean. They know how to wash their hands before they go into the refrigerator to get a glass of water. We changed from using gas to using electricity and also to using running hot water. It was fabulous and I loved it. In the 30 years, I experienced so much change!

I loved it! It was a joy. I have now seen African-Americans marry Africans. Did they have difficult times? Yes, [they did]. Did they have good times? Yes, [they did]. These women found their place. Knowing Christ, they are very happy. They've come back to America because we're in a new millennium now. [Then] you'd fly home every year if you worked in a government school or in a government setup. There are so many Americans that are going to Africa to set up companies. [Nelson] Mandela has been the president of South Africa. Apartheid is lost and gone. The national brethren kept their country together. Ivory Coast experienced a coup, but things were improving. (They weren't improving as fast as people wanted them to, but there was stability there and they were moving forward.)

Because I have a totally different picture of Africa, I would go in any given market and meet Americans who had married and moved over to West Africa to set up their businesses. The logistics of walking through the government and through all the paperwork that we have in all the countries today is challenging. But they have found their place. I was committed and I've seen young men whom I trained go on to Bible school. They came back changed, on fire, reaching out to others, marrying, praying, and seeking the Lord's face.

I'm continually receiving letters from my young women who are now reproducing [their ministries] and they know how to pray. As for the women's ministry, I've seen the women now in the church where I worked, having their own nationalized women's groups. I've seen the Sunday school grow from meeting in little huts to classrooms with trained teachers, not only in the unifying language, but in the language of their local area. It's really stirring that I've had an input in all this. I feel that my 30 years were very well spent.

My commitment [led to His] fulfillment of things. What the Lord helped me do in my time there was superb. It hasn't always been easy. I wasn't always accepted by my coworkers, whether they were European, American, or Canadian. But that was not a real issue with me because I knew where I was going and I knew what I wanted. [Was I] criticized? [Was I] ostracized? Yes, [I was]. [Was I] left out? Sometimes [I was] but I knew what I wanted and knew what I was about. As I left, I still had input in the life there. This is where God called me to minister from 1969 to 1999.

They said to me, "Why are you leaving us?" It was time to move on. If they needed my help I would still be there. The women's ministry has grown beautifully. These girls have kept themselves pure. When I came home, one of my brethren said, "Tizan, when I get married, I want a beautiful white wedding dress." Before I had left Ivory Coast, I had 25 wedding dresses given to me by my sisters in America and Europe. I was able to wash them in dish detergent, lemon juice, and salt. [Then] our women's group started making local soap. I was able to wash the wedding dresses that I still send to the women's group. Now the women's group plans open up a salon and rental shop for these wedding dresses. I also am praying that they will be able to host a two-week training course for girls that are getting married. This training would consist of a couple talking to these women about marriage, along with information about housekeeping and entertaining. This is my dream. I'm always about moving one step forward.

Did I feel fulfilled? Yes. Did I get married? No. Did I have children? Yes, many spiritual children and grandchildren. Lord willing, I will soon have spiritual great-grandchildren.

What kind of changes did I see in Africa? In my 30 years, we moved from hauling water to turning on taps; seeing banking systems being established in our local town; telephones and electricity. I saw e-mails and faxes right in my own town. Faxes would come from my friends in America.

In 1975, more young women poured into the government schools. They said to me, "Where are the black brothers? Tell them to come." This is our [African-American's] time in missions. This is our time in outreach. By the year, 2010 there will be more people of color than any other race. It's our time!

I also question, "Where are the brothers?" We tell the brothers to come. We tell the black sisters to come. It's fabulous to see young black men like Carl Williams studying French to do translations. Since 1960, it has changed. Mission boards need to realize that they need more blacks integrated in missions. I am now representing WEC and their outreach to the African-American community, seeing young people willing to go for short-term mission trips in different parts of the U.S. and Canada. I'm excited to see what's going to happen in this new millennium--new beginnings--a new generation. We can do it! We need to be awakened, especially with the amount of money we have. It has changed. China, Portugal, and Europe need missionaries, too.

God has moved us up from the 1960s into the new millennium. There is plenty for us to do. The doors are off the hinges. Single black males need to go. We need to be there because we also have a part in that Great Commission. The Lord said to "compel" them. The feast is ready. Let's go and pass out the invitations. We as African-Americans need to be there on the firing line. Carl is going back to the Ivory Coast. There's another young man there doing translations. We need to see them move out like a mighty giant waking up, like a might army ready to attack.

Marilyn Lewis, who had such a vision for blacks in missions, recently went home to be with the Lord. We need to take up the slack for Marilyn Lewis, myself, Brian Johnson, and Donald Canty. We need young couples. The Polks and Williams are there. We need to see more young people moving in full-time service. We have a part in this Great Commission.

I recently learned that some of the young people I previously mentored are now missionaries. To God be the glory! He's still shaking off the shackles and mentalities of slavery. Abundant Life came out seven years for missions. They worked beside me. They were people of color. The people didn't want them to go back.

I am not saying that the other brothers [and sisters] didn't have certain different experiences, but times have changed. Blacks need to come back to the Motherland. I had a great time [serving]. I didn't want my name up in lights. I wanted to be a part of sharing

Christ with others, that they might know this great opportunity. African-American brothers and sisters, think about a career in missions. You'll have good days and bad days, but it is fulfilling. You will understand the calling God has given you.

I'm [back] here in America, but I'm still involved in missions. I'm shaking the African-American community gently so we can wake up. This summer, I'm taking two teens to Nova Scotia with Joe Jeter's *Have Christ Will Travel* ministries. We're also going to Mississippi. I look forward to this missionary assignment. Maybe next year we'll go to Haiti. Whatever God wants, I am available. That's what the Lord wants from us: to be available!

Central Asia: Cross Cultural Perceptions and Experiences

Cecil Stewart

The first 23 years of my life were spent in Jamaica. The Jamaican context prepared me to easily adapt to life in the U.S. and to thrive in Asia. I grew up in a culture where my teachers were black. The majority of pastors, policemen, bus drivers, mailmen, doctors, lawyers, judges, engineers, and laborers were black like me. At the same time, I was surrounded by family and friends who were black, white, Chinese, and Indian. We went to school, church, and work together. I [later] grew up in a country whose motto was "Out of many, one people." I grew up confident, supported, and loved.

In 1996 God moved my family to Central Asia to live among the peoples of Kazakstan. In retrospect, the move from the U.S. to Kazakstan was not nearly as hard as the previous move from Jamaica to the U.S. For much of my life I've been reconciled to the fact that I could easily fit into Jamaican–American culture. I've often told my wife that I felt that I could live anywhere in the world. At the same time, I knew that Heaven is my homeland and I look expectantly for the return of the King of the Earth.

In Kazakstan I felt that I belonged, too. I belonged to the Kazaks, the Russians, the Chinese, and the Uighurs. My blackness was a magnet to all and gave me access. People would cross the street to get a better look at me and I learned to exploit their curiosity. I would turn to meet them with my hand outstretched in greeting and they would always smile and shake my hand.

It seemed that the only Russians who could speak Kazak were the school children or the former secret police. My choice of Kazak as a language caused confusion for some Russians. Why would anyone want to speak Kazak? To the Kazaks though, it provided me access.

I was invited by strangers to come visit their homes. One day I went shopping with my wife. As we walked among the aisles, I saw two Kazak women, a mother and daughter, looking at us. After we bumped into each other for the second time, I greeted them in Kazak. We spent several minutes talking together. Right there on the spot hey invited us to come to their house for fellowship.

In Kazakstan I felt safer walking down the street at midnight than I felt walking in my middle-class neighborhood in the U.S. In Kazakstan someone might stop me to ask for money. They would have even assaulted me and taken it,

Cecil Stewart and his wife, Dedra, and their three children live in Raleigh, NC. Cecil serves as an elder at Christ Covenant Church of Raleigh. He works as a computer network engineer. He and his family lived for two years in Kazakstan.

but they didn't because I was black. Sometimes we were living in a tension-filled, unpredictable environment, yet there was never a concern that someone would choose not to recognize my presence because of my blackness.

To be hospitable, especially to strangers, and to be respectful to elders is engrafted into the Kazak psyche. I sat on the floor with many different families and enjoyed their bread, and drank their tea. They could hardly afford sugar for the tea, yet they entertained a stranger and made him a part of their family. These are godly traits that I admire. I felt at home.

I felt safe because people were genuinely interested in who I was as a person. As a result, I felt free to show interest in them. They wanted to know who my father was. How old was he? Did he have more or less hair on his head than I? How long was he married to my mother?

Many who had much less than I did gave gifts, opened up their homes, and invited us to spend time with their families. Beside the desire to see God's kingdom expand in Kazakstan, this "safety" that I felt among the Kazaks caused me to want to remain among them. The friendships I made and the experiences we shared around a meal will drive me back someday.

I would have to be mentally or emotionally deficient not to know and acknowledge my African origins, but, I admit, seldom was I more confronted with it than during my two-plus years in Kazakstan. People would ask, "Where are you from?" When I would respond, "I am from America," they would assume that puzzled look and say, "No, you can't be. Tell me, really, where are you from?" Frustrated by the U.S.A. answer, they would move on to "What is your birth country?" or "What is your nationality?" No answer was acceptable unless it had "Africa" in it. The trouble is, I know that my ancestors were from West Africa, but I cannot be more specific. No matter how hard I try, I may never be able to say with any certainty, "I'm from Ghana," or "I'm from this or that place." This leaves me with a sense of not belonging, but in my heart I know that this, too, is God's doing. He has put in it's place a longing for Heaven.

As the Kazaks say, "Mening Otannim Aspanda": my homeland is in Heaven.

The Missing Black Missionary

Dick Hillis

Charles Richard "Dick" Hillis is a a graduate of Bible Institute of Los Angeles, CA, and attended Dallas Theological Seminary, TX. He received an honorary doctorate from Biola College in 1956. Dick Hillis is founder and general director of Overseas Crusade (or OC) International. His missionary career began in China in 1933 and included 18 months in Communist-controlled China. He stayed there until 1949. He spent 10 years in Taiwan and has made many missionary journeys to South American and the Far East. He has been a member of the board of directors for World Gospel Crusade, Steer, Inc., Missionary Supply Lines, and Preaching Print, Inc.

Reprinted with permission from World Vision Magazine, *January 1969.*

How many American black foreign missionaries have you ever met? Can you count them on two hands?

Yet the American black man makes up more than 10 percent of the U.S. population. And is he not more *religious* than his white brother? The National Baptist Convention, U.S.A., Inc. (Negro) reports 6.3 million members and the National Baptist Convention of America (Negro), 3.5 million. Numerous independent Negro churches and some smaller conventions also must be added to that number.

Are 10 percent of our evangelical missionaries Negroes? If not, why not? Is there something we can do about it?

Does Christ expect Caucasian Christians alone to evangelize the world? No! The first-century church had great Negro missionaries. According to tradition, the Ethiopian eunuch was used of God to write glorious church history across North Africa. Why then the mini-army of American Negro missionaries today?

Has God rejected the witness of the Christian Negro? Has God refused to our black brothers the gifts of the Spirit? Modern history proves quite the opposite. Take Billy Graham's associate evangelist, the Rev. Howard O. Jones, for example. Every place in Africa where the sole of his foot has trod the church has felt the quickening of the Holy Spirit and those outside the church have been irresistibly drawn to the Savior.

But while we might expect an American Negro evangelist to have a successful ministry in Africa, would Howard Jones or any Negro missionary be accepted in countries outside the black continent? The fact that Mr. Jones' ministry has been accepted and effective worldwide should put that question to rest.

Jones himself says,

Many Negro young people today would launch out in a missionary ministry if they honestly felt that their churches would faithfully stand behind them. Instead, these young people are discouraged that many of our wealthy and prospering black churches are without a vision for missions and fail to fulfill their financial responsibility to support missionaries. It is equally disheartening when they see the poorer congregations that are not able to support sufficiently their ministers and the work of the church. If we expect to see an increase of black missionaries on the foreign fields, the Negro churches in America must awake to their own financial obligations to their missionaries.

A little over a year ago [1960s] Overseas Crusades' Negro missionary evangelist Bob Harrison and his family moved to the Philippines. Some of his supporters raised their eyebrows. Would the church in Asia welcome Harrison's help and ministry? The fact that the Harrisons have had to extend their tour of duty in Asia speaks for itself.

First Negro in 103 Years

A missionary in the Philippines writes,

A new trail has been blazed from Taipei to Singapore in Southeast Asia by Bob Harrison, one of the most respected and well-known American Negro singers and evangelists. Everywhere this 'man of color' has gone in the cities of Taiwan, the Republic of the Philippines, Malaysia, and Singapore, he has met with eagerly enthusiastic crowds and in many cities attendance records have been broken.

Harrison completed a one-week crusade in Cebu City, the oldest city in the Philippines. Crowds of excited Filipinos thronged into the 15,000-seat Cebu Coliseum to hear this gifted Negro missionary sing and preach.

In the past year Harrison has conducted crusades in nearly a dozen cities in Asia and has seen more than 3,000 come forward to make personal decisions for Jesus Christ. Crowds jammed the site of each crusade. In one city, local officials stated that his meetings attracted more people than any public meeting held before--either political or entertainment.

A leading Chinese churchman in Taipei, Taiwan explained the great response by saying: 'This is our first Negro evangelist in the 103-year history of the church in Taiwan. His renditions of the Negro spirituals spoke to our hearts. The suffering and disappointments that his people have suffered in the past are similar to our own.'"

Harrison speaks directly to the needs of the people. Many old-time pastors compare Harrison's ministry to that of the famous Chinese evangelist, John Sung, who stirred up Asia and especially China back in the early 1930s.

Harrison agrees with Jones that the Negro churches in America must awaken to their financial obligations to their missionaries. The small number of missionary recruits from the evangelical Negro churches is partially due, he feels, to the absence of a missionary program and vision in the church. But a good percentage of Harrison's support comes from Negro churches, large and small. He believes that if black Christians are given the right missionary exposure and are challenged with the opportunity they will respond generously and often sacrificially.

To deal honestly with the problem before us we have to face an embarrassing fact or two. Part of the reason for the lack of Negro missionaries is due to their conviction that "missionary societies would not consider sending Negro talent to foreign fields even if they applied." At this point the shoe may pinch some mission boards.

Then doctrine plays a larger part in the lack of Negro missionaries than we would like to admit. There is no lack of Negro congregations, but how many of these churches are evangelical? This leads Negro song leader, evangelist, and author Bill Pannell to observe:

"You can check the yearbooks of major Christian Bible colleges and liberal arts schools and I am sure there will be less than 100 Negroes."

The failure, according to Pannell, is that the white evangelical church has channeled its missionary zeal overseas and has abdicated its responsibility to evangelize his Negro neighbor. As white evangelical brothers we must not hesitate to accept the major share of the blame.

"A visitor from outer space would have to conclude that there is one God for white people and another God for black people," Pannell told college students in Seattle. "We'd rather be Americans than Christians. In some grotesque way we believe God is really a segregationist. It's embarrassing and shameful."

A native of Detroit, Pannell is author of the book *My Friend, The Enemy* and is a veteran of evangelistic work in troubled Newark, NJ. He also served as a representative of Youth for Christ International.

"There are times to pray, but this isn't one of them," he said, making reference to racial disorders. He said God demands first that Christians uncover the sin in their camp.

Negro students in some of our finest Christian colleges have admitted to me privately that they are often made to feel unwelcomed. As deeply as we may regret it, white racism is still a part of the outlook of too many evangelicals. Is not the fact that we have separate Negro and white churches and colleges a scandal before the world and an affront to God?

Are there other reasons for lack of missionary participation by the American Negro? Foreign missions in this generation are for the most part directed by white men. I could list a dozen names of outstanding missionary leaders, and the well-informed white evangelical would immediately tell me what mission each belonged to and state his position in that mission. The average black evangelical, by contrast, has little or no knowledge of the evangelical foreign missionary leadership of our day. He is almost totally ignorant of what missions are doing abroad. Why?

Whose fault is it that our Negro brothers remain ignorant? A large share of the responsibility is ours. How often does a missionary leader speak in a Negro church or address a chapel in a Negro college? Have you ever seen a foreign mission advertisement in which it was made clear that their manpower wants included Negroes and other minority groups? When did you last read an article describing the work of a Negro missionary in any country but Africa?

Harrison says, "Some missionary organizations have said that they want qualified Negro personnel, but practice has seldom matched profession."

Missions must do more than make declarations–they must practice what they preach. *The Negro young person is not asking for favors, but one who has been excluded for so long cannot be expected to run to every mission and knock down the door trying to get in.* If he is called and qualified, any evangelical mission should accept the black candidate as quickly as the white one.

Solving the Mystery

We are now faced with the practical question of what churches and missions can do to help solve the mystery of the missing black missionary. The fact that we cannot do everything to correct this situation does not excuse us from doing something.

Bob Harrison feels that Negro pastors need to see what God is doing in Asia so he is taking some key Negro pastors to Southeast Asia to give them a firsthand view of the oriental welcome and show how the Negro can be used in missionary endeavor. New missionary interest on the part of the pastor will lead to a stronger missionary appeal to his people when he returns to America.

Mission agencies must provide speakers and literature for Negro churches. They must also assure Christian Negro youth that they are prepared to accept qualified Negro missionaries on exactly the same basis they accept anyone else.

Evangelical mission leaders must meet with the leaders of the National Negro Evangelical Association and formulate concrete guidelines to educate and stimulate the local black churches in the whole area of missionary privilege and responsibility.

Outstanding Christian Negroes such as Howard Jones, Dr. Edward Hills, the Rev. George Perry, the Rev. Tom Skinner, Bill Pannell and others of similar spiritual caliber should be encouraged and helped to go abroad for a short significant ministry so as to relate more adequately to the American Negro churches the need for Negro missionaries.

Specific pastors' conferences should be held with missions as the focal point. Missionary conferences should be organized in Negro churches and Bible schools.

The embarrassing question

Even more basic is the embarrassing question, "Why is the church divided?" Does the entire structure of the evangelical church and mission "establishment" make Negro involvement in the areas of leadership almost impossible? Would a confession of bigotry on the part of church and mission leaders be helpful or even the starting point? If segregationist structure in evangelicalism were brought crashing to the ground in our churches would not black forget they are black and white forget they are white? Our Christian youth would then march together in obedience to the Great Commission.

Bill Thomas, an American Negro serving in the Congo with the British Baptist Missionary Society, says, "I don't believe that the major mission societies are going to be able to encourage many young Negroes to 'sign up' for overseas work until they have become part of the regular fellowship of the churches at home, for, after all, if you aren't happy about my worshipping in your church with you, you wouldn't be happy about my working with you on the mission field."

Christ's love is for every tribe and tongue and nation. Christ's command to preach the gospel was given to every child of God irrespective of color, skin, race, or socioeconomic groupings.

All God's children are to obey Christ's command...and *all God's Church* is to send God's children.

Connecting to Africa
and Other Nations

COMINAD and the Adopt-a-Village Initiative:

Mobilizing the African-American Church for Missions

and Demonstrating Reconciliation to the World

Brian Johnson & Jack Gaines, Sr.

Brian Johnson is the National Coordinator for COMINAD. He has served as Pastor, Bible college professor, Christian school teacher, and a foreign missionary. He has worked for Carver International missions, World Relief Cooperation, and the International African-American mission Mobilzation project. While in Africa he was the principal of the Monrovia Bible College, Field Supervisor of Carver Missions Liberia, Secretary General of the Association of Evangelicals, and the Country Director for World Relief. His work responsibilities were:, micro-enterprise development, war trauma counselor, ethnic reconciliation, and relief assistance. World Relief honored him with its Helping Hands award, 1997. Brian Johnson & family reside in Virginia Beach, VA. He continues to do ministry in Africa.

Jack Gaines, Sr., is the Assistant Pastor and Missions Director at Calvary Evangelical Baptist Church, Portsmouth, VA, and a member of COMINAD. He also serves as the Assistant Chaplain of the Southeastern Correctional Ministry. Currently enrolled at Angelos Bible College, he also attended Norfolk State University. He played 9 years of professional baseball with the Pittsburgh Pirates and Boston Red Sox. He helped spearhead the Reconciliation Conference held in Benin.

Perhaps one of the greatest failings of the African-American church is our lack of missionary initiative. This is due in large part to our history of suffering and injustice on this continent. Rejected by the rest of society, blacks found in our own churches acceptance and safety from the hostile environment that surrounded us. As a result, our outreach initiative was very narrow. We became, in effect, our own mission field.

But I believe God has a greater plan for African-American churches. If we black Christians can develop a perspective that places our suffering in the light of God's plan for history, I believe He will use our experience to demonstrate the power of reconciliation to the nations of the world. Armed with such a perspective and a biblical theology of missions, African-American churches can step onto the world stage and show the world that our history can be redeemed in such a way that God gets all the glory.

That's why in 1998 several other black ministers and I founded an organization to mobilize African-American ministries to help fulfill the Great Commission. The Cooperative Missions Network of the African Dispersion, or COMINAD, is a collective of church and parachurch organizations working together to increase the missionary vision among Christians who are descendants of enslaved Africans.

COMINAD's hundreds of ministry volunteers from all races maintain their own ministries but offer their resources and talents to help the African-American church reach its full missionary potential.

COMINAD's initiatives are helping black churches increase our missionary activity, as well as use the power of forgiveness to model biblical reconciliation. It's already begun. In fact, it began before COMINAD even was formed. Let me tell you what God has done so far and where we believe He is taking us.

The Benin Reconciliation Conference

In 1994, Romain Zannou, a pastor from Benin, West Africa, called my colleague, Jack Gaines. Romain was in the U.S. trying to tell African-American pastors about his desire to see their churches send and support workers to tell Africans about Jesus Christ. But Romain was confused and hurt at the cool reception he encountered. Jack met with him and explained that he might have experienced some of the anger and resentment that many African-Americans have towards African nations that participated in the slave trade and sent their ancestors to this country in bondage.

Romain listened to what Jack said and went home disappointed. Two years later, though, he called Jack again and asked if he could speak in some African-American churches so he could offer repentance for the activities of his forefathers. But before they could make it happen God put a twist in their plans.

In 1997, Jack and I were attending an evangelism conference in Johannesburg, South Africa, when we received an urgent message from Romain that he had arranged for us to meet with Benin president Matthieu Kerekou. President Kerekou was greatly distressed about his country's past involvement in the slave trade and he had a deep desire to see repentance and reconciliation take place. He told us how God spoke to him through the story of Joseph, the biblical character who was sold into slavery by his brothers, and how he had a vision to host a reconciliation conference in Benin by the year 2000.

In 1998 and 1999 President Kerekou visited the U.S. and spoke in several African-American churches, apologizing for his ancestors' practice of selling other Africans into slavery and presenting the challenge of holding a reconciliation conference in Benin. Through those talks we were able to establish a planning committee of several African-American, European, and Benin church leaders and government officials.

President Kerekou spared no expense on the conference, spending almost $1 million. Despite pressure from his closest advisers to include discussions about foreign aid and development, he kept the focus strictly on reconciliation. His greatest desire for the conference was to see reconciliation between the descendants of the perpetrators and the victims of the slave trade.

To that end, President Kerekou brought in 25 representatives from European nations that had participated in the slave trade; he invited all the tribal chiefs and kings in Benin whose ancestors had participated in the slave trade; he invited the presidents of all the nations of West Africa; and, he brought in 125 representatives of the African Dispersion whose ancestors were victims of the slave trade. U.S. Representatives Tony Hall and Frank Wolfe and U.S. Senator James Inhoff also attended.

It is difficult to describe the powerful impact of that conference. God moved in a tremendous way as the participants modeled reconciliation and experienced its true benefits. Representatives of the nations that participated in the slave trade took responsibility for the actions of their ancestors and asked forgiveness from those whose ancestors were victims of slavery. The victims' representatives then offered their forgiveness and a wave of tears and heart-wrenching sobs shook the participants as they were released from the deep wounds of the past. ["Noble Desire video available through WHRO Television Services. Call (757) 889-9412.]

From that conference has come a flow of activity advancing the cause of reconciliation. President Kerekou sent 19 representatives from Benin to the U.S. to discuss the effects of reconciliation with business leaders, government officials, and church leaders. In Richmond, VA, they addressed a meeting on diversity and race relations where representatives of the Ku Klux Klan and the Nation of Islam also aired their views. Many were impressed with the way that the Benin delegation professionally and respectfully responded to tough questions asked by the participants.

And, perhaps best of all, a new initiative was created that will allow African-American churches to participate in evangelizing the nations of West Africa.

The Voyage Back and the Adopt-A-Village Concept

With the backing of President Kerekou, COMINAD is putting together an event to help African-American churches reconnect to their roots and experience a release from the anger and bitterness that have bound them. The Voyage Back is a plan to charter a cruise ship to take as many black pastors as possible to Benin to pass back through "The Gates of No Return" through which many of their forefathers passed when they were sold into slavery. We are planning to make the trip in the near future.

President Kerekou has promised to rename the gates "The Gates of Return" and to have on hand representatives of hundreds of tribal villages to greet the pastors. The wonderful aspect of this part of the plan is that the African-American pastors will be able to choose a village for their church to "adopt" by supporting indigenous missionaries to work among the people. This will be a great opportunity for the pastors not only to reconnect with their roots but also to demonstrate forgiveness toward the descendants of those who helped enslave their ancestors. It will also help them begin fulfilling the Great Commission by giving them an opportunity to put their resources into an effort to preach the gospel to individual villages.

President Kerekou himself initiated the Adopt-A-Village program and he personally is supporting missionaries to at least one village. The missionaries are natives of Benin and build relationships by working and living among the people and being good neighbors. For instance, if a farmer gets sick, one of the missionaries will take care of his farm until he recovers. Or when a woman has a baby, one of the missionaries' wives will help take care of her house until she can return to work. When the village people see these expressions of love it arouses their curiosity and gives the missionaries an opportunity to tell them about the love of Jesus Christ. Many people have responded to the Gospel message through their witness.

The impact is phenomenal and the growth of the Gospel exponential. As a result of just one village being involved in the program, seven others asked to have missionaries come to their village. Now, as those villages are being blessed by the Gospel, 30 more villages have expressed an interest in the program. When The Voyage Back arrives in Benin I believe there will be hundreds of villages that will be ready for adoption.

Churches don't have to take part in The Voyage Back to participate in the Adopt-A-Village program. Through COMINAD they can make contact with and visit a village any time they are ready. Currently there are almost 100 missionaries waiting for an assignment.

Adoption involves several steps: making contact with the village, introducing yourself to its people, exchanging the names of your church members with those in the village, showing a videotape of the village to your church, and pledging to pray for the village. Later there will be opportunities to start development projects under the supervision of national missionaries and to see that the people are evangelized and discipled. The great part is that when churches begin to grow in the villages they soon begin sending out their own missionaries to reach other villages.

Demonstrating the Ministry of Reconciliation

The conference, The Voyage Back, and the Adopt-A-Village initiative are only preliminary plans for the many things God wants to do using the African-American church. I believe the Lord will use these as tools to let the world see what true reconciliation looks like and to reveal that our ability to reconcile with other people is directly related to our need to be reconciled to God.

Building relationships between villages in Africa and churches of the African Dispersion in the West is a tremendous way to demonstrate the reconciliation that God desires between all men and, indeed, between man and Himself. If we just can practice what He has done for us through Jesus Christ, then we can have peace and reconciliation between the tribes of all men.

The ultimate source of the problem, of course, is man's conflict with God. But Satan's deceptions make us believe that these problems are caused by race, economic status, tribal conflicts, or religious disagreements. But we, the Church, the Body of Christ, have the tremendous opportunity to be used by God to let the world see what true reconciliation is. When we demonstrate how Jesus Christ has reconciled us to God, we can demonstrate how His peace and power within us can allow us to be reconciled to those who abused us in the past and that we can be reconciled despite all the problems.

President Kerekou's initiative recognized a great truth: that slavery was not just a black-white issue. Historically and morally, Africans' participation in the slave trade was every bit as vile as Europeans. As an African, by asking forgiveness of African-Americans for his country's participation in the slave trade, President Kerekou removed color from the reconciliation equation. He focused on what the church should see as the true problem: sin.

Of course, if the world tries to use the same principles President Kerekou implemented, they will run into a stumbling block. Without God they will not be able to foster true repentance. As they meet that obstruction, the church can help them understand why it exists and that it can be overcome only by the power of God. The Body of Christ can share the truth that true reconciliation can come only from a converted, regenerated spirit, from the Holy Spirit living within us. This is a tremendous opportunity to model to the world what real reconciliation looks like.

The same principles that have worked between Africans and African-Americans can work in Bosnia and Serbia. They can work for Rwanda and Burundi. They can work in Northern Ireland. They can work anywhere in the world there is conflict. When I look around the world, the one thing I see more clearly than anything else is the need for reconciliation between peoples.

But the key is forgiveness and forgiveness must come first from the party who has been harmed. In the Bible, when Adam and Eve sinned against God, it was God who initiated forgiveness. And it was God who sent Jesus Christ to take man's sin away and clear the way for reconciliation with Him. Jesus, who was completely innocent, said of those who crucified Him, "Father, forgive them for they know not what they do." Forgiveness is the key and only victims really have control over granting forgiveness.

This is what I hope the African-American church will realize through The Voyage Back and the Adopt-A-Village program. Slavery and oppression were great evils, but even in the midst of abuse, God has had a providential purpose. He is still working it out. By understanding our power to forgive and reach out to those who have hurt us, the African-American church can play a great role in demonstrating the power of God's love and forgiveness. As we model reconciliation, we testify to the world what biblical reconciliation looks like. It's time that we begin!

How Black is the Harvester? A Profile of the African-American Missionary Force, The Extent of the Problem

Jim Sutherland

Jim Sutherland, has a Doctor of Philosophy, Intercultural Studies, from Trinity Evangelical Divinity School, IL; M.Div., New Brunswick Theological Seminary, NJ, and BA, English Major, Psychology minor, Hope College, MI. His career is complemented with his heart for African-Americans and missions. He has been Pastor at Bergen Memorial Church (biracial), AL and Chaplain at Southern Normal School, AL. He has been a missionary with Cedine Bible Mission and Inner City Ministries, TN. He has been an instructor at Southern Normal School, AL; Inner City Ministries, TN, Bible institutes in Uganda, and Covenant College. His major areas of study/teaching interest are: Intercultural Studies, African-American Missions, World Religions, Cults, Missions, Evangelism, Urban Ministry, and Personal Financial Management. He has held positions of Founder, Director, Reconciliation Ministries Network; U.S. Director, Africa Christian Training Institute; Seminar Field Representative & Referral Counselor, Christian Financial Concepts, GA; and Program Director, Urban Ministries Network, TN. He has also produced 50 10-minute radio programs on mission, WMBW, TN, and written papers on missions published by the SE Region of Evangelical Missiological Society, US Center for Word Mission, and Moody Bible Institute, as well as this doctoral dissertation found at http://www.RMNI.org.

How many African-American intercultural missionaries have you personally met? A great many blacks have never met one. Anthony Johnson, one of the few African-American missionaries, wrote that there is a "complete cultural disconnect" between African-Americans and global missions. The African-American church usually transposes "missions" to mean "missions to African-Americans"—often equated with what the uniformed and gloved ladies who usher in church do during the week—visiting the sick or delivering flowers or food baskets. While this ministry is certainly valid, how quickly would the world be evangelized through it?

Virtually anyone who knows the African-American church and believes in the validity of the Great Commission would admit that African-Americans are underrepresented among intercultural missionaries, although people differ as to how long the problem has existed. Joseph Washington, who is an African-American, wrote in *Black Religion*:

> It is this widespread absence of a sense of mission among [black] religious societies which provides such a sharp contrast between them and their fellow Protestants. The very heart of the Christian faith is missing in these communities, be they segregated independent or dependent religious societies. The obvious absence of mission among [black] religious organizations is a phenomenon which deserves more serious attention than it has received (Hughley, 1983, p. 34).

At minimum the problem has existed for more than 50 years. Just before World War II a survey found that 8,000 white missionaries were in Africa, but only 300 African-American missionaries (Roesler, 1953, p. 63), which is 3.7 percent of that African missionary population. One could reasonably argue that under-representation has existed since shortly after the Emancipation Proclamation in 1863 and the fuller emergence of the indigenous African-American church. In fact, the African-American intercultural missionary enterprise has existed since the late 1700s with George Liele (c.1782), considered by some to be America's first missionary (Trulson, 1977, p. 4). Scarce indeed are those who have addressed the problem in popular literature in the last 30 years, and scarcer are scholarly studies in the last 50 years.

Those black Christians called and obedient to the Great Commission are probably most sensitive to the problem. A few who have contributed to this writer's research have been most encouraging.

A female African-American missionary respondent to a questionnaire, who contributed 15 names and addresses of African-American missionaries, added this note:

> I have been aware of the tremendous shortage of African-American missionaries. I am very interested in the results of the research. Just recently, I have wondered if anyone has researched the contributions of African-American missionaries to fulfilling the Great Commission.

The African-American church has been termed a "sleeping giant," but the necessary environment and resources exist.

Estimates of the Current African-American Intercultural Population

African-American candidates do not join white or black evangelical missions in significant numbers (Hughley, 1983, pp. 42, 48; Pelt, 1989, p. 28). The major black denominations support exceedingly few missionaries (Hughley, 1983, p. 17). Hard data on current black missions involvement is elusive. Crawford Loritts, National Director of Urban Ministries for Campus Crusade for Christ, estimated that there were "less than 300 minority members involved in the major U.S. parachurch groups and mission agencies," as of 1987 (Sidey, 1987, p. 61).

My 16 months of research into why there are so few African-American missionaries uncovered at least 102 African-Americans who have served primarily those who are not African-American for at least one cumulative year.

As a proportion of total population, if there were as many as 300 African-American cross-cultural missionaries in 1996, that would be 0.0009% of the approximate 34,000,000 black population. Among whites, 33,000 white missionaries in 1992 would be would be 0.017% of the approximate 194,000,000 total whites (1996).

Earlier Estimates of African-American Intercultural Missionaries

In March 1996 there were an estimated 33.9 million African-Americans (civilian, non-institutional population), or about 12.8 percent of all Americans (Bennett, 1997). But African-Americans hardly approach 12 percent of the U.S. missionary force. Robert Gordon wrote in 1973.

My research shows that out of 30,000 U.S. missionaries, there are about 240 blacks serving in 30 foreign nations. This represents .8 of one percent of the total U.S. missionary force. These results, based on a random sample [emphases supplied] of known U.S. foreign missionary-sending agencies, also indicate that 137 of 450 Protestant sending bodies have at least one black on their staffs (Gordon, 1973, pp. 267-68)

Sylvia Jacobs estimated that between 1820 and 1980, 250,000 to 300,000 Americans served in Africa, the continent most likely to receive African-Americans, and that perhaps 600 of these were African-American (Murphy, Melton, and Ward, 1993, p. 22). This is .2 percent of that total force. Of the 600, black missions sent about half, about half were men, and about half went to Liberia (another 25 percent went to Ghana, Nigeria and Sierra Leone). Most of the 20 destination countries in sub-Saharan Africa were English-speaking (Murphy, Melton, and Ward, 1993, p. 22).

If these estimates are correct, there has never been a numerically strong African-American mission movement, even to Africa, where most mission effort was invested. The observation of a decline in the 1900s, even from previous numbers, draws some consensus. Robert Gordon wrote:

> Though it is not yet possible to graph accurately the black involvement in foreign missions, it appears that there was a significant decline shortly after the beginning of the 20th century (Gordon, 1973, p. 271).

Leslie Pelt, an African-American missionary to Nigeria, who completed a survey for this current research, wrote, "[I]n this century the vision seemed to die and the missionary force dwindled" (Pelt, 1989, p. 28).

Kenneth Scott Latourette concluded his chapter on "The Negroes" in the period of 1800-1914:

> Nor did the Negroes reach out much beyond their own country and race in an attempt to spread their faith. In spite of the fact that by 1914 the proportion of Negroes possessing a church affiliation was about as high as that among the whites, practically the only organized efforts which the Negro churches made to propagate their religion beyond the members of their own race in the United States were missions to coloured peoples in the West Indies, Guiana, and Africa. Even these enterprises were small. . . . As yet this Negro Christianity was not looking much beyond its own borders. . . . Even though its foreign missions were not so extensive as those of the white churches, it initiated and maintained them, and by the gifts of a constituency from the lower income levels of the nation. This was more than was done by the Indians and Negroes of Latin America (Latourette, 1970, p. 364).

The significant contributions of African-American missionaries seem to be located more with outstanding individuals than with large missionary populations or organizations, as various historical surveys illustrate (Seraile, 1972; Hughley, 1983; Martin, 1982, pp. 63-76).

Historical Summary

Only God can assess the spiritual impact of African-American missionaries to Africa—we can only lament their scarcity, sometimes for reasons outside their control. Jacobs, a fine historian of African-American missions, summarized:

> Because of the small number of American missionaries in Africa before 1945, the impact of black American missionaries was severely limited. Afro-American missionaries were an insignificant percentage of the total American missionaries stationed in Africa before 1960, and they were restricted to certain areas of the continent (Jacobs, 1982, p. 225).

Donald F. Roth concluded,

> As noted earlier, in terms of the number of missionary years in Africa, the [African-American missionary] movement barely existed. Yet this area of black activity was a significant one (Roth, 1982, p. 36)

But many strong reasons for hope now exist.

What Is the Portrait of an African-American Missionary?

Black missionaries are almost alien to their culture. What sets them apart? They are well-educated, counter-cultural, risk takers—akin to the Army Rangers. They are secure in their family of origin. Their self-reported grade point average was 3.19 on a 4.0 scale. Forty-six percent are college-educated and 42 percent have some graduate schooling. Seventy-eight percent of them perceive that risks from missionary service (financial, physical, etc.) deterred African-Americans in general, but 64 percent of them had perceived little risk before their missionary service. The risks seen in retrospect (2.73 of 5.0—highest possible) actually were greater than in prospect (2.43 of 5.0).

As counterculturals, 32 percent of respondents (94 persons) were criticized by African-Americans for serving those who were not African-American. In contrast, white missionaries serving cross-culturally have celebrity status in the church, compared with those serving at home. Criticizing a foreign missionary for being a foreign missionary is unthinkable among white Christians.

With Whom Do African-American Missionaries Serve?

Seventy-two percent of the African-American missionaries (71 persons) either had served, or were serving, in predominately white mission organizations. The three largest missionary-sending groups represented are Campus Crusade for Christ, Carver Foreign Mission (a black mission), and the Southern Baptist Convention, in this order. The three largest denominational affiliations are Baptist [various] (53 percent), independents (20 percent) and the Assemblies of God (7 percent).

What Motivated Them?

If it takes the equivalent of a dynamite blast to free African-Americans for crosscultural ministry, what ignited the fuse? Someone significant in their lives motivated 70 percent of the 42 persons who answered. Just under half the time, this person was a missionary who had extraordinary recruiting influence. However, only a total of six persons of the total 102 surveyed were motivated by their pastor. Considering the black pastor's immense influence over the flock, the best conclusion is that they are a disincentive to global missions, generally.

Ironically, 60 percent of respondents said that they were called to missions while their pastors each week preached expository sermons (i.e., sermons which deeply analyze and apply a specific biblical text). The power of God's Word is evident, despite the lack of pastoral encouragement. Only five percent were called through the influence of a church member or a local church. Considering how pervasive is the influence of the African-American church in the life of a member, the African-American church appears to be a disincentive generally. No doubt a lack of missions exposure and education have a role, but why is there a lack of exposure and education?

Short-term mission trips motivated most missionaries, after that, a significant person. Fifty-six percent of the 39 persons answering caught the vision through seeing the mission field, the prime destination being Africa, followed by Asia. Mission trips or private visits are the most effective recruitment strategy, apart from being discipled by an important person.

Twenty-four missionaries were motivated simply by God's call, illustrating the importance of asking the Lord of the Harvest to recruit workers (Luke 10:2). The entire group of missionaries surveyed is highly orthodox. One hundred percent believe that Jesus Christ is the only way to salvation. This conviction is essential to a biblically evangelistic ministry. Given the exceptionally few African-American workers, both in the past and today, it appears that: God either is calling incredibly few African-Americans—[which is] doubtful; many are disobedient to that call; or the obstacles overwhelm the hearts of those called, which is tragic.

What is the Preferred Destination of African-American Missionaries?

Africa was the primary destination. Africa pulls upon [the heart of] her [ethnic] sons and daughters. If African-Americans will go anywhere—agencies take note—it will be to their ancestral home. Studies on the perception of risk show that African-Americans' perception of some environmental and health risks are greater than for whites and Hispanics. The need for American slaves, and their ancestors, simply to survive, explains this. So when African-Americans prefer to serve in more-Westernized countries, as 57 percent of respondents did (compared with 15 percent who did not), this resonates. But the seeming inexorable drawing power of serving their own people [U.S.] exerted by their church and culture, but also influenced by age and other factors, resulted in only 38 percent of even those with an intercultural background still working primarily with non-African-Americans at the time of the survey (all 102 responded to this question—the older the missionary, the greater the likelihood of working among African-Americans).

Conclusion: Reasons for Hope

Despite the many historical, cultural, and spiritual challenges, the African-American church has never been closer to rousing herself to the Great Commission. In fact, at least 12 factors combine to give great, but sober, optimism: (1) Africa and other nations are wide open to African-American missionaries. (2) Civil rights legislation is in place in America. (3) White mission agencies and schools welcome African-American candidates. (4) Evangelical Christian Bible institutes and colleges not only welcome minorities, but some provide special funding for minority attendance. Thus, proper preparation for the field is far more available today. (5) New African-American nondenominational mission agencies have arisen. (6) Racism is newly and increasingly unpopular among white Christians, as illustrated by the pledge of the Promise Keeper movement. (7) The necessity of the African-American church serving interculturally has a higher profile through indigenous efforts such as The Destiny Movement (especially through 1992) and COMINAD (The Cooperative Mission Network of the African Dispersion). (8) Independent and other churches are committing to a foreign missions program. The writer knows of at least four conservative black churches in Chattanooga, TN, which have decided within the past three years to give 10 percent of their total income to missions outside their church. (9) Black income has risen in the past 20 years and black church income is fully sufficient to fund missions. (10) Black clergy also have access to the aforementioned schools, which hopefully impacts their pulpit teaching and preaching ministry, including evangelical missions theology. (11) The world is getting over, in Crawford Loritts' words, "white idolization," and other ethnic groups are both accepted and are picking up the mission torch. (12) Opportunities for short-term mission exposure abound—a very potent recruitment tool.

Study Questions

1. Do you agree that the African-American church is a disincentive to global missions? Why or why not?

2. What factors have contributed to the great underrepresentation of African-Americans in cross-cultural ministry, in your opinion?

3. On the basis of the African-American missionary profile provided [in this study], what recruitment strategies would you advocate?

Reference List

Bennett, Claudette. 1997. "The Black population in the United States: March 1996 (Update)." In *Current Population Reports: Population Characteristics*. (June 1997). U.S. Department of Commerce, Bureau of the Census. Accessed 18 October 1997. Available from   HYPERLINK http://www.census.gov/prod/2/pop/p20/p20-498.pdf;   http://www.census.gov/prod/2/pop/p20-498.pdf; Internet.

Gordon, Robert. 1973. "Black Man's Burden," *Evangelical Missions Quarterly* 9, 1973. no. 5: pp. 267-76.

Hughley, Clyde E. 1983. *An analysis of Black American involvement in world missions*. Th.M. thesis, Dallas Theological Seminary, TX.

Jacobs, Sylvia M., ed. 1982. "Black Americans and the missionary movement in Africa." Contributions in *Afro-American and African Studies.* No. 66. Westport, CT: Greenwood Press.

Janssen, Al., ed. 1994. *Seven promises of a Promise Keeper.* Colorado Springs, CO: Focus on the Family Publishing.

Latourette, Kenneth Scott. [1941, 1969] 1970. "The United States of America: The Negroes." Chapter 9 of *The Great Century in Europe and the United States of America: A.D. 1800-A.D. 1914.* vol. 4. In *A History of the Expansion of Christianity*. Grand Rapids, MI: Zondervan Publishing House. Contemporary Evangelical Perspectives Series: pp. 325-66.

Martin, Sandy Dwayne. 1982. "Black Baptists, Foreign Missions, and African Colonization, 1814-1882." In *Black Americans and the Missionary Movement in Africa*. ed. Sylvia M. Jacobs. Contributions in *Afro-American and African Studies*. no. 66. Westport, CT.: Greenwood Press. pp. 63-76.

Murphy, Larry G. 1993. "Religion in the African American community." In *Encyclopedia of African American Religions.* ed. Larry G. Murphy, J. Gordon Melton, and Gary L. Ward, xxxi-xxxv. NY: Garland Publishing, Inc.

Pelt, Leslie. 1989. "Wanted: Black Missionaries, But How?", *Evangelical Missions Quarterly* 25. no. 4: pp. 28-37.

Roesler, Calvin Lewis. 1953. *The American Negro as a Foreign Missionary*. M.A. thesis, Columbia Bible College, Columbia, SC.

Roth, Donald F. 1982. "The Black Man's Burden: The Racial Background of Afro-American Missionaries and Africa." In *Black Americans and the Missionary Movement in Africa*. ed. Sylvia M. Jacobs. Westport, CT: Greenwood Press. pp. 31-38.

Seraile, William. 1972. "Black American Missionaries in Africa: 1821-1925." *The Social Studies 63*. no. 5: pp. 198-202.

Sidey, Ken. 1987. "Missing: Minorities in Ministry." *Moody Monthly*. (July/August). pp. 60-63.

Sutherland, James W. 1998. *African American Underrepresention In Intercultural Missions: Perceptions Of Black Missionaries And The Theory Of Survival/Security*. Ph.D. dissertation., Trinity Evangelical Divinity School, Deerfield, IL.

Trulson, Reid. 1977. "The Black Missionaries." *HIS Magazine 37*. no. 9: pp. 1, 4-6.

Author's Notes

The principal ones are those of Wilbur Harr in 1945, Bodine Russell in 1945, Calvin Roesler in 1953, Robert Gordon in 1973, Sylvia M. Jacobs in 1982, and Clyde Hughley, 1983.

African American Underrepresention In Intercultural Missions: Perceptions Of Black Missionaries And The Theory Of Survival/Security, Ph.D. dissertation, Trinity Evangelical Divinity School, Deerfield, IL, 1998. Available online at www.reconciliationnetwork.org/dissertation/default.htm; Internet.

Based upon the 13.6 percent ratio of surveys returned from those who were either not African-American, or who had not served at least one year in Intercultural service (16), an estimated additional 140 persons for whom a mailing address could be determined (and to all but two of whom a survey was sent) are both African-American and Intercultural. Only 38 (38 percent) of the 101 qualifying to answer this question and, presumably, of the estimated 140, (or 53) were currently serving primarily African-Americans.

If you know of African-Americans currently serving crossculturally, please send that information to:

HYPERLINK http://www.ReconciliationNetwork.org/research.htm or email jim@RMNI.org. This help would provide better information as to the true extent of current African-American outreach, and possibly help those interested in supporting an African-American missionary working in a particular region or among a specific people group.

This information comes from 102 questionnaire returns (primarily in 1997) from African-Americans who had served a minimum of one year in intercultural ministry. Not all respondents answered all questions. The respondents were equally divided between men and women. Their average length of service was eight years.

Their average Likert Scale response was 3.77 out of 5.0 (the most secure).

See dissertation, ch. 2, Personal Efficacy/Locus of Control

"A Promise Keeper is committed to reaching beyond any racial and denominational barriers to demonstrate the power of biblical unity." The Seven Promises of a Promise Keeper.

A History of Christianity in Africa

Mark R. Shaw

The growth of the church in Africa is one of the most surprising facts of 20th century church history. From an estimated 4 million professing Christians in 1900 African Christianity had grown to nearly 300 million adherents by 1995. [In] the year 2000 one out of every five believers in the world lives in Africa, according to recent [estimates]. What accounts for such growth? The common notion that 19th century missionary efforts explain African Christianity's recent explosion is an oversimplification. The true story behind these statistics reaches back to the very earliest centuries of Christian history.

Beginnings

The roots of African Christianity are to be found in the four regional churches of Africa in the Roman era--Egypt, North Africa, Nubia, and Ethiopia. The origins of Christianity in Egypt are obscure. Eusebius records the tradition that St. Mark brought the faith to Egypt. No reliable historical evidence supports this tradition however. The first documentary evidence of the existence of an Egyptian church dates from A.D.189 with Bishop Demetrius (d. 231), overseer of a number of churches and patron of a thriving theological school associated with the names of Clement (d. 215) and Origen (d. 254). By the time of Demetrius Egyptian Christianity was undergoing radical Hellenization as orthodox teachers like Origen and heretical Gnostic teachers like Basilides demonstrated. Persecution in the third century caused the faith to spread down the Nile into rural Egypt among the Coptic-speaking population where it found a new champion in Antony, the father of monasticism. After a period of syncretism in the fourth century, symbolized by the Arian controversy that opposed the heretical Arius and the orthodox Bishop Athanasius, a mature Coptic church emerged in the fifth century under the leadership of independently minded monastic leaders such as Shenoute (d. c. 466). The signs of an indigenous Christianity rooted in the language and life of the people were everywhere evident. Coptic-speaking clergy, Coptic translations of the Scriptures and Coptic liturgies abounded. Rejecting Chalcedon's two-nature Christology, Coptic Christianity grew increasingly hostile to the colonial intrusions of the Byzantine Empire, which failed in its attempt to impose Chalcedonian ortho-

Mark R. Shaw is a lecturer at Nairobi Evangelical School of Theology. He is editor of the *Africa Journal of Evangelical Theology* and has contributed articles on African church history to the second edition of the *New Twentieth-Century Encyclopedia of Religious Knowledge*. He holds a Th.D. degree from Westminster Theological Seminary.

Taken from *Evangelical Dictionary of World Missions*, edited by Scott Moreau, Baker Book House, 2000. Used by permission.

doxy. Coptic Christians were not entirely op-posed to the Arab invasion of 642 and the promise of increased religious freedom.

North Africa

While Egyptian Christianity was a testi-mony to the importance of a contextualized Christianity, North Africa was a sober re-minder of the fragility of a faith insufficiently rooted in the life of the people. The Roman segment of North Africa embraced the Gos-pel with vigor but the Punic and Berber peoples were never adequately penetrated. The brilliance of North African Christianity cannot be doubted. The genius of Tertullian (d. 225), Cyprian (d. 258) and Augustine (d. 430) is well known. Yet even their brilliance could not prevent the decline of a church troubled by separatism (Donatism) and per-secution (under the Arian Vandals in the fifth century). Byzantium briefly regained control in the sixth century, only to yield in the sev-enth and eighth centuries to the armies of Al-lah. Despite the failure of North African Christianity to contextualize the faith, Augustine's observation that the story of the African church is the story of the clash of two kingdoms, the City of God and the City of Man representing God's gracious love and man's selfish love respectively, would con-tinue to illuminate African Church history.

Ethiopia

Solid evidence for the conversion of Ethio-pia appears in 350. Before that date King Ezana, ruling from his capital city of Axum, ascribed his early victories to Astar and other gods of the Axumite pantheon. But by 350 Ezana credited his achievements to the "Lord of All, Jesus Christ who has saved me." Cru-cial to this change was the ministry of Bishop Frumentius (Abuna Salama, "Our Father of Salvation"), who had been commissioned by Athanasius of Alexandria as a missionary to Ethiopia. The precedent set by Athanasius became entrenched and Ethiopian Orthodox Church continued to receive its Abun (Bishop) by appointment of the Egyptian Coptic patriarch. By Ezana's death in 400 Christianity was firmly rooted at court but had made little impact on the countryside.

That changed in the sixth century with the coming of a new missionary force from Syria. The *tesseatou Kidoussan* ("nine saints") estab-lished monasteries in the rural areas and en-gaged in widespread evangelism. Linked with the Egyptian Coptic Christianity and armed with the Scriptures in the vernacular the Christians of Ethiopia entered the Middle Ages where they "slept near a thousand years, forgetful of the world, by whom they were forgotten" (Edward Gibbon).

Nubia

Like Ethiopia, Nubia (now modern Sudan) was never a part of the Roman Empire. The Christianity that infiltrated Nubia began a re-ligious revolution in Nubia that transformed both people and prince by the sixth century. Archaeological evidence that came to light only in the 1960s has revealed the vigor of Nubian Christianity. The great churches un-covered in the more than 40 digs conducted in that decade bear witness to the depth and breadth of the new faith throughout Nobatia, Makurra, and Alwa, the three constituent kingdoms of Nubia. Two sixth century mis-sionaries from Byzantium, Julian and Longinus, are credited with officially intro-ducing the Christian faith, in its monophysite form, to this kingdom along the Blue Nile.

The African Middle Ages

These four original sources of African Christianity faced their greatest challenge during the African Middle Ages. The first challenge, which inaugurated the African Middle Ages, came from a new religion—Is-lam. The second challenge, which brought the African Middle Ages to an end, came from the kingdoms of European Christendom represented by the Portuguese and the Dutch.

North African and Nubian col-lapse

The rise and spread of Islam across Africa's northern shore by soldier and sultan in the seventh and eighth centuries was fol-lowed in the 10th and 11th centuries by a southward expansion led by the merchant and the missionary. North Africa was most dramatically affected by this expansion of Islam. The Donatist Berbers of North Africa eventually converted to Islam even as the Roman segment evacuated to other parts of the empire. The decline of North African Christianity was nearly total by the 16th century. Attempts by the Fourth Crusade (1215) to liberate North Africa politically and Franciscan attempts to revive it spiritually ended in failure. A faith only lightly rooted in the life of the people faded into memory. Nubia proved more resistant.

During the eighth through 10th centuries, while Islam continued to expand in Africa, Nubian Christianity reached its height. So confidant was Nubia during these centuries that it even invaded Muslim-controlled Egypt in 962 and won concessions from the Caliph of Bagdad. But in 1272 Muslim Turks sent by the legendary Saladin overthrew northern Nubia. In 1504 the southernmost kingdom, Alwa, was conquered by a tribe from the south recently converted to Islam. The last word from Nubian Christianity occurs in 1524 when they wrote to the Coptic patriarch of Egypt for help to meet their critical shortage of clergy. The lack of indigenous church leaders combined with the failure to evangelize the tribes to the south conspired to undermine Nubian Christianity.

Egyptian and Ethiopian Survival

In Egypt, Christianity survived the onslaught of Islam but not without losses. Caliph Umar had forbidden new churches or monasteries but under the Umayyids (661-750) this law was not enforced. Other forms of pressure, however, were applied. In 744 the Muslim governor of Egypt offered tax exemption for Christians who converted to Islam. Twenty four thousand responded. Throughout the African Middle Ages the Coptic church suffered from a lack of trained leadership, discriminatory laws and a stagnant ritualism in worship. Nonetheless, it survived. By 1600, Egypt was a "country of dual religious cultures."

Ethiopian Christianity also followed the path of survival. After a crisis in the 10th century when the pagan Agau nearly toppled the king, Ethiopian clergy began to work for reform and revival of the national faith. One movement of renewal brought a new dynasty to the imperial throne of Ethiopia. The Zagwe dynasty was installed in the 13th century. Its most popular leader, Lalibela, strengthened Ethiopia's religious patriotism by building a New Jerusalem in the Ethiopian highlands and strengthening the belief that Ethiopians were the new Israel through whom God would bring light to the nations. In the 13th century Yekunno-Amlak (d. 1285) restored the Solomonic line. The appearance of the *Kebra-Nagast* ("Glory of kings") renewed Ethiopia's messianic nationalism (and the claims of the new Solomonic dynasty) by chronicling the traditions about Solomon and Menelik and about the transfer of the Ark of the Covenant from Jerusalem to Axum. Under the missionary monk, Tekla-Haymanot (d. 1312), Ethiopian Christianity experienced revival. New missionary efforts among the Shoa of the south met with success. Emperor Zara-Yaqob (d. 1468) brought Ethiopia to new heights of glory but by 1529 the kingdom was in decline. Ahmad Gragn, a crafty Muslim leader, successfully overthrew the Christian kingdom of Ethiopia but his reign was short-lived. Within a few years Christian Ethiopia was restored, this time with the help of a new player on the African stage—the Portuguese.

The Portuguese

Inspired by their visionary leader, Prince Henry "the Navigator", the Portuguese embarked on two and a half centuries of aggressive expansion between 1450 and 1700. This expansion led to the European discovery of Africa and the establishment of a trading empire that spread from Lisbon to India. Christian communities were established in West Africa (especially Ghana and Benin), Angola, Mozambique, and Mombasa but Portuguese missions enjoyed its greatest success in the ancient kingdom of Congo where the king, Afonso I (d. 1540), promoted the new faith aggressively. Yet the missionary efforts of the Catholic missionaries were eventually undermined by the commercial interest of Portuguese merchants, who quickly saw potential for a profit in the slave trade. Hatred of the Portuguese trader soon was directed at the Portuguese priest. The missionary could do little, however, to stop the traffic in human lives. Slavery had been authorized by both Pope and king. By the time of David Livingstone's travels in the mid-19th century few vestiges of Portuguese Christianity could be found.

Dutch Expansion

In 1652, 100 representatives of the Dutch East India Company landed on Africa's southernmost tip and proceeded to establish a way station for company ships traveling from Amsterdam to Batavia in the Pacific. From this modest beginning came Cape Town and the beginnings of the nation of South Africa. The first church established was that of the Dutch Reformed Church but by 1800 Lutherans and Moravians had begun their work [as well]. The churches of the settlers soon came into conflict with a missionary Christianity spawned by the wave of "Great Awakenings" that were sweeping North America, England, and Europe in the 18th century. An early representative of this new evangelical movement was the Moravian George Schmidt, who began work among the Khoisan of the Cape in 1738. He soon came into conflict with the established church and was stopped from further mission work in 1748.

African Christianity in the 19th and early 20th Centuries: the Antislavery Crusade

While Schmidt was struggling with the stubbornness of his Dutch hosts, English evangelicals began to struggle with the issue of slavery. John Wesley (d. 1791) condemned slavery in a 1774 pamphlet and a number of his followers took up the cause. Early opposition to slavery came from Granville Sharp, Thomas Clarkson, and William Wilberforce (d. 1833). Wilberforce in particular, through the support of his upper-class evangelical friends (popularly known as the "Clapham Sect"), led the fight against both the slave trade and the institution of slavery itself. Though a number of important court victories had increased the number of freed slaves in London (particularly following the Somerset case of 1771) there was still the need for legislative reform. Slavery was such a crucial part of the British economy that ef-

forts by Wilberforce and others in the 1790s were thwarted. The first breakthrough came in 1807 with the passage of a bill prohibiting the slave trade. Ownership of slaves, however, was still permitted. By 1833 legislation was passed abolishing slavery everywhere in the British Empire.

British evangelicals have opposed slavery both on humanitarian grounds as well as missiological ones. They realized that their desire to engage in missions in Africa (witnessed to by the formation of a number of new agencies in the 1790s such as the Baptist Missionary society in 1792, the London Missionary Society in 1795, and the Church Missionary Society in 1799) would be seriously thwarted by the existence of slavery. The missionaries that English societies sent out to Africa were, therefore, equipped with the dual message of "Christianity and commerce." Western-style commerce would make slavery economically unnecessary, thus permitting the message of Christianity to make its way deep into the lives of the hearers. The effectiveness of this dual message would first be tested in West Africa.

The Growth of Christianity in Western Africa

In 1787, 411 freed blacks left London to found a new colony in Africa. Through the assistance of Claphamites Granville Sharp and Zachary Macaulay, Sierra Leone became a haven for freed slaves from all over the British Empire. It also became an outpost for the spread of the Gospel throughout West Africa. The first arrivals called their settlement Freetown. In 1792, their efforts were aided by the arrival of 200 former slaves from Canada. Like the Puritans who settled New England, these early settlers burned with religious zeal. Freetown became a Christian commonwealth, which inspired similar Christian communities further down the coast in the Nigerian towns of Abeokuta and Badagry. "Recaptives" (slaves liberated by the British Navy) added to the population of Freetown. Many converted to the Christian faith and found an opportunity for training at Freetown's Fourah Bay College, established in 1827.

One of the most outstanding graduates of the college was a young recaptive named Samuel Ajayi Crowther (d. 1891). Crowther was eventually ordained in London in 1843. In 1864 he became Africa's first Anglican bishop. The Church Missionary Society (CMS) recognized in Crowther the leader they needed to further the spread of Christian in West Africa. Under the visionary leadership of its secretary, Henry Venn, they adopted an aggressive program of africanization, which called for the immediate building of self-supporting, self-propagating, and self-governing native churches. Crowther was asked to implement this strategy in the Nigerian interior. Through the failure of some members of his team and through the hostility of white missionaries opposed to Venn's policies, Crowther was forced to resign. Leadership of the CMS work in West Africa fell into white hands. This led to a number of African Independent Churches that formed in protest. Anglican Nigerians like James "Holy" Johnson found themselves caught in the middle, neither fully at home in the Anglican church nor comfortable in the ranks of the separatists.

Despite these disappointments in Nigeria, Christianity did take root throughout West and Central Africa. The work of Jehudi Ashman, Lott Carey, E.W. Blyden, and Alexander Crummell in Liberia; Thomas Birch Freeman; Johann Zimmerman, and J.G. Christaller in Ghana; Alfred Slaker, George Nkwe, and Thomas Johnson in Cameroon; and the outstanding Roman Catholic missionary efforts of the Holy Ghost Fathers (founded by Francis Liebermann in 1841) in Gabon and Senegal should be noted. Zaire [now the Congo] was the main arena for Catholic missions that established a large and effective presence, as did various Baptist bodies.

Southern Africa

While West Africa was evangelized largely by Africans [abroad] returning to their motherland, South Africa from the very earliest days of Christianity was dominated by the white expatriate. Despite the common denominator of white domination, there was little unity in South African Christianity.

Three distinct and mutually hostile expressions of Christianity emerged in 19th century South Africa.

The first expression was that of Afrikaner Christianity and the Dutch Reformed Church (DRC). After England gained control of South Africa in 1815, conflicts between Boer farmers and English administrators multiplied, which led to mass migrations of Afrikaner families to northeastern regions of South Africa. One small party of "voortrekkers" encountered an army of Zulu warriors. Their surprising victory at the battle of Blood River in 1838, coupled with the tradition that the trekkers had made a special covenant with God prior to the battle, fueled the belief that Afrikaner Christians were an elect nation endowed by God with both a right to rule the land and a right to resist the non-elect. Under the leadership of men like S.J. du Toit (d. 1911) this tradition became a political and cultural force that found expression in both the Boer War of 1899-1902 and in the formation of the Afrikaner Nationalist Party, which came to power after World War II.

A second expression of South African church life in the 19th century was a "missionary Christianity," which often came into conflict with the faith of the Afrikaner. Though the DRC had a missionary wing that worked among the colored population of the Cape (and eventually other African tribes) other mission agencies made a more significant impact. The missionaries of the London Missionary Society, like J. van der Kemp (d. 1811), Robert Moffat (d. 1883), David Livingstone (d. 1873), each of whom openly criticized the Boer community, and John Philip (d. 1851), who worked for native rights, seemed adept at alienating the settler churches. Livingstone's fame exceeded that of all other 19th century missionaries in South Africa as well as in the continent as a whole, despite his failure as an evangelist (he made only one convert who eventually fell away) and church planter. His achievements as an explorer, an antislavery crusader, and missions promoter more than made up for his shortcomings.

The fastest-growing churches in 19th century South Africa belonged to the Methodists. Particularly effective among the agents of Methodism was William Shaw (b. 1798). Francois Coillard of Missionaries from the Paris Mission Society worked with success among King Moshoeshoe and his Basotho kingdom as well as among the Barotse of Zambia.

Though the missionary Christianity tended to emphasize an inward piety and a broadly evangelical theology that stood in contrast with the more reformed Afrikaners by the late 19th century, attempts were made to bridge the gap. Most successful was Andrew Murray, Jr., (d. 1917), moderator of the Dutch Reformed Church and a champion of both evangelical piety and missions. His emphasis on "absolute surrender" and the formation of new agencies such as the South Africa General Mission (eventually the African Evangelical Fellowship) acted as a corrective to the more culturally oriented Afrikaner Christianity. This missionary Christianity made major inroads into the Xhosa community, producing outstanding believers such as the hymn writer Ntsikana and the African Presbyterian leader Tiyo Soga (d. 1872). Such African leaders encouraged the missionary-dominated churches to engage in programs of training. Lovedale College (1841) was one such training school, as was Fort Hare University, both associated with Presbyterian missionary James Stewart.

A third expression of South African Christian was that of the "social gospel." Championed by men like the Anglican Bishop John Colenso (d. 1893) and John Jabavu (d. 1921), the emphasis of this form of Christianity was upon economic and political justice. Colenso combined liberal views of the Bible with egalitarian views about the Zulu and their rights. He also opposed the Afrikaner and English messianic nationalism, which he saw at the root of injustice in South Africa. Colenso's clash with Bishop Robert Gray of Cape Town ended with the formation of an independent Anglican communion in South Africa, where Colenso's views could be promulgated. Like Colenso, John Jabavu regarded politics as an appropriate arena for Christian involvement. A tireless campaigner for African rights he founded his own independent newspaper, *Imvo Zabantsundu* ("Views of the Bantu People"). This third expression of Christianity would become a major force in the years following South Africa's Sharpville massacre of 1960.

Despite the fragmented witness to the kingdom of God provided by South African Christianity, this region entered the 20th century as the bastion of Protestantism and one of the most Christianized regions in all of Africa. Yet white domination of the churches would eventually spawn a vigorous movement of "Ethiopianism," separatist churches that demanded respect from the Westerner and a greater share of church leadership.

Eastern Africa

The 19th century witnessed the reintroduction of Christianity into the former Nubia (Sudan) and in Mombasa (Kenya) where Augustinian friars had labored in the 16th century. Ethiopian Christianity was also revitalized during the century. Additionally the lands of Tanzania and Uganda saw the initial introduction of this ancient African faith among their own people.

Ethiopia and Sudan

In 1830 the Church Missionary Society arrived in Ethiopia. Originally working within the Coptic Church, Protestant missionaries such as J. Ludwig Krapf (d. 1887), Samuel Gobat, and Christian Kugler clashed with church authorities over the veneration of Mary. When theological differences combined with fear that the missionaries might be agents of British colonialism the CMS was expelled in 1843. The Catholic Justin de Jacobis (d. 1860) exercised a remarkable ministry in Ethiopia. His efforts to bring reunion between Roman Catholicism and the Ethiopian Orthodox Church were eventually brought to ruin by Abuna Salama (d. 1867). When the Ethiopian army under Emperor Menelik II (d. 1913) defeated both a resurgent Islam at his borders, as well as an invading Italian force at Adowa in 1896, Ethiopian Christianity experienced a new surge of life and entered the 20th century carefully guarding its dearly won political and religious independence. In Sudan, Catholic work under the leadership of Daniel Comboni and his Verona Fathers was swept away by the Islamic Mahdist movement.

Kenya

J. Ludwig Krapf began work in Kenya in 1844 after his expulsion from Ethiopia. Together with his colleague Johann Rebmann, Krapf envisioned a chain of mission stations across the continent, linking up with Freetown in [Sierra Leone,] West Africa, in order to penetrate the great inland areas with the Gospel. His vision would guide numerous mission agencies for the next century. Though he attempted to establish the eastern link of this chain at Rabai Mpyia it was the later formation of Freetown in 1874 as a refuge for runaway slaves that gave Christianity its firmest foothold in British East Africa. Outstanding Christian leaders came from the community at Freetown such as Ismael Semler, George David, John Mgomba, William Jones, and David Koi, Kenya's first Protestant martyr.

These missionary efforts on the coast were soon augmented by a new thrust inland. The Presbyterian missionary Dr. James Stewart of Lovedale College in South Africa was recruited by Livingstone to establish an industrial mission in the Kenyan interior in 1891. The CMS began work among the Kikiyu of Kenya's central highlands in 1901. Peter Cameron Scott and his newly founded Africa Inland Mission began churches among the Kamba people in 1895. The Holy Ghost Fathers began a work in Nairobi in 1899.

Tanzania

Catholic missionary efforts centered on the formation of a "Christian village" at Bagamoyo (1868) where 300 freed slaves found a place of refuge. Protestant work was conducted by the Universities Mission to Central Africa (UMCA) who were vigorous in their opposition to the Arab slave trade that was decimating the inland tribes of Africa's Great Lake region, where the London Missions Society and CMS had established a presence. Through the intervention of Germany the Arab slave trade was broken and a number of German mission agencies introduced Lutheranism.

Uganda

More dramatic than in any other part of East Africa was the response to the Gospel in Uganda. Christianity was introduced by the CMS in 1877 and flourished under the zealous leadership of Alexander Mackay (d. 1890). White [Catholic] Fathers introduced Catholicism in 1879. Despite the indifference of King Mutesa I and the violent hostility of his son Mwanga, Protestant and Catholic Christianity eventually produced a religious revolution in Uganda that spilled beyond the borders of the kingdom of Buganda into the smaller kingdoms that make up the modern-day nation of Uganda.

The Missionary Factor

The colonial era (1885-1960) brought sweeping changes to African Christianity. The most notable change was the proliferation of missionaries and agencies from the West and the corresponding growth of African Christianity. In 1900 there were an estimated 4 million Christians spread throughout the continent, compared with 60 million Muslims. By 1914 the number of professing Christians stood at 7 million. By 1930 there were an estimated 16 million Christians. By the autumn of colonialism in 1950 the number of African Christians had reached 34 million.

The missionaries of the colonial era were, on the whole, a remarkable lot. Like Roland Bingham of the Sudan Interior Mission, they were a tough-minded breed who often buried their colleagues and kept going. Like George Grenfell of the Baptist Mission Society of Congo, they were tireless explorers and enemies of the slave trade. Like Dr. Albert Schweitzer of Gabon, they were often humanitarians who sought to deliver the African from sickness. Like Mary Slessor of the Calabar mission, many were single women who gave their entire lives to the work. Like P.A. Bennett, acting secretary of the CMS in Nigeria, some were incorrigible racists, but like Archdeacon Dennis, also of the CMS in Nigeria, they more often opposed racism with equal vigor. Like Father Shanahan of Nigeria, they aggressively founded schools. Most important, like Carl Christian Reindorf of Ghana, they mastered the vernacular languages of the people and like George Pilkington of Uganda they translated the Scriptures and trained native evangelists.

This last factor, vernacular translations and the training of national evangelists accounts for the remarkable church growth that took place during the colonial decades. As Roland Oliver has observed "The main lesson of African ecclesiastical history is that the core message tended to run far ahead of this expatriate preachers. Most African societies first received the Gospel from fellow Africans."

Independent Religious Movements

But these African preachers were not always slavishly devoted to the White missionary. One reaction to the missionary factor was the birth of independent religious movements led by Africans. These independent religious movements tended to fall into three distinct groupings. Some were *Ethiopian* in nature, primarily concerned with African leadership and only secondarily concerned with changing missionary theology or worship.

A second grouping was the *Spirit or Prophet* churches, which emphasized healing and the supernatural. Armed with Scriptures in their own languages they struck out on their own, like William Wade Harris of Liberia whose preaching in Ivory Coast and Ghana between 1913 and 1915 claimed over 100,000 adherents. Others like Simon Kimbangu of Zaire [now the Congo] broke away from the Baptist missionaries and founded his Church of Jesus Christ on Earth through the prophet Simon Kimbangu. In some cases these prophet churches moved clearly outside the bounds of orthodoxy. Such was the case with Isaiah Shembe (d. 1935) and his Church of the Nazarites. After his death in 1935 his followers proclaimed that he had risen from the dead and was in fact the true Christ for Africa.

A third category covers *movements of revival* within established denominations. The passion in these type of independent movements was neither struggle with white leadership or Christianity in Independent Africa nor a desire for miracles and healing. The controlling passion was the discovery of a vital Christianity to replace a numbing nominalism in the church. The outstanding example of this third type of movement is the East Africa Revival that swept much of East Africa from 1930-1960 and is associated with the names of Simeoni Nsibambi, Joe Church, Blasio Kigozi, and William Nagenda.

Christianity in Independent Africa

In 1960, 14 African nations achieved selfhood and inaugurated a new era within African Christianity. Henry Venn's vision of an African Christianity that was self-governing, self-propagating, and self-supporting was at last realized. In denomination after denomination African leaders replaced the missionary. The new leaders faced a number of new challenges in the modern era. Five challenges in particular dominated African Christianity in the closing decades of the 20th century:

Church and State

The overarching fact of modern African life since the late 1960s was widespread disillusionment with the nation-state. As the promise of the new African ruling elite turned sour in the '60s, criticism began to mount. The common response of the ruling elite to the growing chorus of criticism was tightened control, promotion of personality cults and messianic nationalism, and growing conflict with the Church. Kwame Nkrumah's tragic rise and fall in Ghana was all too typical. Zaire's [now the Congo] Mobutu Sese Seko, Liberia's Samuel Doe, Uganda's Idi Amin, and Ethiopia's Mengistu Haile Mariam were typical of leaders who saw the church as a dangerous independent voice. Church responses have varied from silent partnership with the ruling elite (Roman Catholicism in Rwanda, Dutch Reformed Church in South Africa) to critical protest of state injustice ([Archbishop] Desmond Tutu in South Africa, National Council of Churches Kenya). Occasionally the state has lashed out violently against the church, as in the cases of the martyred Archbishop Janani Luwum of Uganda and the numerous imprisoned pastors of Mengistu's Ethiopia.

Unity and Diversity

Statistician David Barrett documented more than 5,000 different independent churches in Africa by the late 1960s. These groups claimed over 7 million members drawn from 290 tribes all over the continent. By the 1990s, 10,000 such groups had been identified. Organizations like the All Africa Conference of Churches (AACC) and the Association of Evangelicals in Africa (AEA) have sought to bring some unity to the fractured Body of Christ in Africa. A series of Pan African Christian Leadership Assemblies (PACLA) have sought to bring additional harmony by bring leaders of the AACC and AEA together. Parachurch agencies have played their part in bridging denominational dividing lines.

Theology and Culture

Though Cardinal Joseph Ratzinger has dismissed African theology as more a "project than a reality" great effort has gone into the formation of a Christian theology that would adequately address the modern African context. Early voices in this movement include Roman Catholics such as Tharcisse Tshibangu, Englebert Mveng, Nginud Mushete, Anselme Sanon, Eboussi Boulaga, Charles Nyamiti, Laurenti Magesa, and Benezet Bujo. Protestant contributions have come from Edward Fashole-Luke, John Pobee, Kwesi Dickson, Bolaji Idowu, John Mbiti, Jesse Mugambi, Ukachukwu Chris Manus, and Harry Sawyerr. An African liberation theology has been formed with the encouragement of the World Council of Churches-related Ecumenical Association of Third World Theologians (EATWoT). Cameroonian Jean-Marc Ela and Ghanaian Mercy Amba Oduyoye (from a feminist perspective) have promoted an African liberation theology. An African black theology came to expression in South Africa in the writings of Allan Boesak, Manas Buthelezi, Desmond Tutu, and Stephen Biko. The movement's high point came with the publication of the Kairos Document of 1985. African evangelical theology is still emerging but important voices have been Tite Tienou, Byang Kato, Tokunboh Adeyemo, and the *Africa Journal of Evangelical Theology*.

African Missions and Church Growth

In the 1970s Kenyan Presbyterian leader John Gatu called for a moratorium on Western missionaries in order to foster "selfhood" within the church. The outcome of this debate has been a decrease in mainline missionaries (5,000 in 1959 to 3,000 in early 1970). At the same time there has been a resurgence of missions in three other groups. In 1974 a Synod of Bishops at Rome rejected the call for a moratorium and pledged 100,000 new missionaries by the year 2000. Evangelical missionaries from the faith missions grew from 11,000 in the 1970s to more than 16,000 in the late 1980s. In addition dozens of new African mission agencies emerged in the 1970s, '80s and '90s. The most dramatic story of church growth in Africa, however, was the expansion of Pentecostal and charismatic preachers, evangelists, and missionaries in the closing decades of the 20th century. The gospel of health, wealth, and wholeness accounted for much of the appeal of this form of Christianity.

Discipleship, Leadership and Nominalism

The greatest challenge facing African Christian leadership was the challenge not of the unreached but of the undiscipled. If one accepts the statistics that African Christianity has grown from an estimated 4 million professing Christians in 1900 to nearly 300 million adherents today, then one is forced to ask about how these huge numbers of people can be discipled. Though the promise of African Christianity is great, the church of Africa must wrestle with the dilemma of a Christianity that may be "expanding at the periphery" even while it is "collapsing at the center" (Roland Oliver). Leadership development and the training of the laity seem to be the crucial needs of this continent "shaped like a question mark" (Ali Mazrui).

Bibliography

Baur, John. *2000 Years of Christianity in Africa: An African Church History 62-1992.* Nairobi: Paulines Publications Africa. 1994.

de Gruchy, John. *The Church Struggle in South Africa.* Grand Rapids, MI: Erdmans. 1979.

Gray, Richard. *Black Christians and White Missionaries.* New Haven, CT: Yale University Press. 1990.

Groves, C.P. *The Planting of the Church in Africa.* 4 volumes, London: Lutterworth. 1948-1958.

Hastings, Adrian. *The Church in Africa: 1450-1950.* Oxford: Clarendon Press. 1994.

Isichei, Elizabeth. *A History of Christianity in Africa From Antiquity to the Present.* Grand Rapids, MI. 1995.

Sanneh, Lamin. *West African Christianity The Religious Impact.* Maryknoll: Orbis Books.

Working in Unity

Brian Johnson

Brian Johnson is the National Co-ordinator for COMINAD. He has served as Pastor, Bible college professor, Christian school teacher, and a foreign missionary. He has worked for Carver International missions, World Relief Cooperation, and the International African-American mission Mobilzation project. While in Africa he was the principal of the Monrovia Bible College, Field Supervisor of Carver Missions Liberia, Secretary General of the Association of Evangelicals, and the Country Director for World Releif. His work responsibilities were:, micro-enterprise development, war trauma counselor, ethnic reconciliation, and relief assistance. World Relief honored him with its Helping Hands award, 1997. Brian Johnson & family reside in Virginia Beach, VA. He continues to do ministry in Africa.

There are three partners in global missions today: the sending church, the national church, and the mission agency. The sending church is involved in the edifying and nurturing of its members, preparing for its involvement in the Great Commission. The leaders of these churches have understood that the Great Commission is a command, and not an option, for all believers. Sending churches take practical steps to expose their people to what is going on around the world with a view toward getting involved in winning lost people to Christ.

The national church is the church that is located within separate geopolitical boundaries around the world. For example, the church that is in the U.S. is the Church of Jesus Christ located in the U.S.. The church located in Colombia, South America is the Church of Jesus Christ located in Colombia, South America.

The collective national leadership within each country is the church leadership of that nation. These leaders are those whom God holds responsible for shepherding His flock in their country.

The mission agencies are organizations that help to facilitate and transport the sending churches' resources, both human and otherwise, to the world.

There are times when the three partners experience strained relationships; nevertheless, this has been the way the Western church has contributed to the establishment of the Church around the world during this modern missions era. But, nowadays there has been more direct contact between the sending churches and the national church and more cooperation among mission agencies.

The African-American Christian and Missions

The good news of the Gospel is to be proclaimed to the lost world by every believer. Those who receive the Gospel are to be discipled in the ways of Christ Jesus (Matt. 28:19-20), and, in turn, those disciples are to make disciples of others (2 Tim. 2:2).

The Lord Jesus knew that if believers were faithful in discipling people and motivating them to disciple other people, He would be proclaimed to the whole world. The problem has been, and is today, as Jesus Christ said, "the laborers are few." What Jesus hoped would happen is not fully happening around the world. There are many Christians who are not making disciples in the world, as our Lord commanded.

African-American Christians, for the most part, are strangely absent from mission fields around the world. Almost all of the mission activity of the African-American Christian is local in nature. Local mission is good, but our Lord commanded that the Gospel should go to the ends of the earth also.

There are many reasons why there are not many African-Americans involved in reaching the world, but what is certain is that there are many good signs from around the U.S. that show the African-American Christian is moving toward greater involvement in world missions.

The Powerful Voice of Unity

As the African-American Christian is being mobilized, it is important that African-American sending churches, mission agencies, and national churches work harmoniously together. If they don't work together the message of Christ could suffer great harm.

It is very important for godly Christians to work very hard to see that the new army of African-American sending churches and Western mission agencies, which are, for the most part, white, work together. In some cases African-American church leadership does not share my desire to partner with white mission agencies. Therefore, African-American church leaders go directly to the national church and bypass mission agencies all together. This desire of African-Americans not to partner was brought on by racism on the part of whites toward blacks in the U.S..

National churches within countries all over the world experience deep division. This hinders the work of making Christ known to the world. Mission agencies and national churches also experience strained relationships which hinders the work of Christ.

The Lord Jesus prayed a remarkable prayer in John 17:20-23, Amp:

> Neither for these alone do I pray—it is not for their sake only that I make this request— but also for all those who will ever come to believe in (trust, cling to, rely on) Me through their word and teaching; So that they all may be one just as You, Father, are

in Me and I in You, that they also may be one in Us, so that the world may believe and be convinced that You have sent Me. I have given to them the glory and honor which You have given Me, that they may be one, (even) as We are one: I in them and You in Me, in order that they may become one and perfectly united, that the world may know and (definitely) recognize that You sent Me, and that You have loved them (even) as You have loved Me."

The Church of Jesus Christ has experienced positional oneness, because all believers belong to one body, but experientially Christians are divided. This division is hurting Jesus and His message to the world. This is because the message that Christ has to present to the world is a message of reconciliation (2 Cor. 5:18-19). This message, if accepted, can produce the power necessary to reconcile sinful man to God and man to man.

The evidence that a person has been reconciled to God also demonstrates man's reconciliation to his fellow man. It is through this reconciliation message (believer loving believer) that the world will believe that the Son of God has come to earth in the flesh and died for all men. The Lord makes it clear that the empirical evidence for whether a person is a disciple of Christ, in the eyes of the world, is if we Christians have love among ourselves (John 13:35).

Therefore, when missionaries proclaim the reconciling message of Christ to a lost and unreconciled world, it is more believable when presented from people who once were visibly unreconciled, but now speak with the powerful voice of unity. Without a display of reconciliation the message of Christ could be easily rejected by those whom the Lord wants to reconcile to Himself.

As African-American Christians pursue global missions, they must study carefully what God has been doing through other African-Americans and Christians of other ethnic groups around the world. After gaining a clear understanding of what God has been doing in the past and what He is doing today, they can be a great blessing to the Lord and to the world.

The Ministry of Mediation

One of the most vital roles that African-American Christians can play in missions (especially among national churches, mission agencies and the world in general) is in the area of mediation. Satan persistently tries to hinder the work of God by causing division among God's people. When Satan succeeds in dividing believers on the mission field, in many cases the work of missions is hindered and could even stop altogether. It is at this time that God uses Christians to begin a process of mediation in order to restore unity within His church so His work can continue.

The African-American Christians' unique life experiences make them more suited to be mediators than many other Christians around the world. African-Americans have experienced racism, suppression, segregation, poverty, and humiliation, along with verbal, physical, and emotional abuse. In this same context, African-Americans have grappled with Christ's commands to be meek, humble, and gentle. Living in a society where white Christians saw themselves as superior was bad enough, but teaching that God cursed blacks, making them inferior to whites in intelligence and spirituality, was hard to deal with. Some black Christians endured paternalism, patronism, forced servitude, indentured servitude, and psychological servitude, yet in the same lifetime experienced economic prosperity and affluence. Although not all African-American Christians have gone through this roller coaster of experiences in one lifetime, many have. These experiences help black Christians to understand where people are coming from and allow them to put themselves in other Christians' shoes when mediating disputes. From my experience, mediation is high on the list of vital needs in missions today and one of many roles for which African-American Christian missionaries are well suited.

The African Christian Fellowship, U.S.A.
Strategic Links with the Diaspora and the World

Elijah O. Adeoye & Matthew N. O. Sadiku

Edited by Frank E. Gainer

Elijah O. Adeoye is from Nigeria and resides in Norman, OK with his lovely wife, Victoria, and their four children: Seyi, Segun, Dotun and Tosin. Mr. Adeoye is a long time member of the African Christian Fellowship (ACF) and serves as a member of the National Board of Directors for ACF, USA. He is one of the pioneering members of the organization for Mission work in Africa and he is currently the Director of Missions and Reconnecting with the Continent. He served very dynamically for two terms as the South Region President 1991-1995.

Matthew N. O. Sadiku is from Nigeria. He was an assistant professor at Florida Atlantic University and a professor at Temple University. Since July, 2001, he has been with Boeing Satellite Systems as a senior scientist. He is the author of over 100 professional papers and 20 books. Some of which have been translated into Korean, Chinese, Italian, and Spanish. He was the recipient of the 2000 McGraw-Hill/Jacob Millman Award for outstanding contributions in the field of electrical engineering.

Edited by Frank E. Gainer. He resides in Indianapolis, IN, and is a member of Trinity Baptist Church. He holds a Ph.D. in Analytical Chemistry, Iowa State University. He is a retired chemical analyst after 25 1/2 years with Eli Lily & Company.

The African Christian Fellowship (ACF) is an inter denominational body of believers who are dedicated to working together for the realization of God's plan and purpose for the continent of Africa and peoples of African descent worldwide. Even though the ACF has been organized in the U.S. since 1976, it is a little-known entity among mainstream evangelicals. It was only recently (1994) that ACF began to focus on mission activity. Even though ACF does not have a long history of mission involvement, their unique nature and current commitment to reclaiming Africa for Christ justifies their presence in this publication.

The fellowship has restructured itself and has developed a strategic vision to provide ministry direction for the 21st century. In addition, ACF has placed missions as a core value under its strategic vision and has the potential to be a dynamic force in the shaping of world evangelization as its vision is fully realized. This chapter presents a brief overview of the African Christian Fellowship including its history, organizational structure, activities, and strategic vision.

Perhaps the best way to position ACF (in the reader's mind) as a viable entity in world evangelization is to highlight some findings relative to one of the strategic initiatives at this point.

The Building Bridges Initiative --The creation of a vitally needed cooperation under this initiative will have a tremendous impact on the world. It is a linkage being formed between immediate descendants of Africa and African-Americans. Since it is rather obvious, based on skin color, that African-Americans are descendents of Africa that truth can hardly be denied. Even though it is an indictment against both groups, Africans and African-Americans do not always acknowledge that common heritage. The absence of behavioral factors that create and cultivate healthy relationships tend to support the indictment.

Operatives such as mutual acceptance, openness of communication, freedom of interaction, willingness to partner, and unity of purpose appear to be lacking *in toto* between Africans and African-Americans. African-Americans have been privileged to be members of ACF over the years but there has not been a deliberate effort by either party to bridge the gap. Fortunately, during the past three to four years and unknown to each other, both the ACF and some mission minded African-Americans have recognized the gap between the two groups and have pondered ways to bring about greater connectivity. Perhaps a turning point in history took place in 1997 at the ACF National Conference in Valley Forge, PA, as the ACF began to unveil its core strategic areas to its members publicly.

As God would have it, an African-American Christian, attending an ACF conference for the first time, heard the initiatives being recited. Unknown to ACF the African-American had attended the conference for the express purpose of beginning dialogue with African Christians about the need to bridge the gap. As the conference progressed, so did dialogue, and it became clear that God was honoring the earnest desire of both parties to further His kingdom by *Building Bridges*. Thus, the die was cast for a journey that has the potential of empowering the African Diaspora to become a stronger advocate and participant in evangelism and missions on the world scene during the 21st century.

Both Africans and African-Americans historically have been recipients or objects of evangelistic and mission efforts. They have been target groups to be reached by other ethnic groups, primarily the Anglo-Saxons. ACF and a growing segment of African-American Christians realize that they must become more involved in reaching the lost for Jesus Christ during the 21st century. More involvement on the part of the African Diaspora is not only a biblical mandate, but also it is a reasonable and timely mandate. Neither the world as a whole, nor Christendom, has seen large scale involvement of the African Diaspora in world evangelism and missions in modern times. Supporting missionary activities in Africa is a core value under the ACF initiative of *Reconnecting with the Continent*. Implementation of this strategic initiative should result in much fruit being harvested for the kingdom.

Implementation of the *Building Bridges* strategic initiative via collaboration and partnership with African-Americans will have a synergistic effect on world evangelism and missions by the African Diaspora. Collaborative missions by the African Diaspora on the continent of Africa alone have potential for a great harvest. Imagine the empowerment of sub-Saharan African Christians to evangelize northern Africa and the impact that would have on world evangelization. Stretch your imagination a bit more to foresee collaboration of ACF with other Christian groups outside of the African Diaspora. It is exciting to see that the *Building Bridges* initiative opens the door for a multitude of collaborative and partnership efforts for reaching the unreached.

The ACF has already created a *Building Bridges* committee consisting of both Africans and African-Americans to begin development of the framework under which the corresponding initiative will operate.

History

The U.S. has always had a glamorous appeal and attraction to a lot of students worldwide, especially those from the continent of Africa. A large number of these students are Christians who maintain a good relationship with the Lord Jesus Christ at home. While some remain strong in their faith, others backslide in the U.S. because of cultural shocks and cool acceptance or outright rejection in some churches.

As some of these Christians attended Urbana conferences sponsored by InterVarsity year after year, they discovered that there were more African Christians from various African countries studying in the U.S. than they had thought. As they gathered and got to know each other more intimately, they began to share their experiences of spiritual and social isolation due to cultural and environmental differences in the U.S..

Therefore, the need arose to form a fellowship where African students of like background could come together and relate, while encouraging and supporting one another. Initially, the objective of the fellowship was to provide a medium whereby Africans Christians could fellowship together, maintain their faith, and be taught to live holy lives so that they would not backslide or be tossed here and there by the new environment. In the early days, the scope and the objective of the fellowship changed as its leadership changed locally, regionally, and nationally.

God has His own timing in fulfilling His purposes, and the establishment of the African Christian Fellowship is a good example. Proposals made at InterVarsity's Urbana conferences to form an African Christian Fellowship were turned down year after year. In 1976 the hour had come. God was moving from different directions. At Urbana 1976 held at the University of Illinois, Urbana, the African Christian Fellowship in the U.S. and Canada was formally inaugurated.

In April 1977, about 50 African Christians students met at Madison, WI, and founded what was then called African Christian Student Fellowship (ACSF), USA & Canada. Some African Christian students from Canada wanted to be a part of this Fellowship and that wish was granted. The next few years were spent forming chapters on various U.S. campuses.

The adoption of the name ACSF was significant because it was organized by students who were seeking to have fellowship with one another. The primary objective of the ACSF was for African Christians to come together to encourage one another in a culture foreign to their own or one they were used to.

Since the beginning of ACSF, there has been a proliferation of ministries started by Africans in the U.S.. At the 1988 ACSF national conference at Tulsa, OK, the group's name was changed to African Christian Fellowship, USA, (ACF). In order to reflect the demographic constitution of the Africans; the words *Student* and *Canada* were dropped.

Organizational Structure

To ease management, the African Christian Fellowship, USA, has been divided into five regions with each region comprising of local chapters. The ACF, a nonprofit organization, is incorporated as a national organization with affiliated local chapters and regions under a central leadership of a national board of directors. Each region and chapter is as unique as the individuals that formed it and the circumstances that led to its formation.

National Board

The board of directors is solely responsible for the management of ACF at the national level. The board consists of two elected representatives from each of the five regions and up to two additional members appointed by the elected members of the board. The board meets on a regular basis, makes decisions on behalf of the body, and passes decisions by the elected representatives down to the regions and chapters .

Regions

Five regions are provided for in the ACF Constitution.

Established in 1983, the Midwest Region is comprised of Illinois, Indiana, Iowa, Kansas, Kentucky, Michigan, Minnesota, Missouri, Nebraska, Ohio, and Wisconsin.

Formed in 1985, the South Region is comprised of Alabama, Arkansas, Florida, Georgia, Louisiana, Mississippi, North Carolina, Oklahoma, South Carolina, Tennessee, and Texas.

Inaugurated at a meeting in Delaware, March 1991, the East region is comprised of Connecticut, Delaware, Maine, Maryland, Massachusetts, New Jersey, New Hampshire, New York, Pennsylvania, Rhode Island, Vermont, Virginia, and West Virginia, and the District of Columbia.

The West Region is comprised of Arizona, California, Colorado, Hawaii, Nevada, New Mexico, and Utah.

Northwest Region (not functioning when this article was written) is comprised of Alaska, Idaho, Montana, North Dakota, Oregon, South Dakota, Washington, and Wyoming.

Chapters

The chapters are the backbone of the African Christian Fellowship. Without them, there is no ACF. All the action happens there. Each chapter is autonomous and unique in its establishment. Some started as a prayer group and became a chapter with many activities. Some groups were recruited as chapters through introduction by friends, acquaintances, national executives, regional executives, or local chapters. Each chapter is run by the local executive officers: the President, Secretary, Treasurer, and others. There are chapters located in many cities of all sizes throughout the country, each tailored to meet the needs of its local constituents.

Membership

ACF Membership is not restricted to persons of African descent and includes members from across Africa, the Caribbean Islands, and the U.S.. Membership is over 2,000 adults and youths, with representation from more than half the countries in Africa. The African countries represented include: Angola, Cameroon, Congo, Cote d'Ivoire, Egypt, Ethiopia, Gambia, Ghana, Kenya, Liberia, Nigeria, Rwanda, Sierra Leone, South Africa, Tanzania, Togo, Uganda, Zambia, and Zimbabwe.

It is open to individuals and groups (churches, organizations or ministries). Each has accepted and confessed Jesus Christ as their personal Lord and Savior. Most adult members of the ACF are born-again Christians with college degrees; more than half have graduate or professional degrees.

Finance

The fellowship is a nonprofit organization. ACF depends primarily on voluntary contributions by its members and conference revenues for its operations. This approach made it very difficult to raise enough money to run the organization in earlier days since many of its members were students.

In recent times the organization has devised and continues to pursue other ways to raise money. In 1980, ACF made its first budget and set a specified allotment amount for each chapter to pay. Since approval of the 1990 budget and modifications to the allotment system, the finances of the organization have improved considerably. The allotment system encourages and enables each chapter to contribute a specified amount to the national budget based on its membership.

Activities, Meetings, and Conferences

Mission Activities

ACF's mission work began in Africa in 1994 out of a desperate effort to render help to the refugee camps built up as a result of the Rwandans fleeing the massive genocide in their country. Since the Rwandan project, ACF through the regions and chapters has been involved in mission work to other Africans including the Kanuri in Nigeria and Central African Republic, and to other parts of the world, such as India and South America.

The ACF East Region maintains a scholarship program for the training of missionaries through CAPRO's Institut Interafricain de Formation Missionaire, based in Abidjan, Cote d'Ivoire, and YWAM's School of Frontier Missions, based in Lome, Togo.

Other Activities

ACF is an active organization. Most ACF activities take place at the local level with conferences and mission projects conducted at the regional and national levels. Local and regional meetings are held at the discretion of the respective groups, but all groups seek to promote activities that support ACF's core values.

Meetings

In accordance with the organizational structure, every ACF chapter is headed by its elected officers. These leaders work as an executive body to take care of their members. They are responsible for organizing meetings and events.

Conferences

The ACF national conference is held every two years, generally in the late July and early August and usually in a major U.S. metropolitan area. The national conference provides a natural venue to enable leadership to inform membership, discuss, and resolve ACF business matters.

Families, [extended families,] and individuals are encouraged to attend. Each conference, influenced by the leadership, has a unique setting. Depending on the denominational persuasions of attendees, the conference may be loud, quiet, or anywhere in between. The conference is normally very well attended from across the U.S. and sometimes from overseas. This conference also is used as a platform to address spiritual and physical growth, and development. Preachers, teachers, and professional experts are invited to preach, teach, and give seminars and symposiums on various subjects that affect the sociospiritual and socioeconomic needs of members.

Families are encouraged to use this conference for a relaxing and learning vacation time. Recognizing that this may be the only vacation for some attendees, the activities are designed to include tourist attractions, provide opportunities for friendship and networking, and opportunities for families to share their experiences on raising godly, positive children in a today's negative and wild world.

Concurrent sessions of seminars and workshops cover a wide range of topics.

Strategic Vision

A working document has been developed by the fellowship to guide ACF's activities in the coming years. The document is consistent with ACF's constitution and is subject to revision as the need arises. The document maps out plans and strategies to implement at the various levels of the fellowship. The strategic vision consists of four strategic areas:

Strategic Area I: Building the Family and ACF Community

The intent of this area is to build and preserve a stable, functional, and harmonious community that effectively addresses its spiritual, physical, social, and emotional needs, and recognizes their diversity. At its best, this strategic plan will empower ACF to teach, apply, and implement consistent biblical principles on individual responsibility, marriage, and the family. It will also require ACF to teach and encourage effective communication among family members and consistently apply biblical principles of economic stewardship at family and fellowship affairs. It will further cause ACF to recognize and account for the cultural and environmental factors that impact on its values, performance, and effectiveness.

Inherent in this initiative is a consistent effort to increase the total membership of the fellowship by at least 10 percent per year.

Indices of progress or success include, but are not limited to, absence or minimal levels of divorce among members, retention of visitors to the fellowship, absence of or few quarrels at home, a high level of confidence and peace for children in their families, and positive futures, behavior, and manners for children.

Strategic Area II: Reconnecting with the Continent

This intends to initiate and maintain active and relevant connections with the continent and peoples of Africa to maximize the benefits of Africa's spiritual, social, economic, and cultural resources. It involves supporting missionary activities in Africa; promoting economic investments in Africa; mobilizing relief efforts for Africa; enhancing the health and social well-being of peoples in Africa; educating ACF members on current issues and needs in Africa; and recognizing and promoting positive African culture.

Strategic Area III: Passing on the Legacy

This initiative has focused primarily on how to develop ACF's youth and energize their interest in the activities of the fellowship. It is designed to inculcate ACF's children with an appreciation of the vision and values of the ACF, thereby equipping them to effectively serve God's purpose in their generation.

This core initiative includes the following categories:

• *Spiritual:* Demonstrate to ACF's children the reality of godly living by equipping ACF parents to consistently demonstrate practical Christian living before their children.

• *Education & Training:* Nurture and maintain the value and purpose of the African Christian heritage while facilitating the contextual implementation of the ACF Vision.

• *Social & Physical:* Promote and provide opportunities for social and physical development.
ACF Vision: Train the youth to understand, accept, and articulate the ACF vision clearly.

• *Missions:* Encourage the contextual application of the Great Commission.

Strategic Area IV: Building Bridges

The objective of this strategic plan is to establish viable, sustainable, and productive relationships with Africans and other groups in the U.S.. ACF achieves this by:

- fostering reconciliation, unity and understanding with Christian groups and persons;
- fostering collaboration and partnership with appropriate organizations, agencies and persons;
- acknowledging and enhancing positive mutual perceptions of Africans and other people groups; and
- increasing and maintaining the membership and participation of all African countries in the fellowship.

Acknowledgments

The authors would like to thank Sam Umunna and Richard Ehriawarien for providing pieces of information for this chapter. They are also very grateful to ACF Southern California for the information on its trip to Central African Republic and ACF-USA. for allowing them to use the information on their website (http://www.acfusa.net).

The African-American Church and African Mission in the 21st Century

The African-American Church and African Mission in the 21st Century

The Challenges of an Effective Missionary Strategy

Chinaka S. DomNwachukwu

The material presented here is an adaptation of one of the main papers at Speaking for Ourselves! The State of Christianity in Africa: A Consultation on Christian Mission in the 21st Century Africa. *The author has revised, adapted, and refined the aspect that he feels might speak to the African-American mission-minded church, for this publication.*

C hristian mission as done in Africa in the past years has had its unique characteristics. The picture about Africa most prevalent in the West is that Africa is "dark," "poor," "illiterate," "helpless," and "Godless." Much of Western missionary activity in Africa has been carried out with the same air of superiority and imperialism that has characterized Western interaction with Africa since the colonial years. Whereas many Africans have come to accept the fact of the Western ethnocentrism, not many of them expect that attitude from African-Americans.

Africans do not see African-Americans the same way they view white Americans. They see the African-Americans as brothers and sisters, people with whom they share a common ancestry, as well as a common experience of exploitation and dehumanization. They come into their interaction with the African-Americans believing that they stand on equal ground, given their shared history and experiences. It is unfortunate, however, that many African-Americans involved in the African mission often encounter this same attitude that has characterized white interaction with Africa for years. Many African-Americans view themselves as more privileged and more "civilized" than Africans, so they come with a superiority complex, which is often repulsive to the Africans.

Like their predecessors, white Americans, our African-American brothers feel more privileged than the African brothers, which to an extend is justifiable--they live in an industrialized culture and make the same mistakes of the early missionaries. They fail to try to understand the culture and people with whom they are interacting.

African-Americans are even more disadvantaged on the African mission field because of the color of their skin. Africans expect African-Americans them to know them, failing to realize that these blacks are not the same generation taken from Africa hundreds of years ago. We Africans often

Rev. Chinaka Samuel DomNwachukwu is an ordained Southern Baptist Minister, from Nigeria and a member of the Nigerian Baptist Convention. He is currently president and executive director of Global Mission, Incorporated, a nondenominational mission agency targeting unreached parts of Africa. He and his wife, Nkechi, are committed to leadership development, mission education, and mobilization for the ripe African mission field. He holds a Doctor of Philosophy degree (Ph.D.) from Fuller Theological Seminary in Pasadena, CA, and serves as a professor of leadership and intercultural studies at Azusa Pacific University, Azusa, CA.

expect them to like our food, to like our ways, and to understand us better than the whites. This places the African-American missionary in a more difficult place when attempting to serve God in African mission fields.

Another crises of the African-American mission is that most African-Americans churches realize that life in America is more comfortable than life in Africa. This is expected, given the many pictures of poor and starving children and war refugees that fill American media. As a result they resort to sending money, food, and clothing as immediate release from the guilt of living comfortably while their ancestral brethren are suffering in the motherland.

Some of these churches are criticized for sending just monetary resources and not even going to these places to see the needs for themselves. They believe they are ensuring that they do not perpetuate an age-long issue of dependency that has characterized Western mission in Africa.

For African-American involvement in African mission to be effective, therefore, they must understand this issue of dependency, as well as some of the new challenges that are emerging from within African churches that often attract Western attention.

Dependency Theory: Its Facts and Its Flaws

A fact that must be accepted is that the African mission field is so vast that the African church cannot reach it alone. They are unable to fund meaningful mission activities on their own, especially in the midst of Islamic aggression, which is strong and richly funded from the Arab world, as well as within the current level of economic inequity, which characterizes our global economy in the 21st century.

Most Western-established churches in Africa are weak, unable to embark on meaningful mission enterprises. This is because missions as they know it was done by Westerners and the resources and manpower for mission came from the West. Many of these churches do not see missions as an intrinsic aspect of their mandate, which has created a problem in Africa. In areas where

they see missions as a vital aspect of their existence as a community of God's people, many are unable to fund it due to the very low per capita income for which most parts of Africa are known.

Glenn Schwartz, a former missionary to Zambia, has been bold enough to address this issue of dependency. His position can be summarized as follows:

1. Africa is not lacking in money and highly qualified and gifted leaders.
2. Financial dependency has less to do with wealth and poverty than with a mentality of dependence that accompanied the spread of the Gospel.
3. The complex foreign structure of Christianity introduced into many areas of Africa, created and built with foreign dollars, has been hardly reproducible.[1]

Schwartz also traces the history of dependency to the early missionary era when the Western missionary went to Africa and other parts of the world and tried not only to replicate the Christianity of the Western societies, but also attempted to replicate the culture and lifestyle of the West in African societies. At the Westerners' departure, the nationals inherited a burdensome responsibility of maintaining these Western structures, and to do so they have had to depend on Western money. Schwartz blames the people's lack of commitment as the major problem, hence his emphasis that the African church needs to be taught how to give.

Mission Frontiers carried a discussion between Schwartz and Chuck Bennett, President of Partners International. In his response to Schwartz, Bennett agrees that "unhealthy dependency is not to be encouraged." But he cautioned Schwartz to face the fact that "the Scriptures are full of admonitions that members of the Body of Christ should be interdependent." He argues, "To refuse to share our resources with overseas brethren because there have been abuses is like saying we should outlaw marriage because some husbands beat their wives."[2]

Bennett goes further to state emphatically: "I admire Glenn's passion and I agree in principle with his concern. But his experience has been mostly limited to some of the worst cases."[3]

The problem as presented by Schwartz sounds simplistic, but the challenge his work poses to the course of Christ is fearful. We cannot throw the baby out with the bath water. Christian missions must always be seen as a collective mandate for the Church of Christ.

The African-American church, therefore, has a valid spiritual mandate to enter the ripe mission field of Africa for, indeed, the laborers are few. The caution they must observe, however, is to avoid a transplantation of the home-baked ideas of missions and church planting, which often will not work in African situations.

The African-American church needs to enter the mission field, boldly but cautiously. We need the African-American church to join forces with us in confronting the challenge of Islam and the need for the knowledge of God in Africa. However, for them to do the job better than their white predecessors, they must be willing to listen to us Africans, dialogue with us, and to work hand in hand with us. They are not to create unhealthy dependency, neither are they to pack their luggage and go home telling themselves that Africans can do it without them.

Islam in Africa

Islam came to Africa from the Arab world through trade, diplomacy, and warfare. Africa had been engaged in trade with the Arab world for centuries before Islam, and those trade routes soon became viable avenues for the transmission of Islam into Africa. Islamic propagation in Africa has been calculated and consistent. Muslims approached the Islamization of Africa with a ruthless and persistent force. Where diplomacy and trade proved unsuccessful, Islam used coercion and military force both to subdue and to subjugate the people where possible. This has continued until today; Sudan is a living example of this.

The Islamic agenda in Africa also has been based on a determined effort to make Islam an African way of life. In a recent write-up, I contended that Islam cannot claim to be an African religion, just as Christianity cannot.

They are both newcomers to Africa. But unlike the Western Christianity that came to Africa, Islam came with Islamic culture and language. It made concerted efforts to contextualize the religion in Africa. This has reached the point that most African Muslims are unable to see the Arab influences that have gradually eroded their African heritage. This has been possible because Islam insists on being seen as a way of life rather than a mere religious expression.

In the 21st century, Islam remains one of the strongest religious influences in Africa. The Islamic agenda for the 21st century Africa is to plant a mosque within walking distance of every major African city. This agenda has been preached and pursued vigorously, well aided by the Arab petrodollars pumped into many poor African communities daily.

This is a major challenge that the Christian church is either unaware of or seems impotent to combat. The lack of an organized program of confrontation with Islam is causing Christianity to lose ground in many parts of Africa. Some parts of Africa that about 20 years ago did not have a single Muslim now have mosques filled with worshippers. Most of these worshippers are bought [won] over by money. The Islamic petrodollars are a force that African Christians alone are incompetent to engage unless by a miraculous outworking of God's intervention. This becomes all the more reason why Christians from the West need to get involved in the battle for souls in Africa.

And the Islamic aggression of today is not just an African problem, but is now a global threat. Europe and America are now confronted by Islamic propaganda more than ever before in history.

Unfortunately, many Western Christians are asleep to the reality of this encounter. For this reason God is raising missionaries from both Western and non-Western countries, crisscrossing them at a global level to awaken a sleeping church to the final onslaught of the enemy. It is my prayer that every Christian who reads this document will begin to see the work of missions in the 21st century as a spiritual power encounter. Our involvement is mandatory, not optional.

New and Challenging Open Doors for African Mission

Management and Money

Another challenge that the African-American church must be acquainted with as she enters the African mission field is the emerging trend of abuse of power and finances. Some missionary groups have accused many African churches of money laundering. Many from the old missionary camp excuse their unwillingness to let go of power and empower the nationals with accusations that the nationals cannot manage the money and resources the missionaries leave behind.

Whereas this must be seen as an unfair generalization and as scapegoating, there may be valid cases of mismanagement which have characterized certain Christian groups in Africa. But these incidents are not absent in Western churches. As much as the Western church embarking on missions in Africa must be aware of these trends, they should not form the basis for their decision as to whether or not to go to Africa. Instead, they should inform the missionary towards strategies that the African-American church will map out for her work in Africa.

African Independent Churches

In a recent paper presented at a consultation on African missions for the 21st century, one of the points I made is that God has made available to us some significant open doors for missions in the 21st century Africa. Among these open doors is the emergence of the African Independent Churches. These are churches which are authentically African. They are started mostly by Africans and have little or no connection with the missionary-established churches. Worship is spontaneous, and worship forms and practices are African. These constitute the fastest-growing Christian groups in Africa today. Many of them are charismatic and often Pentecostal in their doctrinal leanings. They grow very rapidly, to the extent that some have called them "mushroom" churches.

This group constitutes the thrust of human resources needed for missions in Africa today. They have many young men who are enthusiastic and daring, willing to take the Gospel anywhere, if they can be sent. A group may start in Nigeria, and before you know it there is a branch in Ghana, Kenya, and Tanzania. I have often seen this type of group as the lifeblood for an authentic African missionary force. I still believe they are.

Given the fact that many African-American churches involved in missions in Africa lean towards charismatic or Pentecostal, they quickly identify with these new groups and tend to collaborate more with them. There are, however, some ills within some of these groups which any Western church that plans to do missions in Africa must be aware of and be prepared to address.

Some, not all, of these churches have been founded on the wrong footing. Some bad elements have taken advantage of African Christians' desire for their own way of worship and have proliferated churches for personal gain. Some have even come to see church planting as an economic undertaking.

Many critics have rightfully attributed the heavy emphasis on money that we see in some African Independent Churches to the influences of American televangelists like Jim Baker, Jimmy Swaggart, and others regularly seen on the Trinity Broadcasting Network. Assuming that a number of African Independent Churches have been influenced both positively and negatively by American Pentecostalism and prosperity theology, mission strategist must be aware of this. These problems, though, are not uniquely African, and should not become the criteria for missionary decisions about Africa.

It is important to mention that in most of these churches, the lack of any long-standing ecclesiastical order leaves room for abuse. It is even unfair to expect the same level of organization and management evident in a 300-year-old denominations from churches that are only a few years old. Western churches need to be objective in looking at these challenges as they embark upon the work of missions in Africa. This way they can take their time and study the projects to which they are committing and make certain that they are on the right track.

Closing Remarks

We need the African-American church to come to us in a spirit of love, humility, and gentleness. If African-Americans would come back to Africa as brothers unto their own brothers and come knowing that we need them to combat a common enemy, the devil, we will welcome them. Then we know that they are, indeed, our own and together we can get the work done. This way the kingdoms of this world will then become the kingdom of our God and of His Christ.

Endnotes

1. Glenn Schwartz, "Its Time To Get Serious About The Cycle of Dependency in Africa," *Evangelical Missions Quarterly*, vol. 29, no. 2, April 1993, pp. 126-130.

2. Chuck Bennett, "Two Christian Leaders Discuss Dependency," *Mission Frontiers*, vol. 19, no. 1-2, January-February 1997, p. 25.

3. Ibid.

Jesus in African Culture

(a Ghanaian perspective)

Kwame Bediako

Christian Faith and African Traditional Religion in Retrospect

One of the most telling commentaries on the presentation of the Gospel of Jesus Christ in Africa is the following statement:

> Christ has been presented as the answer to questions a white man would ask, the solution to the needs that Western man would feel, the Savior of the world of the European worldview, the object of the adoration and prayer of historic Christendom. But if Christ were to appear as the answer to the questions that Africans are asking, what would he look like?[1]

It was made by one of the more perceptive and sensitive missionaries to Africa of our time and describes neatly the general character of Western missionary preaching and teaching in Africa since the arrival of missionaries on our continent during the 19th century. It also raises a question which must be faced by African churches and African Christians of today who are convinced that Jesus Christ is the *Universal* Savior, and thus the Savior of the African world, and who feel that the teaching they have received so far is inadequate.

And yet the negative side of missionary history in Africa must not be exaggerated for several reasons. First, the vitality of our Christian communities bears witness to the fact that the Gospel really was communicated, however inadequate we now may consider that communication to have been. There is always more to the "hearing" of the Word of God than can be contained in the actual preaching of it by the human agents;[2] the Holy Spirit also is present to interpret the Word of God directly to the hearers. Therefore we must allow the mercy and providence of God to override the shortcomings of human achievements.

Second, African theological thinkers now share in the inheritance of the Gospel as the Apostle Paul proclaimed it, the Gospel that set the early Gentile Christians free from Jewish Christian attempts to impose upon them the regulations of the Jewish Law.[3] Paul grasped firmly the universality of the Gospel of Jesus the Messiah, and by insisting that the Gospel includes all peoples without reserve, gave Gentile Christians the essential tools for assessing their own cultural heritage, for making their own contribution to Christian life and thought, and for testing the genuineness and

Kwame Bediako is director of the Akrofi-Christaller Memorial Centre for Mission Research and Applied Theology based at Akropong-Akuapem, Ghana.

First published in 1990 by Asempa Publishers in Accra, Ghana.

Used by permission.

Christian character of that contribution. For many years now African theologians have refused to accept the negative view of African religion held by Western missionaries and have shown consistently the continuity of God from the pre-Christian African past into the Christian present.[4] They have therefore, like the Apostle Paul, handed to us the assurance that with our Christian conversion, we are not introduced to a new God unrelated to the traditions of our past, but to One who brings to fulfillment all the highest religious and cultural aspirations of our heritage. In this way the limitations in our missionary past need no longer hinder the growth of Christian understanding and confidence in our churches.

A further reason touches on the nature of African traditional religion itself and its encounter with the Christian faith. The common Western missionary view of traditional religion was that it formed "the religious beliefs of more or less backward and degraded peoples all over the world"[5] and that it held no "preparation for Christianity." Yet in more recent years, it has been shown that Christianity has spread most rapidly in "societies with primal religious systems,"[6] that is, religious systems akin to African traditional religion. These societies are the Mediterranean world of the early Christian centuries, the ancient peoples of northern Europe, and the modern "primalists" of black Africa, Asia, South America, and Oceania. This fact of history has led to the question whether there might be "affinities between the Christian and primal traditions?" It shows clearly that the form of religion once held to be the furthest removed from the Christian faith has had a closer relationship with it than any other.[7] Indeed, since primal religions have been "the most fertile soil for the Gospel," it has been argued that they "underlie, therefore, the Christian faith of the vast majority of Christians of all ages and all nations."[8] John Mbiti, probably the best-known African theologian outside of Africa, has repeatedly argued that Africa's "old" religions have been a crucial factor in the rapid spread of Christianity among African peoples.[9] They were a vital preparation for the Gospel.

This argument stands the Western missionary view of African religions on its head and so opens the way for a fresh approach to how we may understand the relation of Jesus as Lord and Savior to the spiritual realities of our context.

Christ and Spirit Power

Jesus as Divine Conqueror in the African World

On the wider African scene, John Mbiti has written two articles that deal with African understandings of Christ, drawn largely from evidence from the Independent churches. His view was that it is within these churches that African Christians have been able to express more freely their experience of the Christian faith than in the mission-dominated or historical churches (that is, the mainline denominations).[10] Though the distinctions between "independent" and "historical" churches are now less meaningful than they once were,[11] Mbiti's articles did indicate that there was something to write about, that there are characteristically African understandings of Christ. In this area, as in much else, he has been a pioneer.

By way of illustration I shall highlight two major points he makes in those studies. The first is that Jesus is seen above all else as the *Christus Victor*, Christ supreme over every spiritual rule and authority. This understanding of Christ arises from Africans' keen awareness of forces and powers at work in the world that threaten the interests of life and harmony. Jesus is victorious over the spiritual realm and particularly over evil forces and so answers to the need for a powerful protector against these forces and powers.

The second important point is that for African Christians the term "our Savior" can refer to God and sometimes to the Holy Spirit, as well as to Jesus. Jesus, as our Savior, brings near and makes universal the almightiness of God. This means that He "is able to do all things, to save in all situations, to protect against all enemies, and is available whenever those who believe may call upon Him." It also means that the humanity of Jesus and His atoning work on the Cross are in the background, and Jesus is taken to belong essentially to the more powerful realm of divinity, in the realm of Spirit-power. Though Mbiti considers this view of Christ as inadequate, he does stress that the methods and context of present-day evangelism need to be reexamined and that there needs to be also a "deeper appreciation of the traditional African world, whose grip is so strong that it exercises a powerful influence on the manner of understanding and experiencing the Christian message, however that message may be presented."

These considerations bring us near the heart of the problem that confronts us now: how to understand Christ authentically in the African world. To make my reflections more concrete, I propose to relate them as far as possible to the religious belief and worldview of the Akan peoples. Being an Akan myself, I shall be dealing with realities with which I can easily sympathize. For I believe such reflection can be authentic only in context. I shall be setting forth some of my own concerns with regard to my own Akan world of ideas and beliefs.

Jesus and the Ancestors in Akan Worldview

Accepting Jesus as "our Savior" always involves making Him at home in our spiritual universe and in terms of our religious needs and longings. So an understanding of Christ in relation to spirit-power in the African context is not necessarily less accurate than any other perception of Jesus. The question is whether such an understanding faithfully reflects biblical revelation and is rooted in true Christian experience. Biblical teaching clearly shows that Jesus is who He is (i.e., Savior) because of what He has done and can do (i.e., save), and also that He was able to do what He did on the cross because of who He is (God the Son), cf. Colossians 2:15 ff. Since "salvation" in the traditional African world involves a certain view of the realm of spirit-power and its effects upon the physical and spiritual dimensions of human existence, our reflection about Christ must speak to the questions posed by such a worldview. The needs of the African world require a view of Christ that meets those needs. And so Who Jesus is in the African spiritual universe must

not be separated from what He does and can do in that world. The way in which Jesus relates to the importance and function of the "spirit fathers" or ancestors is crucial.

The Akan spirit world, on which human existence is believed to depend, consists primarily of God, the Supreme Spirit Being (*Onyame*), Creator and Sustainer of the universe. Subordinate to God, with delegated authority from God, are the "gods," (*abosom*), sometimes referred to as children of God (*Nyame mma*) and the ancestors or "spirit fathers" (*Nsamanfo*). The relative positions of the "gods" and the ancestors are summed up by Dr. Peter Sarpong, the Catholic Bishop of Kumasi and an authority on Akan culture:

> While God's power surpasses all others, the ancestors would appear to tilt the scale in their favor if their power could be weighed against that of the lesser gods. After all, are the deities not often referred to as "the innumerable gods of our ancestors," the spokesmen of the human spirits?[12]

John Pobee formerly of the University of Ghana, also has underlined the importance of the ancestors in the religious worldview of the Akan. He has devoted a whole book to developing some aspects of an Akan Christian theology. He concludes that:

> Whereas the gods may be treated with contempt if they fail to deliver the goods expected of them, the ancestors, like the Supreme Being, are always held in reverence or even worshipped.[13]

We shall not discuss here whether ancestors are worshipped or simply venerated. We need only to recognize that the ancestors form the most prominent element in the Akan religious outlook and provide the essential focus of piety. Pobee's comment on the ancestors is therefore well-founded:

> Perhaps the most potent aspect of Akan religion is the cult of the ancestors. They, like the Supreme Being, are always held in deep reverence or even worshipped. The ancestors are that part of the clan who have completed their course here on earth and are gone ahead to the other world to be elder

brothers of the living at the house of God. Not all the dead are ancestors. To qualify to be an ancestor one must have lived to a ripe old age and in an exemplary manner and done much to enhance the standing and prestige of the family, clan or tribe. By virtue of being the part of the clan gone ahead to the house of God, they are believed to be powerful in the sense that they maintain the course of life here and now and influence it for good or ill. They give children to the living; they give good harvest, they provide the sanctions for the moral life of the nation and accordingly punish, exonerate or reward the living as the case may be.[14]

Ancestors are essentially clan or lineage ancestors. So they have to do with the community or society in which their progeny relate to one another, and not with a system of religion as such, which might be categorized as the Akan religion. In this way, the "religious" functions and duties which relate to ancestors become binding on all members of the particular group who share common ancestors. Since the ancestors have such an important part to play in the well-being (or otherwise) of individuals and communities, the crucial question about our relationship to Jesus is, as John Pobee rightly puts it: "Why should an Akan relate to Jesus of Nazareth, Who does not belong to his clan, family, tribe and tradition? "

Up to now, our churches have tended to avoid the question and have presented the Gospel as though it was concerned with an entirely different compartment of life, unrelated to traditional religious piety. As a result, many of our people are uncertain about how the Jesus of the Church's preaching saves them from the terrors and fears which they experience in their traditional worldview. This shows how important it is to relate Christian understanding and experience to the realm of the ancestors. If this is not done, many of our fellow African Christians will continue to be men and women "living at two levels"—half-African and half-European—but never belonging properly to either. We need to meet God in the Lord Jesus Christ speaking immediately to us in our particular circumstances, in a way that assures our people that we can be authentic Africans and true Christians.

John Pobee suggests that we "look on Jesus as the Great and Greatest Ancestor" since "in Akan society the Supreme Being and the ancestors provide the sanctions for the good life, and the ancestors hold that authority as ministers of the Supreme Being."[15] He considers some of the problems involved, but because he approaches the problem largely through Akan wisdom sayings and proverbs, he does not deal sufficiently with the religious nature of the question. In addition, he does not let the biblical revelation speak sufficiently in its own terms into the Akan situation. He too easily assumes similarities between Akan and biblical (for him "Jewish") worldviews, underestimates the potential for conflict, and so does not achieve real encounter. For if we claim as the Greatest Ancestor one Who, at the superficial level, "does not belong to his clan, family, tribe and nation," the Akan non-Christian might well feel that the very grounds of his identity and personality are taken away from him. It is with such fears and dangers, as well as the meanings and intentions behind the old allegiances, that a fresh understanding of Christ has to deal.

The Universality of Jesus Christ And Our Adoptive Past

I suggest that we should read the Scriptures with Akan traditional piety well in view. In this way we can arrive at an understanding of Christ that deals with the perceived reality of the ancestors. I also recommend that we make the biblical assumption that Jesus Christ is not a stranger to our heritage. I, therefore, start from the universality of Jesus Christ rather than from His particularity as a Jew. By doing this I do not disregard the Incarnation; rather I affirm that the Incarnation was the incarnation of the Savior of all people, of all nations, and of all times. Also, by insisting on the primacy of Jesus' universality, we do not seek to reduce His incarnation and its particularity to a mere accident of history. We hold on to His Incarnation as a Jew because by faith in Him, we, too, share in the divine promises given to the patriarchs and through the history of ancient Israel (Eph. 2:11-22). So those promises belong to us also, because of Jesus. Salvation, though "from the Jews" (John 4:22), is not thereby Jewish. To make Jesus little more than a "typical" Jew is to distort the truth. There is clearly more to Him than Jewishness. His statement in John 8:43-44 that a Jew could have for father, not Abraham at all, but the devil, was outrageous from the Jewish point of view. What counts is one's response to Jesus Christ. Here we find one of the clearest statements in Scripture, that our true human identity as men and women made in the image of God, is not to be understood primarily in terms of racial, cultural, national, or lineage categories, but in Jesus Christ Himself. The true children of Abraham are those who put their faith in Jesus Christ in the same way that Abraham trusted God (Rom. 4:11-12).

Consequently, we have not merely our natural past, for through our faith in Jesus we have also an "adoptive" past, the past of God, reaching into biblical history itself. This also—aptly described as the "Abrahamic link"—is our past.[16]

In the same way, Jesus Christ, Himself the image of the Father, by becoming one like us, has shared our *human* heritage. It is within this *human* heritage that He finds us, and speaks to us in terms of its questions and puzzles. He challenges us to turn to Him and participate in the new humanity for which He has come, died, been raised, and glorified.

The Good News as Our Story

Once this basic, universal relevance of Jesus Christ is granted, it is no longer a question of trying to accommodate the Gospel in our culture; we learn to read and accept the Good News as *our* story. Our Lord has been, from the beginning, the Word of God for us as for all people everywhere. He has been the source of our life and illuminator of our path in life, though, like all people everywhere, we also failed to understand him aright. But now He has made Himself known, becoming one of us, one like us. By acknowledging Him for who He is, and by giving Him our allegiance, we become what we are truly intended to be,

by His gift, that is, the children of God. For He Himself is the Son of God, originating from the divine realm. If we refuse Him that allegiance, we lose that right of becoming children of God. Our response to Him is crucial because becoming children of God does not stem from, nor is it limited by, the accidents of birth, race, culture, lineage, or even religious tradition. It comes to us by grace through faith.

This way of reading the early verses of John's Gospel, from the standpoint of faith in Jesus Christ as our story, is valid and necessary. The beginning of the Gospel echoes the early verses of Genesis 1. We are meant to appreciate the close association of our creation and our redemption, both achieved in and through Jesus Christ (Col. 1:15 ff). We are to understand our creation as the original revelation of God to us. It was in the creation of the universe and especially of man that God first revealed His Kingship to our ancestors and called them and us to freely obey Him. Working from this insight, that our creation is the original revelation to and covenant with us, we, from African primal tradition, are given a biblical basis for discovering more about God within the framework of the high doctrine of God as Creator and Sustainer, which is deeply rooted in our heritage. More significantly, we are enabled to discover ourselves in Adam (Acts 17:26) and come out of the isolation which the closed system of clan, lineage, and family imposes, so that we can recover universal horizons.

However, "as in Adam all die..." (I Cor. 15:22). Adam sinned and lost his place in the garden. Where the biblical account speaks of the expulsion of man (Gen 3), African myths of origins talk of the withdrawal of God, so that He is continually in people's thoughts, yet is absent from daily living in any practical sense. The experience of ambiguity which comes from regarding the lesser deities and ancestral spirits as both beneficent and malevolent, can be resolved only in a genuine incarnation of the Savior from the realm beyond. But Trinitarian doctrine is preserved, for the God who has become so deeply and actively involved in our condition is the Son (John 1:18), whom to see is to "see" the Father (John 14:15 ff; Acts 2:38 f, and this is made possible through the Holy Spirit (John 14:23).

Jesus as "Ancestor" and Sole Mediator

Thus the gulf between the intense awareness of the existence of God and yet also of His "remoteness" in African traditional religion and experience is bridged in Christ alone because "there has been a death which sets people free from the wrongs they did while the first covenant was in force" (Heb. 9:15). How does this death relate to our story and particularly to our natural "spirit-fathers"? Some suggest that ours is a "shame-culture" and not a "guilt-culture," on the grounds that public acceptance is what determines morality, and consequently a "sense of sin" is said "to be absent."[17] This view is oversimplified and is challenged by African theologians and sociologists.[18] However, in our tradition the essence of sin is in its being an antisocial act. This makes sin basically injury to the interests of another person and damage to the collective life of the group. K. A. Busia's comment on the Ashanti is significant: "The Ashanti conception of a good society is one in which harmony is achieved among the living, and between the living and the gods and the ancestors...".[19]

Such a view of morality does not resolve the real problem of the assurance of moral transformation, which the human conscience needs. For the real problem of our sinfulness is the soiled conscience and, against this, purificatory rites and sacrificial offerings to achieve social harmony are ineffectual. And yet the view of sin as antisocial seems to be also biblically valid: sin is, indeed, sin against another person and the community's interest. But human beings are the creation of God, created in God's image, so social sin is also sin against God. The blood of Abel cried to God against Cain (Gen 4). The Good News underscore's the valid insight about the social nature of sin, but brings the need for expiation into a wider context. Sin is more than the antisocial act; the sinner sins ultimately against a personal God who has a will and purpose in human history.

Seen from this angle, our needs in our tradition make the insights about Jesus Christ in the Epistle to the Hebrews perhaps the most crucial of all. Our Savior has not just become one like us; He has died for us. It is a death that has eternal sacrificial significance for us. It deals with our moral failures and the infringements of our social relationships. It heals our wounded and soiled consciences and overcomes, once and for all and at their roots, all that in our heritage and our somewhat melancholy history brings us grief, guilt, shame, and bitterness. Our Savior is our Elder Brother who has shared in our *African* experience in every respect, except in our sin and alienation from God, an alienation with which our myths of origins make us only too familiar. Being our true Elder Brother now in, the presence of God, His Father and our Father, He displaces the mediatorial function of our natural "spirit-fathers." For these themselves need saving, since they originated from among us. It is known from African missionary history that sometimes one of the first actions of new converts was to pray for their ancestors who had passed on before the Gospel was proclaimed. Such an action is an important testimony to the depth of these people's understanding that Jesus is sole Lord and Savior Jesus Christ, "the Second Adam" from heaven (1 Cor. 15:47) becomes for us then the only mediator between God and ourselves (1 Tim. 2:5). He is the "mediator of a better covenant" (Heb. 8:6), relating our human destiny directly to God. He is truly our high priest who meets our needs to the full. (We shall have more to discuss on this all-important epistle of the New Testament, later.)

From the kind of understanding held about the spirit-world, the resurrection and ascension of our Lord also come to assume great importance. He has now returned to the realm of spirit and, therefore, of power. From the standpoint of Akan traditional beliefs, Jesus has gone to the realm of the ancestor spirits and the "gods." We already know that power and the resources for living are believed to come from there, but the terrors and misfortunes which could threaten and destroy life come from there also. But if Jesus has gone to the realm of the "spirits and the gods", so to speak, He has gone there as Lord over them in much the same way that He is Lord over us. He is, therefore, Lord over the living and the dead and over the "living-dead," as the ancestors are also described. He is supreme over all "gods" and authorities in the realm of the spirits. So He sums up in Himself all their powers and cancels any terrorizing influence they might be assumed to have upon us.

The guarantee that our Lord is Lord also in the realm of the spirits is that He has sent us His own Spirit, the Holy Spirit, to dwell, with us and be our protector, as much as to be the Revealer of Truth and our Sanctifier. In John 16:7 ff, our Lord's insistence on going away to the Father includes this idea of His Lordship in the realm of spirits, as He Himself enters the region of spirit. It also includes the idea of the protection and guidance which the coming Holy Spirit will provide for His followers in the world. The Holy Spirit is sent to convict the world of its sin in rejecting Jesus, and to demonstrate, to the shame of unbelievers, the true righteousness which is in Jesus and available only in Him. But He is also sent to reveal the spiritual significance of God's judgment, this time not upon the world, but upon the devil, who deceives the world about its sin and blinds people to the perfect righteousness in Christ. Our Lord therefore, entering the region of spirit, sends the Holy Spirit to His followers to give them understanding of the realities in the realm of spirits. The close association of the defeat and overthrow of the devil ("ruler of this world") with the death, resurrection, and exaltation of Jesus (John 12:31) is significant here. In addition, the thought of the "keeping" and the protection of His followers from "the evil one" forms in important part of Jesus' prayer recorded in John 17:9, which is aptly described as His "high priestly" prayer.

These are some areas for us to investigate when we begin to reflect on the Good News from the standpoint of the worldview of our heritage. Some important insights are in store for us, not from isolated passages of Scripture, but from entire and significant bodies of teaching in the Word of God.

The Lordship of Christ Amid Sacred Power

The Position of the Chief: the Problem of Ambiguity

So as to make concrete the Lordship of Christ in relation to the natural "spirit-fathers" or ancestors, let us focus on the way in which Christ's Lordship may be related to the significance of Kingship in our society. This close connection between the place and role of the ancestors and the meaning of Kingship on the one hand, and the place and role of Christ on the other, is due to the fact that the reigning Chief occupies the stool of the ancestors, particularly his royal ancestors. There is more to the Chief's position than simply succession to the office of his deceased predecessors. In the Akan worldview these do not die but simply go "elsewhere," that is, into the realm of the "spirit fathers," from where they continue to show interest and to intervene in the affairs of the state. The installation of the Chief renders his very person sacred. This is done by bringing him into a peculiarly close contact with the ancestors. The ceremony at which this is effected is known to be quite simple. Upon the ritually preserved stool of his most renowned ancestor, the Chief is briefly lowered and raised three times. Once enstooled in this way, the Chief, as Dr. [Peter] Sarpong explains, is "now more than just a head of state. He is, in a sense, an ancestor himself. From that moment everybody must call him Nana (grandfather)."[20] The Akan royal title Nana is itself an ancestral title. The ancestors are Nananom Nsamanfo, that is, ancestor spirits or "spirit-fathers."

Since the cult of the ancestors is the most powerful aspect of religious life in traditional Akan society, the Chief's sacred office has great religious significance. Because the traditional belief is that the well-being of the society depends upon the maintenance of good relations with the ancestors on whom the living depend for help and protection, the Chief acquires a crucial role as the intermediary between the state and the ancestors. He is the central figure at the organized religious ceremonies that ensure the maintenance of harmony between the living and the spirit-fathers. So closely is religion bound up with Akan kingship that in his authoritative study of Ashanti kingship Dr. Busia concluded:

> No one could be an adequate chief who did not perform the ritual functions of his office. There have recently been elected as chiefs in different parts of Ashanti, men who are both literate and Christian. But they have all felt the obligation to perform the ritual acts of their office. They were enstooled in the stool house, where they poured libations to the ancestors whom they had succeeded... It is as ancestors of the ancestors that they are venerated and their authority respected, and they could not keep the office without maintaining contacts with the ancestors through the traditional rituals.[21]

While Busia rightly insists that "the chief's position is bound up with strong religious sentiments," his conclusions also indicate that there is some ambiguity about the position of the Chief who wishes to embrace the Christian faith. Busia himself points to the enstoolment of men "who are Christian," in order to emphasize the significance of his central point that the institution of Chiefship is basically of a sacral nature. Furthermore, Dr. Busia was well-known for his view that our churches must come to terms with the Akan understanding of the universe and the nature of society, particularly its religious aspects.

Since Busia wrote in the 1950s, the ambiguity that characterizes the relation of the Chief to the Christian community in our society has continued. It has remained as a crucial area of confrontation between the Christian faith, as generally understood in our context, and the religious traditions of Akan culture. When the Moderator of the Presbyterian Church of Ghana inaugurated in March 1981 a committee, charged with the specific responsibility of studying the relation of the Church to traditional culture, he drew attention to the persisting ambiguity of the Chief's position. According to the report, many Chiefs have been baptized and confirmed, but their positions prevent them from becoming full members of the church. The question which he posed was: "What can bring these Chiefs and the church together?"[22]

The Problem of the Chief's Authority

The moderator was not the first to ask that question. Behind the decision to set up this committee lay the desire of some Chiefs, with their traditional Councils, to understand more fully how the Christian faith, which they cannot now ignore, relates to the cultural tradition in which they themselves stand. This is not the first instance of such an initiative by our Chiefs. In 1941 the Chiefs and elders of the Akan state of Akim-Abuakwa sent a memorandum to the synod of the Presbyterian Church that was meeting in the Chief's capital, Kibi. The memorandum criticized the church on several counts, and particularly complained about what the state authorities saw as the disruptive effect of separating Christian converts into a community apart in each town in order to guard against what were considered to be "pagan" influences. This undermined the unified authority of the Chief over his natural subjects.

Another state response to the Christian presence occurred in the same year, 1941, from Ashanti. The Ashanti Confederacy Council decreed that farming on Thursday, the natal day of the earth deity, Asaase Yaa, was to be regarded as an offense. Since the Christian community had, in the meantime, become quite a significant factor in the state, it is understandable that the traditional authorities were disturbed by evidence of increasing violation of this law, mainly on the part of Christians.

The Christian churches concerned responded to the state authorities on each of these points of state criticism. In the earlier case, the church pointed to the social and educational benefits of its work and stressed the Christians' loyalty to the state. In the second case, the Christian churches in Ashanti presented a memorandum to the Asantehene on the relations between Christians and the state. The memorandum asserted the rights of Christian conscience with regard to the law on grounds of Christian belief, and while protesting the loyalty of Christians to the state, attempted to secure a dispensation from the law for Christians. The heart of the churches' argument for our purposes was found in paragraph 6:

> "On the part of the chiefs we would ask that they accept as a fact the existence of Christians as members of their state and lay down ways by which they can show their allegiance to their chiefs without at the same time offending their Christian conscience."[24]

I shall not discuss in detail the issues raised in these two instances of conflict between Akan traditional authorities and the Christian churches within their jurisdiction. But while the Christian faith was obviously attacking the institutions of sacral kingship as well as the position of the Chief in some of its most vital aspects, that is, its specifically religious dimensions, none of the Christian responses seem to have addressed themselves to these issues. The memorandum to the Asantehene tried to apply fully developed Western Christian ideas on church and state to a sacred order, which made no sharp distinctions between religious and political institutions. Busia's comment on this controversy provides a useful insight into the deeper issues at stake:

> In a society in which political and religious office are combined, the chiefs regard the request for the recognition of the existence of Christians and for the adaptation of native law as a request for the surrender of authority. As they see it, the Christian church requests that they should not have power to legislate on certain things for certain members of the community because the church desires the right to legislate on these for those of the chief's subjects who have embraced the Christian faith. Christianity challenges the traditional position of the chief as the religious as well as the political head of his tribe.[25]

The Factor of Christ and the Desacralization of Political Power

Behind this conflict between two authorities—the Christian church and the traditional state—lie two conceptions of power and differing views as to the source of power. In the religious view of the world underlying Akan social organization, the power of the reigning Chief as the channel through which cosmic forces operated for the well-being of the society was based on his position as one "who sits on the stool of the ancestors." The power of the Chief among the living is, therefore, the power of the ancestors, sacral power, just as his title (Nana) is also theirs. Consequently, presentations of Christ that fundamentally undermine and remove the power of the ancestors over the living at the same time undermine the sacred power of the reigning Chief. We may wonder how many of our Chiefs who now desire closer links with Christian churches realize how far their power as well as their own persons, would need to be desacralized. Perhaps some of our natural rulers may rather be men among men. An understanding of Christ, which alters so radically the nature and source of power, carries inevitably immense implications for politics in our societies.

Here I mean politics in a wider sense than the political organization of our sacred states. Historically, biblical faith has had the effect of desacralizing societies,[26] and the story of Christianity in Africa has also demonstrated this quality in the Christian faith.[27] Much of the prestige associated with kingship in the past has been lost in the process of social change. New forms of political administration have been forged with the emergence of the new nation-states and their elected presidents. The natural ruler who sits on the stool of the ancestors is compelled now to seek ways of coming to terms with the new realities.

However, sacralization of political power is not confined to the old order. It can find its way into the new ideology of states as a secular parody of the old, genuinely religious social organism. Some modern African republics need to be understood from this angle. In so many of our modem nation-states, the leaders who achieved political independence often insisted on holding on to power even when they became unpopular. This may well reflect the role of the royal ancestor who never ceases to rule from the realm of spirit-power! Certainly praise-names and titles of some African presidents bear ancestral overtones. When Dr. Kwame Nkrumah accepted the title of "Osagyefo" [President], he must have known what he was doing. Nkrumah was not concerned with promoting the interests of the "old" sacral rulers and he was not from a royal house himself. But the title "Osagyefo" portrayed him as the "Savior" from British colonial rule. Under his presidency, Ghana's coins bore his image and the inscription: Civitatis Ghaniensis Conditor, Founder of the State of Ghana. Nkrumah, for all practical purposes, became an ancestor in the old sacral sense. It is not surprising that the Young Pioneers recited, "Nkrumah never dies!"

I have not drawn attention to the modern secular politics of African societies in order to lessen the significance of the old order. On the contrary, if we are to know how to deal as Christians with the problems of contemporary politics in our societies, we may need to find ways of getting to grips with the forces at work the old order, which have not yet been touched adequately by the Gospel. If there is to be a genuine encounter with the realities behind the traditional institutions at the level at which our people experience them, it is important that the Gospel of Jesus Christ be seen as our story also. If it is true that "the sovereignty of the world has passed to our Lord and His Christ, and He shall reign for ever and ever" (Rev, 11:15, NEB), this must find its meaning also in our context. In terms of the old sacred order, it is understandable that one Asantehene should say, "I am the center of this world around which everything revolves." And one of his subjects is reported to have said of him, "Everything comes out of him; he is holding the source of power, force and generation."[28]

However, what happens when the spirit-fathers who ensure such power to the reigning chief become subservient to Christ the Lord? What happens to the position of the chief, who sits on the stool of the ancestors, when it becomes evident that Christ Himself is the Great Ancestor of *all* mankind, the Mediator of *all* divine blessing, the Judge of *all* mankind and that access to Him is not dependent on inherited right through royal lineage, but through grace and faith and repentance from the heart? Will the chief be a man among men, respected, and honored, but not venerated or worshipped?

All this goes to indicate that the Christian faith has a unique contribution to make towards the development of such forms of political life as ensures an adequate sharing by all persons in *real* power and so enhance stability in any society. The pointer to the Christian contribution is seen in Jesus' attitude to power. When Jesus told Pontius Pilate that His (Jesus') Kingdom was not of this world (John 18:36), He could not have meant that it had nothing to do with this world. If He had meant that, then His coming as *Savior of the world* would have been meaningless. His meaning could only have been that He held a conception of kingship and power which was fundamentally different from that which Pilate was used to and practiced.

The clue to and the logic of what our Lord meant are symbolized in the cross, which He willingly embraced, the symbol of His death which Pilate sanctioned. The Christian Scriptures are quite clear that Jesus won His way to preeminence and glory not by exalting Himself, but rather by humbling Himself, to the point of dying the shameful death on the Cross. In other words, by making Himself of no account, everyone now must take account of Him: "All beings in heaven, on earth, and in the world below will fall on their knees and will openly proclaim that Jesus Christ is Lord, to the glory of God the Father." (Phil. 2:10-11, TEV)

The essential character of Jesus' conception of power is that of power as nondominating. This understanding of power will always remain one of the most significant Christian contributions to politics in any society, particularly to those that are feeling their way towards a true and genuine, open sharing in political power. Faith in Jesus Christ, as alone, Lord and Mediator of blessings and power frees political leaders to become true human beings among fellow humans. It ennobles politics itself into a service of God in the service of our fellow human beings. Without such a conception of power as Jesus held, taught, and demonstrated by the cross, the hope of achieving a real sharing of political power in any society will remain elusive.

The Relevance of Christian History

These problems are not peculiar to our context and are certainly not new in Christian history. The very early centuries of the Christian era are the most instructive for our purposes. Those early Christians were convinced that in the Good News about Jesus Christ and through Jesus Christ they found access to the God beyond the gods, and that Jesus Christ met their spiritual needs and inspired higher hopes.

For this reason they were able to make a definite break within the cult of the emperor. However, many earnest men and women did not make that break, even though they may have disapproved of much in the popular and state cults; they were not gripped by the Gospel. For such people the Gospel was alien, if not distasteful. But not so for the Christians. The Gospel assured them that the, sovereignty of the world had indeed passed to their Lord and so all other claims to sovereignty paled into insignificance. And they won, as John was shown on Patmos, "by the blood of the Lamb and by the truth which they proclaimed; and they were willing to give up their lives and die" (Rev. 12:11, TEV).

The message is quite clear: the heart of the encounter of the Good News with our context is our understanding of Jesus Christ— how our faith in Jesus Christ, crucified and risen, relates to our existence and destiny in the world. With such faith comes a firm conviction that in and through Christ, we have found and been found by ultimate Truth, which is utterly dependable for interpreting our human experience. We also are bound to discover that we are involved in a struggle to the death. It is not with flesh and blood, but with more subtle powers and intelligence who would hinder men and women from perceiving the nearness of Christ as One Who has opened for us a new way, a living way, into the presence of God, through His own body and as one of us! (Heb. 10:20).

Bearing Witness to Christ as a Power Encounter

True witness to Christ, then, has to do with encounter, "pulling down strongholds," "destroying false arguments," leveling "every proud obstacle," taking every thought captive and making it obey Christ (1 Cor.

10:4-5). But this kind of encounter does not wait for the "specialists" and the "experts." It takes place in the normal worshipping, witnessing life of the congregation, as the following incident reported a few years ago shows:

Drumbeat in Church

A sharp conflict recently erupted between the Christian churches and the traditional authorities in the Ghanaian town of Akim Tafo over the violation by the churches of a ban on drumming during a traditional religious festival. During the two weeks preceding the "Ohurm" religious festival, drumming, clapping of hands, wailing, firing of musketry and any other noises likely to disturb the gods is not permitted. But Christian churches in the town ignored the ban and continued to allow drumming during their worship services, arguing that drumming was an essential part of the Ghanaian form of worship.[29]

Obviously it is the fact of drumming in church that, in view of our missionary past, the reporter found most striking. I am more interested in the fact that the controversy took place in the context of worship. We have here an encounter of experiences and of views of reality. We have a power encounter. It is equally interesting that the Christians claim their drumming in church to be "an essential part of the Ghanaian form of worship." They do not say *Christian* form of worship. However, since they are Christians, we have to assume that their worship has to do with Jesus Christ and not with the "gods" of the "traditional religious festival." So, we may ask, who are maintaining the authentic *Ghanaian* form of worship?

Our Christian brethren here have grasped the insight of the early Christians, that the issue at stake is not the confrontation of two religions or religious systems. The Gospel has to do with grace and personality, with God manifesting His love for us in and through Christ, touching our hearts and opening our eyes through His Spirit, so that we can respond to His love where He finds us, in our heritage of culture and religious tradition.

Could it be that in their own way the Akan Christians of Akim-Tafo have understood that Christian identity (for salvation has to do also with identity—God calls us by name). It has to do with the discovery of our true personality in Christ, touching both individual and social levels of our existence, and that this discovery, which is a gift of Christ, itself becomes the basis of confidence.

I doubt whether I have claimed too much for the theological awareness of the Christians of Akim-Tafo. Their attitude seems to have something of the understanding that I have described. This enabled them to confront the traditional authorities on the common ground of a belief in the value of worship and to challenge the devotees of the "old" gods (and ancestors) to recognize that their own *Christian* worship with the aid of drums, even though it might be in violation of a traditional religious ban, is in its own right authentic Ghanaian worship.

Such incidents and actions ought to give us hope. They show me that the approach I outlined above ties in with the Christian experience of those who share in the same cultural heritage.

The Epistle to the Hebrews as OUR *Epistle!*

Now I should like to return to what I indicated earlier about the importance for our situation of the Epistle to the Hebrews. It has often been assumed that the problem of theology in New Testament times was how to relate the Gospel to Gentile cultures and traditions. The meaning of Christ for Jewish religious tradition was thought to be relatively simple. The Epistle to the Hebrews however corrects that error. The writer is aware that some Hebrews might be tempted to turn from the proclamation of the great salvation in Christ. His frequent warnings about the danger of falling away from Christ may sometimes sound theoretical. He balances them with assurances that his readers would not fall away from their Christian discipleship. Yet he is also conscious that he is seeking to give them "solid food" and that some of the readers might not be used to such heavy diet.

The clue to the Epistle's teaching lies in its presentation of Christ. Hebrews is the one book in the New Testament in which Jesus Christ is understood and presented as High Priest. His priestly mediatorial role is fully explored and we are given one of the highest and most advanced understandings of Christ in the entire New Testament.

One of the most significant statements in the epistle must be Heb. 8:4, "If He were on earth, He would not be a priest at all" And yet it is obvious that our Savior does and did fulfill a high priestly function in His redemptive work for us. The problem arises when one has to justify that insight on the basis of Old Testament prophecies and anticipation. The fact is, "He was born a member of the tribe of Judah; and Moses did not mention this tribe when he spoke of priests" (Heb. 7:14). Thus the view of Christ in Hebrews involves making room in the tradition of priestly mediation for One who, at the purely human level, was an outsider to it. How were the Hebrews to take this demonstration? "Why should an Akan relate to Jesus of Nazareth Who does not belong to his clan, family, tribe, and nation?" My suggestion is that a similar question must have occurred to some Hebrews in time past, and the Epistle to the Hebrews was written to answer that question.

The way the writer of the Epistle to the Hebrews approaches the question we have indicated is to work *from* the achievement of Jesus—in the meaning of His death and resurrection—into the biblical tradition of sacrifice and high priestly mediation. In the process, the *universality* of the Lord from heaven, that is, His universal significance as the Savior of *all* people everywhere, comes to form the basis of the call to Hebrew people to take Him seriously as *their* Messiah. Even more striking, the writer shows that the high priesthood of Jesus is not after the order of Aaron, the first Hebrew high priest, but rather after that of the enigmatic non-Hebrew, and greater priest-king, Melchizedek (Heb.7,8 cq'd.). Therefore, the priesthood, mediation, and, hence, the salvation that Jesus Christ brings to *all* people everywhere belong to an entirely different category from what people may claim for their clan, family, tribal, and national priests and mediators. It is the quality of the achievement and ministry of Jesus Christ for and on behalf of *all* people, together with Who He is, that reveal His absolute supremacy. In other words, as One Who is fully divine, He nonetheless took on human nature in order to offer Himself in death as sacrifice for human sin. Jesus Christ is unique not because He stands apart from us; rather, He is unique because no one has identified so profoundly with the human predicament as He has done, in order to transform it. The uniqueness of Jesus Christ is rooted in his radical and direct significance for every human person and every human context and every human culture.

But the specific value for us of the presentation of Jesus in the Epistle to the Hebrews stems from its relevance to a society like ours with its long and deep tradition of (a) sacrifice, (b) priestly mediation, and (c) ancestral function. In relation to each of these features of our religious heritage the Epistle to the Hebrews shows Jesus Christ to be truly the answer to the spiritual longings and aspirations which our people have sought to meet in the ways that our traditions have evolved.

(a) Sacrifice

Sacrifices as a means of ensuring a harmonious relationship between the human community on the one hand, and the realm of divine and mystical power on the other, are regular events in Ghanaian society. It is easy to assume that the mere performance of sacrifice is sufficient, and yet the real problem with sacrifice is whether it achieves its purpose. Hebrews gives us the fundamental insight that since it is *human* sin and wrongdoing that sacrifice seeks to purge and atone for, in real terms, no animal or subhuman victim can stand in for human beings. Nor can any sinful human being stand in for fellow sinners. So it becomes clear that the action of Jesus Christ, Himself divine and sinless, yet taking on human nature in order to willingly lay down His life for all humanity, fulfills perfectly the end that all sacrifices seek to achieve:

> "When Christ went through the tent and entered once and for all into the Most Holy Place, He did not take the blood of bulls and goats to offer as sac-

rifice; rather He took His own blood and obtained eternal salvation for us" (Heb. 9:12).

No number of animal or other victims offered on any number of shrines in the land can ever equal the *one, perfect* sacrifice made by Jesus Christ of Himself *for all time and for all peoples everywhere*. To *reject the worth of the achievement* of Jesus Christ on the grounds of a theory of race, ethnicity, and cultural tradition, as some would counsel, is to act against better knowledge, distort religious truth, and walk into a blind alley. To choose such a path, in the words of the Epistle to the Hebrews, is to court "the fearful prospect of judgment and the fierce fire which will destroy those who oppose God" (Heb. 10:27). There is no need to arrive at such an end.

(b) Priestly Mediation

If the quality of Jesus' self-offering in death sets His sacrifice above all sacrifices and achieves perfect atonement, so also His priestly mediation surpasses all others. Since Jesus had no human hereditary claim to priesthood (Heb. 7:14, 8:4) the way is open for appreciating His priestly ministry for what it truly is. His taking of human nature in His incarnation enabled Him to share the human predicament and so qualified Him to act for humanity. His divine origin ensures that He is able to mediate between the human community and the divine realm in a way that no merely human priest can ever do. As Himself God-man, therefore, Jesus bridges the gulf between the Holy God and sinful human beings and so achieves for humanity the harmonious fellowship with God which all human priestly mediations seek to effect, but can only approximate.

And yet His priestly ministry takes place not in an earthly temple nor an earthly shrine. Indeed, it cannot, since no earthly temple or shrine can ever match the quality of His ministry. Rather, His priestly mediation takes place in the realm where it really matters, and where all issues are truly decided, namely, in the divine presence. "For Christ did not go into a man-made Holy Place...He went into heaven itself, where He now appears on our behalf in the presence of God" (Heb. 9:24).

But the priestly mediation of Christ has done more than acts "on our behalf." It actually brings priestly mediation to an end by bringing also into the divine presence all who by faith associate themselves with Him. The meeting of the perfect sacrifice with the perfect priestly mediation in the same single person, Jesus Christ, is extraordinary, and it means that having identified with humanity in order to taste death on *behalf* of humanity (Heb. 2:14-15), He has opened the way for all who identify with Him to be *with* Him in the divine presence (Heb. 10:19-20).

This unique achievement of the priestly mediation of Christ renders, therefore, all other priestly mediations obsolete, thus revealing their ineffectiveness. To disregard the surpassing worth of the priestly mediation of Jesus Christ for all people everywhere and to choose, instead, ethnic priesthood, in the name of cultural heritage is to fail to recognize the true meaning and end of all priestly mediation, to abdicate from belonging within the one community of humanity, and to clutch at the shadow and miss the substance. The whole thrust of the Epistle to the Hebrews is that such error is not only unredeemable, but also it is utterly unnecessary.

(c) Ancestral Function

Of the three features of our traditional heritage we are considering, ancestral function seems, on the face of it, to be the one to which Jesus Christ least easily answers. Although we have touched upon this subject briefly earlier, we can now treat it more thoroughly.

Ancestors are lineage or family ancestors and so belong to us; they are by nature *ours*. One might claim that whatever may be said in relation to sacrifice and priestly mediation, the cult of ancestors is beyond the reach of Christian argument. In other words, if the cult of ancestors is valid, then here is solid ground on which traditional religion can take a firm stand.

Yet it is precisely here that the problem lies. In what does the validity of the cult of the ancestors consist? Since not all become ancestors but only those who lived exemplary lives and from whom the community derived some benefit, are not ancestors in effect a projection into the transcendent realm of the social values and spiritual expectations of the living community? Since traditional society views existence as one integrated whole, linking the living and the departed in a common life, such a projection is understandable. However, the essential point is that ancestors have no independent existence from the community that produces them. The cult of ancestors provides the basis for locating in the transcendent realm the source of authority and power in the community. It is this that gives to leadership itself a sacred quality, as we noted in our discussion of the religious aspects of kingship (chieftaincy) in Akan society.

Strictly speaking, therefore, the cult of ancestors, from the intellectual point of view, belongs to the category of myth, ancestors being the product of the myth-making imagination of the community. To characterize the cult of ancestors by the word "myth" is not to say that the cult is unworthy of serious attention. Rather, the term stresses the functional value of the cult of ancestors, for myth is sacred, enshrining, and expressing some of the most valued elements of a community's self-understanding. The cult of ancestors as myth, therefore, points to the role of the cult in ensuring social harmony by strengthening the ties that knit together all sections and generations of the community, the present with the past and with those as yet unborn. On each of the occasions of heightened feeling in the community—birth and outdooring of infants, initiation into adulthood, marriage, death, as well as the installation of a chief and celebration of harvests—the cult of ancestors forms an essential part of the ritual ceremonies that secure the conditions upon which the life and continuity of the community are believed to depend.

However, it is also important to realize that since ancestors do not originate, in the first place, from the transcendent realm, it is the myth-making imagination of the community itself which sacralizes them, conferring upon them the sacred authority they exercise through those in the community, like chiefs, who also expect to become ancestors. Earlier we noted Prof. John Pobee's comment that "perhaps the most potent aspect of Akan (traditional) religion is the cult of the ancestors." Now we can state more clearly that the potency of the cult of ancestors is *not* the potency of ancestors themselves; the potency of the cult is the potency of myth.

Once the meaning of the cult of ancestors as myth is granted and its function is understood within the overall religious life of traditional society, then it begins to become clear how Jesus Christ fulfills our aspirations in relation to ancestral function, too. Ancestors are considered worthy of honor for having "lived among us" and for having brought benefits to us; Jesus Christ has done infinitely more. They, originating from among us, had no choice but to live among us. But He, reflecting the brightness of God's glory and He, the exact likeness of God's own being (Heb. 1:3), took our flesh and blood, became like us, shared our human nature and underwent death for us to set us free from the fear of death (Heb. 2:14-15). He who has every reason to abandon sinful humans to their just deserts is not ashamed to call us His brethren (Heb. 2:11). Our natural ancestors had no barriers to cross to live among us and share our experience. His incarnation implies that He has achieved a far more profound identification with us in our humanity than the mere ethnic solidarity of lineage ancestors can ever do.

Jesus Christ surpasses our natural ancestors also by virtue of who He is in Himself. Ancestors, even described as "ancestral spirits," nonetheless remain essentially human spirits; whatever benefit they may be said to bestow upon their communities is, therefore, effectively contained by the fact of their being human. Jesus Christ, on the other hand, took on human nature without loss to His divine nature. Belonging in the eternal realm as Son of the Father (Heb. 1:1, 48; 9:14)—He has nonetheless taken human nature into Himself (Heb. 10:19) and so, as God-man, He ensures an infinitely more effective ministry to *human* beings (Heb. 7:25) than can never be said of merely human ancestral spirits.

The writer of the Epistle of the Hebrews, confronted by the reality of the eternal nature of Jesus Christ, is lost for words and has to fall back on the enigmatic Melchizedek of Gen. 14:17-20 for analogy: without father or mother, without beginning or end, he (Melchizedek) is *like* the Son of God (Jesus Christ). The likeness is only in thought, for Jesus has actually demonstrated, through His resurrection from the dead, his possession of an indestructible life (Heb. 7:16). This can never be said of ancestors. The persistence of the cult of ancestors is owed, accordingly, not to their demonstrable power to act, but to the power of the myth that sustains them in the corporate mind of the community. This means that the presumption that ancestors actually function for the benefit of their communities can be seen to be part of the same myth making imagination which projects departed human beings into the transcendent realm in the first place. We cannot in this study consider in detail the spiritual dynamics of the world of traditional religion, for, indeed, spiritual forces do operate here, too. My point is that ancestral spirits as human spirits which have not demonstrated any power over death, the final enemy, cannot be presumed to act in the way tradition ascribes to them.

Since ancestral function as traditionally understood is now shown to have no basis in fact, the way is open for appreciating more fully how Jesus Christ is the only real and true Ancestor and Source of Life for all mankind, fulfilling and transcending the benefits believed to be bestowed by lineage ancestors. By His unique achievement in perfect atonement through His own self-sacrifice, and by effective eternal mediation and intercession as God-man in the divine presence, He has secured eternal redemption (Heb. 9:12) for all those who acknowledge Who He is for them and what He has done for them, abandon the blind alleys of merely human traditions and rituals and instead entrust themselves to Him. As mediator of a new and better covenant between God and humanity (Heb. 8:6; 12:24), Jesus brings the redeemed into the experience of a new identity in which He links their human destinies directly and consciously with the eternal gracious will and purpose of a loving and caring God (Heb. 12:22-24). No longer are human horizons bounded by lineage, clan, tribe, or nation, for the redeemed now belong within the community of the living God, in the joyful company of the faithful of all ages and climes. They are united in a fellowship which through their union with Christ, is infinitely richer than the mere social bonds of lineage, clan, tribe, or nation, which exclude the "stranger" as a virtual "enemy".

Some Concluding Observations

Reading and Hearing the Word of God In Our Own Language

In the light of the significance of Jesus Christ as taught in the Epistle to the Hebrews, it becomes clear that for the first readers of the epistle, as for us, there is no valid alternative to Jesus Christ. Once this discovery is made, the important question is no longer: why should we relate to Jesus of Nazareth, Who does not belong to our clan, family, tribe, and nation? Rather the question becomes: how may we understand more fully this Jesus Christ, Who, in fact, relates to us most meaningfully and most profoundly in our clan, family, tribe, and nation? One of the helpful ways of growing in this understanding is to seriously read and listen to the Word of God in our own Ghanaian languages.

In matters of religion there is no language that speaks to the heart and mind and to our innermost feelings as does our mother-tongue. The achievement of Christianity with regard to this all-important place of language in religion is truly unique. For Christianity is, among all religions, the most culturally translatable, hence, the most truly universal, being able to be at home in every cultural context without injury to its essential character. For a Scriptural religion which roots religious authority in a particular collection of sacred writings, this achievement is truly remarkable. The explanation for this must lie with Christianity's refusal of a "sacred" language. With the exception of the dominant role of Latin in the European phase of Christianity and in some sectors of Roman Catholicism, Christianity has, in the course of its expansion, developed generally as a "vernacular" religion. The significance of this fact has been most marked historically in Africa, where the early possession of the Scriptures in the mother-tongue meant that many African

peoples had access to the original sources of Christian teaching, on the authority of which they could, if need be, establish their *own* churches. The "mushrooming" of churches is *not* always evidence of the activity of foreign agents; in the majority of cases it indicates how fully at home we Africans have become in the Gospel of Jesus Christ. Each one of us, with access to the Bible in our mother-tongue, can truly claim to hear God speaking to us in our own language!

The importance of this fact is a theological one. Unlike, say, the Qu'ran, which when translated becomes less than its fullness in Arabic, the Bible in the vernacular remains in every respect the Word of God. This Christian belief has its basis in what took place at the very outset of the preaching of the Gospel on the Day of Pentecost. For the Holy Spirit, through the first Christian witness spoke at one and the same time to people "who had come from every country in the world (Acts 2:5, TEV), each in his own language; therefore, is not to be sneered at and left to "illiterates"; rather it is what is required if we seriously seek growth in our understanding of Jesus Christ (Acts 2:1-12).

A final comment on the Epistle to the Hebrews will clarify the point. The second part of Heb. 1:3 in two popular versions of the Bible reads as follows:

> "When He had made purification for sins, He sat down at the right hand of the Majesty on high" (RSV).
> "After achieving forgiveness for the sins of mankind, He sat down in heaven at the right hand side of God, the Supreme Power" (TEV).

The Akuapim Twi version of the same text reads as follows: "Ode n'ankasa ne ho dwiraa yen bone no, okotraa anuonyam kese no nifa so osorosoro" (Apam Foforo).

If Akan speakers read their Bibles only in the English versions, neglecting the Word of God in their *own* language, it is conceivable that they would dutifully attend and participate in every annual *Odwira* Festival without ever coming to the realization that the traditional purificatory rituals of *Odwira*, repeated year after year, have in fact been fulfilled and transcended by the one, perfect *Odwira*. Jesus

Christ has performed once and for *all*, and for all people everywhere, a perfect *Odwira* that has secured an eternal redemption for all who cease from their own works of purification and instead trust in Him and in His perfect *Odwira*. The Twi here is more expressive than the English versions, it is Jesus Christ in Himself, Who has become our *Odwira* (*ode n'ankasa ne ho dwiraa yεn bone no*). The *Odwira* to end all *odwiras* has, accordingly, taken place.

What remains for us is to live to His praise, to pray and to seek for more understanding, and proclaim Him to our people. There is perhaps no better way to bring this study to a close than to quote this simple, artless yet direct adoration of Jesus by Madam Afua Kuma. It expresses the refreshing sense of newness and fulfillment that comes from a real encounter with Jesus. (Her *Prayers and Praises*, both in the original Twi and in the English translation by Fr. John Kirby, are highly recommended.)

Nkwagyesem afa yen kra nnommum
de yEn akotra asase foforo so.
YEne asofo di nhyiam,
adom ne nhyira nko
na yEn nsa aka.

YEaba wiase abEbrE yEn ho,
Yesu mu na yEakc home.

Salvation has taken our souls captive
and carried us off to a new land.
Along the Way we met with asofo;
grace and blessing alone have we received.

We have come to this earth
only to work and wear ourselves out.
But in Jesus we find our rest.[30]

Endnotes

1. John V. Taylor. *The Primal Vision--Christian Presence Amid African Religion*, London: SCM Press, 1963, p.16.

2. John V. Taylor. *The Growth of the Church in Buganda--An Attempt at Understanding*, London: SCM Press, 1958.

3. See Acts 15 and also Paul's Letter to the *Galatians*.

4. See, among others, E. Bolaji Idowu. *Olodumare—God in Yoruba Belief*, London: Longmans, 1962; J.S. Mbiti. *Concepts of God in Africa,* London: SPCK, 1970; G.M. Setiloane. *The Image of God Among the Sotho-Tswana*, Rotterdam: A.A. Balkema, 1976.

5. W.H.T. Gairdner. Edinburgh 1910. *An Account and Interpretation of the World Missionary Conference*, London: Oliphant, Anderson and Ferrier, 1910, p.139.

6. A.F. Walls. "Africa and Christian Identity" in *Mission Focus*, vol. IV, no. 7, (Nov. 1978), pp.11-13.

7. W. Turner. "The Primal Religions of the World and their Study" in Victor C. Hayes (ed), *Australian Essays in World Religions*, Australian Society for the Study of Religions, Bedford Park; South Australia, 1977, p. 37.

8. A.T. Walls. "Africa and Christian Identity", p.11.

9. See John S. Mbiti. "The Encounter between Christianity and African Religion" in *Temenos*, 12 Helsinki, 1976, pp.125-135.

10. See John S. Mbiti. " 'Our Savior' as an African Experience" in B. Lindars and S. Smalley (eds.), *Christ and the Spirit in the New Testament (Essays in Honor of C.F.D. Moule)*, Cambridge University Press, 1973, pp. 397-414.

11. A.F. Walls. "The Anabaptists of Africa? The Challenge of the African Independent Churches" in *Occasional Bulletin of Missionary Research*, vol. 3, no. 2, (April, 1979), pp. 48-51.

12. Peter Sarpong. *Ghana in Retrospect—Some aspects Of Ghanaian Culture*, Accra-Tema: Ghana Publishing Corporation, 1974, p. 43.

13. John S. Pobee. *Toward an African Theology*, Nashville, TN: Abingdon, 1979, p. 48.

14. John S. Pobee. *Toward an African Theology,* p. 46.

15. John S. Pobee. *Toward an African Theology*, p. 94.

16. A.F. Walls. "Africa and Christian Identity", p.13.

17. See F.B. Welbourn. "Some Problems of African Christianity: Guilt and Shame" in C.G. Baeta (ed.), *Christianity in Tropical Africa*, London: Oxford University Press, pp.182-199; cf. John V. Taylor, *The Primal Vision,* pp.166-169.

18. John S. Pobee. *Toward an African Theology*, pp. 102 ff; cf. K.A. Busia, "The Ashanti" in Daryll Ford (ed.), *African Worlds—Studies in the Cosmological Ideas and Social Values of African Peoples*, London: Oxford University Press, 1954, p. 207.

19. K.A. Busia. "The Ashanti" in Daryll Forde (ed), *African Worlds,* p. 207.

20. Peter Sarpong. *The Sacred Stools of the Akan*, Accra-Tema: Ghana Publishing Corporation, 1971, p. 54, cf. p. 26.

21. K.A. Busia. *The Position of the Chief in the Modern Political System of Ashanti (A Study of the Influence of Contemporary Social Changes on Ashanti Political Institutions)*, London: Frank Cass, 1968, 1st published 1951, p. 38.

22. *Christian Messenger,* Accra, vol. IV, no. 4, (April 1981), p. 3.

23. S.G. Williamson. *Akan Religion and the Christian Faith, A Comparative Study of the Impact of Two Religions*, Accra: Ghana Universities Press, 1965, pp. 152-153.

24. See K.A. Busia. *The Position of the Chief.* pp. 220-222; cf. pp.133-138.

25. K.A. Busia. *The Position of the Chief*, p.137.

26. Cf. H.W. Turner. "The Place of Independent Religious Movements in the Modernisation of Africa" in *Journal of Religion in Africa*, vol. 11, 1969, pp. 43-63, esp. pp. 49ff.

27. A.F. Walls. "Towards Understanding Africa's Place in Christian History" in J.S. Pobee (ed), *Religion in a Pluralistic Society, Essays Presented to C.G. Baeta*, Leiden: E.J. Brill, 1976, pp. 180-189.

28. See Eva L.R. Meyerowitz. *The Sacred State of the Akan*, London: Faber and Faber, 1951, p. 57, note 1.

29. *Voice Weekly*, (Sept. 3-9, 1980), p. 6.

30. Afua Kuma. *Jesus of the Deep Forest—Prayers and Praises of Akua Kuma,* Accra: Asempa Publishers, 1981, (Twi and English), p. 25.

Mobilizing the African-American Church for Global Evangelization

Vaughn J. Walston

African-Americans make up about 12 percent of the U.S. population, but less than one percent of the American missionary force to the world. Why is this? What can be done to change it? It has been said that African-Americans are in a position to become one of the most effective mission forces in the world. The need today is mobilization.

The Manila Manifesto held as its motto, "The Whole Church Taking the Whole Gospel to the Whole World."[1] The African-American church is a part of the whole church and the African-American church can relate to a whole Gospel. The problem is that the African-American church is not involved in the whole world. Most African-American churches know little about crosscultural missions and even fewer are involved in crosscultural ministry.

In the pages to follow, I will recap our historical involvement and summarize our current obstacles. To conclude, I propose several recommendations for global impact. We have great potential to do great things for the mighty God we serve, not only in our own communities, but in the world.

Underrepresentation in Missions

The number of African-American missionaries serving cross-culturally has always been proportionately low. What are the reasons for this underrepresentation? Why is it still the case today? What will it take to change it?

History

The modern missions movement of the Protestant church began somewhat officially with the great step of William Carey in 1792. He suggested to the Church that the Great Commission was still applicable. They replied, "When God chooses to win the heathen, He will do it without your help or ours." Carey's reply was a small book, *An Enquiry Into the Obligations of Christians to Use Means for the Conversion of the Heathens*.[2] Carey went on to serve as a missionary to India. Prior to Carey serving in India, the Moravians were the primary missions sending organization. Carey's little book served as the catalyst for the missions thrust of the modern period.

In the late 18th century in the African-American community, there were many slaves and freed slaves starting

Vaughn J. Walston is a missions mobilizer with The Impact Movement, a ministry of Campus Crusade for Christ. He earned his Master of Divinity in Missions at Columbia Biblical Seminary in 2000. He and his wife, Rebecca, reside in Orlando, FL.

churches and pastoring among the slaves. A few freed slaves traveled abroad to carry the Gospel to other blacks in the Caribbean and in Africa. Many African-American Christians during this time had a desire to take the gospel to their ancestors in Africa. Most African-Americans who served as missionaries in the late 1700s and early to mid 1800s were sponsored primarily by white churches and white mission boards since African-American denominations and boards had not yet come into being.

In the late 19th century and into the 20th century, African-American involvement in missions waned. It is hard to know the impact on the actual number of African-American missionaries because there is so little numerical data. Yet, history shows that the African-American church has never recovered from that period.

Sylvia Jacobs records several reasons for the decline of missions involvement among African-Americans.[3] After 1880 and the death of Rufus Anderson (the pioneer mission theoretician of America), American and European missionaries caught the colonial mind and focus shifted from conversion to trusteeship fostered by colonialism. Between 1890 and 1910, East African revolts spurred the colonial powers to discourage the use of blacks as missionaries. They feared that the black missionaries would instigate trouble against the colonists.[4]

With Jim Crow came a distrust and even opposition toward African-American missionaries. The mission boards were being pressured by the European imperialists to recall African-American missionaries from the field. "By 1920, the idea of using black missionaries in Africa was all but dead in the white American religious community."[5]

European colonizers and mission societies rejected blacks as naturally inferior and ruled that Europeans must control churches. This pushed the African-American mission boards out. The president of the Lott Carey Mission Board, the first African-American mission board, lamented, "We are shut out from large areas by the strong arm of human laws. We have little welcome in our fatherland save in the Republic of Liberia."[6]

Marcus Garvey, a Jamaican, wanted the British to leave the West African colonies. His campaign was "Africa for Africans." The colonizers feared that African-American missionaries would promote the philosophy of Garvey and thus upset the colonial status quo.[7] For this reason, the colonists restricted the activity of black missionaries.

"During the 40-year period between 1920 and 1960, few black American missionaries not already in Africa were assigned there by white boards....However, after 1960, white boards again used a number of blacks as missionaries to Africa."[8] One generation was pushed out of missions. The next generation was unaware of missions.

In his article, "Black Man's Burden," Robert Gordon lists seven factors for what he called the decline of African-American involvement in missions in the 20th century.[9] Two areas not already addressed by Jacobs were recruiting and economics.

One area of major missions recruiting has always been among university students. The Student Volunteer Movement was the most influential means of recruiting missionaries, [starting] in the late 19th century (1888-1920). "Recruitment was aimed at university campuses—precisely where blacks were least likely to be found."[10] While thousands of university students were making commitments to give their lives to foreign missions, the African-American community was fighting for its very survival in the U.S.

The economic struggle in the African-American community made it difficult for the African-American church to support missionaries financially. In the 18th century, white agencies supported African-American missionaries, but in the 19th century, that support dropped away. Without the support of white agencies, many African-American agencies and denominations did not have the income to send missionaries.

Current Obstacles

With some background into the historical hindrances among African-Americans in missions, we can now consider the situation today. What is the current involvement of African-Americans in [overseas] missions?

The latest statistics paint a sad picture of the current involvement of African-Americans in missions. Jim Sutherland counted under 300 total African-American missionaries serving crossculturally in 1998.[11] Fewer than 300 were reported by Robert Gordon in 1973.[12] These numbers compare to 33,000 missionaries from the U.S. in 1973 and about 60,200 U.S. missionaries today.[13] African-Americans make up about 12 percent of the U.S. population but less than one percent of the U.S. mission force to the world.

We know that history has played a part in bringing about this shortfall. When several generations were cut off from direct involvement in and promotion of missions, then missions became a nonissue for subsequent generations. But what other factors come into play in today's church situation? In March 1999, a new mission association called The Cooperative Missions Network of The African Dispersion, or COMINAD, held a conference on mobilizing the Christian descendants of Africa to world missions. The conference identified many contemporary obstacles to African-American involvement in missions.

Most African-American pastors are unfamiliar with what is going on in the world today regarding missions. They were never taught about missions and do not know general missions history. They are unaware of the heritage of African-Americans in missions, thus, cannot teach their congregations about missions.

African-American pastors also desire financial stability. They want to bring the money into their churches, not send it out. Since the African-American community historically has been oppressed and deprived of opportunity for financial gain, and now that many opportunities exist, the desire is to bring it in and keep it in the community. Though many African-American churches still struggle financially for their own survival, the statistics indicate that a high percentage of African-American churches are doing very well financially.[14]

Some African-American pastors will discourage, even rebuke, anyone who endorses sending resources outside the black community. The needs of the community over-shadow missions. They cannot see the needs of the world because they are focused on the needs right next door. The church is correct in its concern for the needs of the community, but with almost 2 billion people outside of the reach of the Gospel, we are not released from our responsibility to reach the world.

Historically, the American dream has eluded the African-American community. For many attaining it has become a Christian value. Thus, moving from oppression and want to materialism and comfort are subtle but natural distractions. The African-American community is finally within reach of American prosperity and missions runs counter to that plan.

Also, many African-Americans fear rejection and a lack of emotional support from white mission boards. In the past, African-Americans were accepted to serve with white boards, but on the field were given menial tasks. Blacks were accepted to work, but not to lead.

With a lack of mission education and a priority on home missions, it is no wonder that the African-American church represents only a small percentage of the missions force to the world.

Recommendations for World Impact

In the second of the "Servant Songs," the Lord says through Isaiah, "It is too small a thing that you should be My servant to raise up the tribes of Jacob, and to restore the preserved ones of Israel; I will also make you a light of the nations so that My salvation may reach to the end of the earth" (Isa. 49:6, NAS). In the African-American church, it is too small a thing that we should restore our communities and our own people. The challenge before the African-American church is to mobilize for global impact. God can use the unique experience of the African-American church to restore the community and also to serve as a light to the nations. We can relate to many of the struggles of the Two-thirds World better than the typical Westerner. As minorities, we already know what it means to adapt to a culture not our own.

Work of this type cannot merely report what has happened and leave the reader in dismay. We would be remiss to conclude this work without making some recommendations for the future of missions within the African-American church. I shall make recommendations directed to the African-American church and to the predominately white missions arena including the missions-training institutions and the mission-sending agencies.

To the African-American Church & Pastors

The greatest motivation is a biblical one. The African-American church must walk in obedience to the biblical mandate to fulfill the Great Commission. The church must look inward to train and equip and it must look outward to the world to whom we are sent.

Pastors should seek opportunities to educate themselves and their congregations about missions and the African-American missions heritage. Understanding our heritage is often a motivation to further action.

For example, pastors may invite missionaries to speak at their churches. This can be a very powerful strategy. In the late 19th century, missionary testimonies were instrumental in recruiting. "Some of the missionary volunteers were recruited after listening to the testimonies of other missionaries or missions advocates. William Sheppard, for example, attracted four other Afro-American Presbyterian volunteers during his 1893 trip to the U.S."[15]

Pastors also may seek opportunities to go on short-term vision trips overseas or across cultures. In doing so, they can develop a vision for the needs in other parts of the world and gain some insight into how their church can develop international partnerships for world impact. They can also begin to develop a vision for the unreached.

Finally, pastors should realize that when people from their congregations are involved in short-term missions trips, they return more excited about ministry at home. They usually become the most equipped for ministry and they add depth to the congregation. Missions involvement makes for a stronger local assembly.

To Mission Agencies & Training Institutions

Leslie Pelt, an African-American missionary with SIM recognized that few African-American churches are familiar with any missions boards. Thus, it is no surprise that the churches are not sending candidates to these missions boards. Pelt recommends that mission agencies take the initiative to make contact with and seek to build bridges with the African-American church.[16] In the turbulent 1960s, Dick Hillis was willing to challenge the missions agencies to recruit in the African-American churches and institutions.[17] His challenge also applies today.

[Missions should] recruit at the schools. Even in the late 19th century, many African-Americans were influenced for missions in the schools they attended. "For some of them it was their school experience which set them on the course of becoming missionaries."[18] University students have the mobility to participate in short-term missions trips during summer breaks. This is an ideal time to help students gain a vision for the world.

Recruiters must creatively seek to recruit from African-American institutions. They should attend African-American conferences, schools, and churches. They need to sensitively build rapport in the African-American community.

Institutions also should actively recruit in the African-American community. Most African-Americans are unaware of the many missions training institutions in this country. Bob Harrison, a retired African-American missionary with Overseas Crusades, recommends "the next time your church holds a missionary or Bible conference you ought to invite delegations from black churches to attend and provide a bus to pick them up if necessary."[19] This can apply to churches or training institutions.

The most important relationship that a recruiter can make is with the African-American pastor. If a pastor feels you are trying to take people from his congregation, he will resent you. But, if the recruiter builds a rapport with the pastor and the pastor gains a vision for missions, then a pastor can be your greatest advantage in recruiting and helping to mobilize.

Conclusions

We have looked at some historical and some contemporary obstacles to mobilizing the African-American church for global evangelization. It took a long time to get where we are today. We cannot pretend that change will be easy, yet, we should not run from the task merely because it is difficult.

We must be reminded of the purpose of the Church and the biblical mandate for reaching the world and making disciples of all nations. The whole Church needs to be mobilized to accomplish the task. We must work together using our diverse gifts to accomplish the task.

Many African-Americans have paved the way by traveling to distant lands and overcoming incredible obstacles taking the Gospel to the world. They have shared a vast array of motives, but the primacy of the Gospel overshadows them all. The hindrances of the 20th century have prevented the African-American church from experiencing a missions movement. There are exceptions, but overall the African-American church is not actively engaged in world evangelization today. This situation is not self-correcting. It will require missions agencies, churches, and individuals taking the initiative to be contagious with a vision for missions and infecting the African-American community within its reach.

Closing Remarks

In these pages, a great deal has been said about the African-American presence in world missions. We have seen progress on several fronts and continue to struggle on others. Today, it is our challenge to understand the call and to find creative ways to respond. We should learn from the past and in faith move forward.

I believe that we are a powerful force and that we can rise to prominence as a world missions-sending community. It will require fervency in prayer and a zeal for the souls of men to interact with the message in the Word of God of the Messiah.

Endnotes

1 "Manila Manifesto," *Proclaim Christ Until He Comes*, ed. J. D. Douglas, Minneapolis, MN: World Wide Publications, 1989, p. 25.

2 Ralph D. Winter. "Four Men, Three Eras, Two Transitions," *Perspectives on the World Christian Movement: A Reader*, eds. Ralph D. Winter & Steven C. Hawthorne, Pasadena, CA: William Carey Library, 1992, p. B-35.

3 Sylvia Jacobs. *Black Americans and the Missionary Movement of Africa*, Westport, CT: Greenwood Press, 1982, pp. 20-23.

4 Ibid., pp. 13, 15, 20.

5 Ibid., p. 20.

6 William Seraile. "Black American Missionaries In Africa: 1821-1925," The Social Studies, (October 1972), p. 201.

7 Jacobs, pp. 20; 21. Seraile, p. 201; and Robert Gordon, "Black Man's Burden," *Evangelical Missions Quarterly* (Fall 1973), p. 273.

8 Jacobs, p. 22.

9 Gordon, p. 272.

10 Gordon, p. 272; and Winter, p. B-40.

11 Jim Sutherland. "African-Americans in Intercultural Missions," p. 2. The count was 242. This is from an unpublished statistical report on the current situation of African-Americans in crosscultural missions. A more detailed analysis is available in his Ph.D. dissertation, *African-American Underrepresentation in Intercultural Missions: Perceptions of Black Missionaries and the Theory*

of *Survival/Security*, Deerfield, IL: Trinity Evangelical Divinity School, 1998. His research is current and thorough.

12 Gordon, p. 268.

13 Patrick Johnstone and Jason Mandryk. *Operation World, 21st Century Edition*, Waynesboro, GA: Paternoster USA, 2001, p. 658

14 Sutherland, *Underrepresentation,* p. 109.

15 Walter L. Williams. *Black Americans and the Evangelization of Africa, 1877-1900,* Madison, WI: University of Wisconsin Press, 1982, p. 91.

16 Leslie Pelt. "Wanted: Black Missionaries, But How?" *Evangelical Missions Quarterly,* (January 1989), p. 31.

17 Dick Hillis, "The Missing Black Missionary," *World Vision* (January 1969), p. 24. Hillis was the founder and director of Overseas Crusades, Inc.

18 Williams, p. 87.

19 Bob Harrison. *When God was Black*, Concord, CA: Bob Harrison Ministries, 1978, p. 150.

Resource Pages

U.S. Center for World Mission

1605 Elizabeth St.
Pasadena, CA 91104
626-797-1111
www.uscwm.org

Perspectives on the World Christian Movement

The purpose of the *Perspectives* course is to mobilize and equip Christians to invest their unique abilities to advance the Kingdom, whether locally or internationally. It helps individuals and fellowships discover their strategic place of service. For information about the course and locations nationwide see www.perspectives.org or call (888) 777-3806.

Mission Frontiers

The bulletin of the U. S. Center for World Mission that features critical thinking articles and resources. www.missionfrontiers.org

Global Prayer Digest

This unique devotional booklet gives a glimpse of what God is doing around the world and what still remains to be done. Daily prayer for that still-unfinished task is at the heart of this prayer guide. Each month a different area of the world is featured with inspiring reports, stories, biographies and scripture. To order see www.global-prayer-digest.org or call 626-398-2249.

Noble Desire: A Time for Healing - video

Video produced by WHRO and FOX 43 television, Norfolk, VA. This video features the historic efforts of a small west African country's quest for reconciliation. Benin's President, Mathieu Kerekou, invited representatives of slave merchants as well as victims of the African diaspora to participate in an event where apologies were made for the role of their ancestors in the Atlantic Slave Trade. Europeans and Americans also attended and sought forgiveness from displaced Africans. Three hundred people attended including the President of Ghana, nearly 50 African Kings, two members of Congress, delegations from several European nations, and members of the African diaspora. To order contact WHRO Television Services, 5200 Hampton Blvd., Norfolk, VA 23508, phone: 757-889-9412. One hour video with Discussion Guide is $29.95; Half hour video with Guide is $29.95; and one hour, half hour and Guide is $39.95. Include $6.00 for shipping and handling and mail to WHRO Television Services with check payable to them as well.

Operation World–2001 Edition for the 21st Century

The updated version of this remarkable prayer encyclopedia tells what God has been doing in numerous countries. Factual and very detailed, *Operation World* is also inspiring in its coverage of the powerful reality of God's Spirit at work around the world. To order contact Southeast Regional Office—USCWM at 919-787-3821 or email: bsuscwmse@aol.com

COMINAD (Cooperative Mission Network of the African Dispersion)

For Adopt-A-Village brochures, COMINAD Consultant Training, and conference information, contact info: (757) 467-5803, IAAMM@aol.com, P.O. Box 9756, Chesapeake, VA 23321.

ACMC

Advancing Churches in Missions Commitment
www.acmc.org
1-800-747-7346
Resources for planning missions conferences, short-term trips, establishing or strengthening church missions committees.

AFRICAN-AMERICAN MISSION AGENCY CONTACTS

(partial listing to get you started on your adventure with God)

African Christian Fellowship

Joseph Richardson
jorichardson@na.cokecce
410-536-5371

African Methodist Episcopal Zion Church

Rev. K.J. Degraffenreidt, Sec/Treas.
domkd5@aol.com
212-870-2952

Ambassadors Fellowship

Virgil Amos, Director
102466.2243@compuserve.com
719-495-8180

Carver Bible College

Robert Crummie, President
404-527-4520

Carver International Missions

Glen Mason, Director
carverfm@aol.com
770-323-0772

Christians in Action

Elgin Taylor, President
www.christiansinaction.org
cinamissions@christiansinaction.org
559-564-3762

COMINAD

Brian Johnson, Director
iaamm@aol.com
757-467-0601

Good News Jail & Prison Ministry

Calvin Scott, Director
hq@gnjpm.org
301-292-4952

Great Commission Global Ministries

Bishop David Perrin, President
www.gcgm.org
bishop@gcgm.org
301-316-4132
800-707-3521

Have Christ Will Travel Ministries

Joseph Jetter, Director
215-438-6308

Impact International

A ministry of Campus Crusade for Christ
Vaughn Walston
impactmovement.com
407-826-2542
888-672-2896

International Mission Board of Southern Baptist Convention

African-American relations
David Cornelius
dcornelius@imb.org
804-794-8015

Lutheran Church-Missouri Synod Board for Mission Services

Bryant Clancy, Ex. Director
blackministry.lcms.org
bryant.clancy@lcms.org
314-965-9000
800-248-1930 x1751

Lott Carey Baptist Mission Conv.

David Goatley, Exec. Director
www.lottcarey.org
LottCarey@aol.com
202-667-8493

National Baptist America

John C. Rapheal, Jr., Exec. Director
members.aol.com/nbyc1/nbca.html
214-942-3311

National Baptist USA

Elaine Siryon
berrian2sir@netscape.net
215-843-1949

National Baptist USA

William Shaw, President
www.nationalbaptist.com
615-228-6292

Navigators - African-American ministries

Eugene Burrell, Urban & Collegiate Ministries
home.navigators.org/us/african-american/index.cfm
719-598-1212

Pan African Christian Exchange

Gregory Alexander
galexander_1@msn.com
248-557-2499

SIM USA - African-American relations

Ron Sonius
www.sim.org
803-980-4713

Wycliffe African-American relations

Gertrude Nicholas
www.wycliffe.org
gertrude_nicholas@wycliffe.org
407-852-3600 or 407-852-4113

Youth With A Mission - African-American relations

Orchidy Boyd
orchi41@yahoo.com
501-248-7033

Bibliography

Compiled by Vaughn Walston

Book Bibliography

Banks, William L. *A History of Black Baptists in the United States*. Philadelphia, PA, 1987.

Bowen, J.W.E. *Africa and the African American Negro*. Miami, FL: Mnemosyne Publishing Inc., 1969.

Ellis, Elward. *It's Our Destiny*. Atlanta, GA: InterVarsity 2100 Productions, 1987.

Fitts, Leroy. *Lott Carey: First Black Missionary to Africa*, Valley Forge, PA: Judson Press, 1978.

Fitts, Leroy. *The Lott Carey Legacy of African American Missions*, Baltimore, MD: Gateway Press, 1993.

Gregg, Howard D. *The History of the African Methodist Episcopal Church*, Atlantic City, NJ: AMEC Sunday School Union, 1980.

Hagood, L. M. *The Colored Man in the Methodist Church*, Westport, CT: Negro University Press, 1970.

Harr, Wiber. *The Negro as an American Protestant Missionary in Africa* , Chicago, IL: University of Chicago, 1945.

Harrison, Bob. *When God was Black*, Concord, CA: Bob Harrison Ministries International, 1978.

Harvey III, William J. *Bridges of Faith Across the Seas*, Philadelphia, PA: The Foreign Mission Board of the National Baptist Convention, USA, 1989.

Hughley, Clyde E. *An Analysis of Black American Involvement in World Missions*, Dallas, TX: Dallas Theological Seminary, 1983.

Jacobs, Sylvia. *Black Americans and the Missionary Movement in Africa*, Westport, CT: Greenwood Press, 1982.

Martin, Sandy D. *Black Baptists and African Missions: The Origins of a Movement 1880-1915*, Macon, GA: Mercer University Press, 1989.

Roesler, Calvin L. *The American Negro as a Missionary*, Columbia, SC: Columbia Bible College, 1952.

Sidwell, Mark. *Free Indeed: Heros of Black Christian History*, Greenville, SC: Bob Jones University Press, 1995.

Sutherland, James W. *African American Underrepresentation in Intercultural Missions: Perceptions of Black Missionaries and the Theory of Survival/Security*, Ph.D. dissertation, Deerfield, IL: Trinity Evangelical Divinity School, 1998.

Waite, Montrose. *Waite, A Man Who Could Not Wait*, Detroit, MI: Parker Books, 1988.

Wakatama, Pius. *Independence for the Third World Church*, Downers Grove, IL: InterVarsity Press, 1976.

Walls, William J. *The African Methodist Episcopal Zion Church: Reality of the Black Church*, Charlotte, NC: AMEZ Publishing House.

Williams, Ethel L. *Afro-American Religious Studies*, Metuchen, NJ: Scarecrow Press, 1972.

Williams, Walter L. *Black American Attitudes Toward Africa*, The Missionary Movement, 1877-1900. Chapel Hill, NC: University of North Carolina, 1974.

Williams, Walter L. *Black Americans and the Evangelization of Africa*, Madison, WI: University of Wisconsin Press,1982.

Wills & Newman. *Black Apostles at Home and Abroad*, Boston, MA: G. K. Hall, 1982.

Yates, William L. *The History of the AMEZ Church in West Africa, Liberia and Gold Coast (Ghana), 1880-1900*, Hartford, CT: Hartford Seminary, 1963.

Periodical Bibliography

Andrew, John A. "Betsy Stockton: A Stranger in a Strange Land." *Journal of Presbyterian History* (Summer 1974), pp. 157-166.

Beckner, Verne. "A New Era for Black Missionaries" *Christianity Today*, Oct. 20, 1989, pp. 38-40.

Butcher, Andy. "Cross-Cultural Missions the 'Great Omission' of the Black Church, Study Says." *Mission Frontiers*, April 2000, p.15.

Coan, Josephus R. "Redemption of Africa: The Impulse of Black American Overseas Missionaries," *Journal of the International Theological Center* (Spring 1974) pp. 27-37.

Costen, James H. "A Tale of Two Countries," *Journal of the International Theological Center* (Fall-Spring 1996-1997) pp. 15-30.

Davis, John W. "George Liele and Andrew Bryan, Pioneer Negro Baptist Preachers," *Journal of Negro History*, April 1918, pp. 119-127.

Frame, Randy. "The Call of Destiny," *Christianity Today*, September 4, 1987, p. 64.

Gaines, Adrienne S. "The Apology that Shook a Continent," *Charisma*, March 2000, pp. 77-89.

Gordon, Robert. "Black Man's Burden," *Evangelical Missions Quarterly* (Fall 1973) pp. 267-276.

Hillis, Dick. "The Missing Black Missionary," *World Vision Magazine*, January 1969, pp. 14,15, 24.

Holmes, Edward A. "George Liele: Negro Slavery's Prophet of Deliverance," *Baptist History and Heritage*, August 1965, pp. 27-36.

Isaacs, Harold R. "Back to Africa," *Practical Anthropology*, March-April 1963, pp. 71-88.

Jacobs, Sylvia M. "African Missions and the African American Christian Churches," in the *Encyclopedia of African American Religions*, NY: Garland Publishing, 1993, pp.10-23..

Johnson, Michael. "Are You A Keeper or a Killer?," *Mission Frontiers*, April 2000, pp. 21-22.

Lewis, Marilyn. "Jewel of the Kingdom," *Mission Frontiers*, April 2000, pp. 22-23, 28.

Lewis, Marilyn. "Overcoming Obstacles," *Mission Frontiers*, April 2000, pp. 23-28.

Martin, Sandy D. "Missionary Movements," in the *Encyclopedia of African American Culture and History*, NY: Simon & Shuster, Macmillan, pp.1815-1818.

Martin, Sandy D. "Spelman's Emma B. DeLaney and the African Mission," *Journal of Religious Thought* (Spring-Summer 1984) pp. 22-37.

Martin, Sandy D. "The Baptist Foreign Mission Convention," *Baptist History and Heritage*, October 1981, pp. 13-25.

Martin, Sandy D. "The Debate over Interracial Cooperation Among Black Baptists in the African Mission Movement," *Journal of the International Theological Center* (Spring 1986) pp. 291-303.

Maxwell, Joe. "Destiny '92 Calls Black Christians to the Mission Field," *Christianity Today*, September 14, 1992, pp. 52-54.

Mulholland, Kenneth B. "Legacy and Destiny: A History of Missions. Destiny: The Time has Come," pp. 5-10.

Pelt, Leslie. "Wanted: Black Missionaries, But How?," *Evangelical Missions Quarterly*, January 1989, pp. 28-37.

Quarles, Naima A. "A Wholistic View of Mission," *The AMEZ Quarterly Review*, January 1997, pp. 62-70.

Reapsome, James. "Where are the Black Missionaries," *Evangelical Missions Quarterly*, July 1987, pp. 296-297.

Sanneh, Lamin. "Prelude to African Christian Independency," *Harvard Theological Review*, January 1984, pp. 1-32..

Seraile, William. "Black American Missionaries in Africa," *The Social Studies*, October 1972, pp. 198-202.

Symposium, "Negro Missionary Reaction to Africa," *Practical Anthropology*, March-April 1964, pp. 61-70.

Trulson, Reid. "The Black Missionaries," *HIS Magazine*, June 1977, pp. 1, 4-6.

Walston, Vaughn J. "Ignite The Passion," *Mission Frontiers*, April 2000, pp. 14-20.

Wilmore, Gayraud S. "Black Americans in Missions: Setting the Record Straight," *International Bulletin of Missionary Research*, July 1986, pp. 98-102.

Wimberly, Anne Streaty. "Called to Witness, Called to Serve: African-American Methodist Women in Liberian Missions" *Methodist History*, January 1996, pp. 67-77.

Compiled by Vaughn Walston, vjwalston@juno.com

Index